Malindy's Freedom

THE STORY OF A SLAVE FAMILY

BY MILDRED JOHNSON AND THERESA DELSOIN
EDITED BY STUART SYMINGTON, JR., AND ANNE W. SYMINGTON

MISSOURI HISTORICAL SOCIETY PRESS
ST. LOUIS
DISTRIBUTED BY UNIVERSITY OF MISSOURI PRESS

09 08 07 06 05   1 2 3 4 5

LIBRARY OF CONGRESS CATALOGING-IN-PUBLICATION DATA

JOHNSON, MILDRED, 1916-
     MALINDY'S FREEDOM : THE STORY OF A SLAVE FAMILY / BY MILDRED JOHNSON AND
     THERESA DELSOIN ; EDITED BY STUART SYMINGTON, JR., AND ANNE W. SYMINGTON.
          P. CM.
     INCLUDES BIBLIOGRAPHICAL REFERENCES.
     ISBN 1-883982-53-7 (HARDCOVER : ALK. PAPER)
1. WILSON, MALINDY, B. CA. 1820. 2. CHEROKEE WOMEN--BIOGRAPHY. 3. CHEROKEE
INDIANS--MIXED DESCENT. 4. WOMEN SLAVES--UNITED STATES--BIOGRAPHY. I.
DELSOIN, THERESA. II. SYMINGTON, STUART, JR. III. SYMINGTON, ANNE W. IV. TITLE.
     E99.C5W65 2005
     306.3'62'08997557077863--DC22
          2005002751

DISTRIBUTED BY UNIVERSITY OF MISSOURI PRESS

DESIGN: STEVE HARTMAN, CREATIVILLE, INC.
PRINTED AND BOUND BY SHERIDAN BOOKS

TABLE OF CONTENTS

This book is dedicated to the authors' great-grandparents, Malindy and Charlie Wilson. They and their children suffered under the oppression of slavery in the area of Gray Summit, Franklin County, Missouri. We fervently bow to all people, then and now, who have become captives because of the greed of slave masters, their lack of compassion for humanity, and their failure to recognize God's plan, which is free will and freedom for all human beings.

When I discover who I am, I'll be free.

—*Ralph Ellison*

MALINDY'S FREEDOM

FOREWORD

W e are not so far from slavery. Just outside Charleston, South Carolina, a plantation called Drayton Hall has been restored by the National Trust for Historic Preservation. On a recent tour of the grounds I was among a group that included several African Americans. One woman was accompanied by a teenage boy, probably her son, who was just a little bored by the whole excursion. "Because," she patiently explained to him, "we have to find our roots so we can get to know ourselves and keep on living." I spoke to the woman a little later; her name was Drayton.

Malindy's great-granddaughters Mildred Johnson and Theresa Delsoin know their roots and share the memory of being enslaved. They come from a strong storytelling tradition, passed down from Malindy and her ancestors. Many cultures, especially pre-literate ones, use this storytelling technique to preserve their histories and transmit their values, sending them with their children into the future. Ms. Johnson and Ms. Delsoin have conducted Malindy's story not only into the future but into the whole community through its publication. This "painful yet meaningful journey," as Theresa writes, now becomes part of our own story, an opportunity to discover our roots and the roots of our community.

When Stuart Symington, Jr., brought me the manuscript of *Malindy's Freedom*, I was struck by the immediacy and the intimate detail that the narrative included. I understand the value of multigenerational reminiscences and how such a story could survive intact for more than 180 years. "Slave narratives" were often a nineteenth-century propagandist's product or a substantially rewritten interview with a freed person. But *Malindy's Freedom* came from a different tradition, and the authenticity of the stories from this tradition is not suspect. A Native American woman once told me that when she was a child, her grandmother would tell her the stories of her youth and her ancestors' and make her recite those memories until she could repeat them word for word. Grandmother's stories, and thus her tribe's, were successfully and authentically passed down through many generations. Malindy, a member of the Cherokee Nation and an African through bondage and marriage, followed this tradition, and we are all the beneficiaries.

—Robert R. Archibald, Ph.D.
President, Missouri Historical Society

PREFACE

———◆———

Freedom is about making choices. Over a period of 260 years in America, white men committed massive crimes against humanity. Avaricious, vicious, white men, with the Christian Bible, sword, and whip, conquered the Native Americans and enslaved millions of Africans. The slave trade and enslavement of blacks in the United States of America were tragedies of such magnitude that it is difficult to imagine, much less comprehend, such inhumanity. Many Africans refused to be slaves or to allow their children to live as slaves. Some took their own lives; others fought and died in the quest for freedom. Millions surrendered, accepting existence as chattels. Our ancestors were a part of that group. They were survivors who thrived in a wretched environment. We owe them our lives and are grateful to them for their choice to survive and prevail. Knowledge of their struggle continues to make a profound difference in their descendants' lives each day.

Our great-grandparents passed on a courageous history and a remarkable legacy. Their daughter, my grandmother, told me about their lives in slave times. She always emphasized the concept that being descendants of slaves was not a disgrace. On the other hand, the legacy left by the slave masters to their descendants was full of disgrace and shame. I have always believed that we must never either forget slavery or be crippled by the massive afflictions of the past. Most of my life, I have been haunted by the story told to me by my grandmother of her mother's life. It left an indelible impression on my soul and mind.

On November 28, 1948, I started on a journey to re-create my ancestors' lives with a commitment to tell their story to the world. As my family lived in the present and planned for a brighter future, I also embraced the past. When slavery is spoken about in this country, some folks, both white and black, want it left in the time capsule of the past or swept under the rug. "We must forget the past and move on," is the common expression. The question for me has always been, "Can we deal with ourselves and heal our wounds with evasion and half truths without ever really knowing our past?"

Ellen Buckner, my grandmother, made sure that I knew the real story, the truth. She was tireless and strong. She always read the Bible to me before bedtime and explained the works of God and how He rescued the Negroes from the atrocities of slavery. Many nights, I combed my grandmother's long black hair and washed her tired feet as she talked for hours about her experience as a slave in Missouri. She told me in vivid color about the "peculiar institution" as it existed in this God-fearing nation, the United States of America, good land of the free and home of the brave. She prayed to God with appreciation that her children and grandchildren were free in the state of Missouri, where as a child she had witnessed her mother, Malindy, being whipped by their master.

Until the very day my grandmother died in 1941, she lived under the Jim Crow policies of Missouri. Nevertheless, she felt that it was far better than slavery. She died a good, righteous Christian, forgiving of the whites who enslaved and demeaned her people. Her mother and father, Malindy and her husband, Old Free Charlie, passed this great legacy of forgiveness to her. When she told the saga of the slaves' ordeal, it was never with malice. Therefore, we tell her story without malice.

My sister and I reached into the past to give a factual account of our family's life in slavery from 1820 to 1865. We explored their love and their struggles to survive and thrive in a horrid place and time that did not make any sense. We walked the journey with our ancestors, white, African, and Native American. We summoned the strength to delve deep into our own spirits, to feel and recall our forebears' thoughts and emotions as we became one with them. It was like gliding through a time capsule, cautiously and with great humility. Our ancestors' emotions and thoughts became ours as we formulated them into written expression on the pages of this book.

Malindy, my great-grandmother and Ellen Buckner's mother, was a full-blood Cherokee, unlawfully enslaved by a Franklin County, Missouri, farmer. In this book, Cherokee culture is explored and described to identify the influences that shaped Malindy's identity and behavior throughout her life. The similarities between the Cherokee and Negro belief systems and cultures are discussed, to give Malindy's descendants a broader understanding of their cultural backgrounds and to explain how Malindy integrated easily into the black slaves' society.

More questions are answered. Were our ancestors and other slaves as lazy and dumb as the white men said they were, or were they really the economic backbone of the slave states?

Some people still perceive Missouri as having been a free state. Others claim Missouri was a "good" slave state, not like "down home in Dixie." This book clears up that misconception, describing Missouri as being at least as repressive as any other slave state. In Missouri, as in the Deep South, Negroes, poor whites, and freed blacks had no voice in civil society.

Malindy was robbed of her Cherokee identity and unlawfully enslaved, just as her Cherokee people were oppressed and robbed of their lands. Her husband, Old Free Charlie, was deprived of the right to be a full man. Her children were denied education, a childhood, and, perhaps worst of all, compensation for years of hard work on the master's farm. And yet, they never attempted to harm, much less kill, their oppressors.

The debasement our ancestors endured could have snatched their souls clear out of their bodies. Nevertheless, they lived with overwhelming faith in the Creator, and they always believed that their power came from the Creator. Power did not come from their tormentors, the slaveholders, nor did it come from the government. God would be the ultimate decision maker.

This book explores how our ancestors used the white man's religion to survive in his Hell. The biggest mistake the slaveholders made was to civilize the "black, nasty savages" by giving them the Holy Bible and Christ. This effort provided the ancestors with a valuable weapon with which to fight back against oppression. They organized secret religious meetings, which are often referred to as the "invisible institution" or the "plantation mission," right under the noses of the slaveholders. The ancestors embraced the Bible and its story of Moses and the liberation of the Jews. The Bible provided them with the hope and courage to stand strong and pray for freedom.

Will there ever be an apology or some form of reparations for all of the free labor done by slaves? Do all the European countries, along with the United States of America, who participated in the slave trade and acquired wealth from the cotton, tobacco, and other products from American farms and plantations owe an apology to Africans and African Americans for the poverty inflicted on their slave ancestors as whites prospered from their sweat, blood, and tears for centuries? This wealth has been passed on to white descendants from generation to generation.

Our ancestors should be honored with a national monument. We must never forget who picked the cotton and breast-fed the master's children. Our ancestors taught their descendants forgiveness and compassion for white men. As we wrote this book, we had to bring forth all the forgiveness that had been taught to us.

Masters can enslave bodies, but not the spirit. Our enslaved ancestors were bold and courageous. Their history gives us strength to explore who we are and the courage to live each day. As Ralph Ellison said, "When I discover who I am, I'll be free."

We encourage all folk to honor and remember our ancestors, our teachers, as we move into the pages of this story from long ago. We can learn from their mistakes and triumphs. Let us bring our ancestors to life in our thoughts and listen to their stories with understanding and love. Most of all, let there be malice toward none and freedom, always, for all.

Incantation by a Spanish writer

I am already given to the power that rules my fate,

I cling to nothing to defend.

I have no thoughts,

So I will see.

I fear nothing, so I will remember myself,

Detached and at ease.

I will dart past

The Eagle to be free.

Mildred Johnson

Editors' Note

As pointed out by William L. Andrews, E. Maynard Adams Professor of English at the University of North Carolina, *Malindy's Freedom* is technically a biographical slave narrative. Unlike an autobiography, it is not told in the first person. Unlike a fictionalized or neo–slave narrative, it is true, to the best of the authors' recollection.

The authors have made a remarkable contribution to the slave narrative tradition. Their book is notable not only for what it contains, but also for what it lacks. It deals with the standard stations of the cross visited daily during slave times by slaves and masters alike. We observe many of the basic themes discussed by Henry Louis Gates Jr. in his introduction to *The Classic Slave Narratives* (New American Library, 1987). Most important is the overriding desire of slaves to be free, educated, and human. Within this framework, we see what it meant to discover one was a slave, the deprivation of the slaves' hallmarks of identity, and the barbaric, casual sadism inflicted by both slave master and mistress on their human property.

Mildred Johnson has recorded her recollections of what her grandmother, Ellen Buckner, told her about life in slavery. Her sister, Theresa, has painted the historic backdrop for the drama of their ancestors' lives. Hence, the narrative is both black and female. It explores the feelings of the female slave who speaks for herself and her gender, the hard choices she faced, the centrality of her bonding experiences with other female slaves, her fear of being torn from her children, and the strength, dignity, and nobility of her family.

The authors have cast new light on the subject of miscegenation in the slavocracy. Malindy, the protagonist, was a full-blood Cherokee Indian, unlawfully enslaved. Her husband, Old Free Charlie Wilson, was half Irish, a quarter African, and a quarter Native American. We see how three cultural traditions, Native American, African, and European, influenced the lives of Malindy and her family.

The profound lesson that the authors teach us is that we are all human, and that skin color is irrelevant to the core values of human existence. In so doing, the authors have placed their narrative at the cutting edge of social development in the United States today. As a nation, we are just now beginning to acknowledge and accord a decent respect to our ancestors, whatever their skin color may have been.

In his introduction to *The Classic Slave Narratives*, Professor Gates suggests that many authors of classic slave narratives honed their stories on the antislavery lecture circuit before putting them on paper. Even then, they wrote only after "reading and re-reading the telling stories of other slave authors who preceded them." But the authors of this authentic narrative have told Malindy's story in all its powerful starkness and simplicity, just as Ellen Buckner told it to Mildred Johnson, without reliance on rhetorical devices. Thus, the light this narrative casts on slave times in Missouri is purer and more intense. It makes very real for us the travails of the many thousands of slaves in Missouri, a Union state, who did not escape slavery by the Underground Railroad, who were not liberated by Lincoln's Emancipation Proclamation of 1863, and who only gained their freedom in 1865.

A word about the dialect spoken by Malindy and her children. No one living can claim to speak a dialect spoken more than 150 years ago. For guidance, we have looked to Mark Twain. Readers will recall that in an "Explanatory" in *The Adventures of Huckleberry Finn*, Twain said, "In this book a number of dialects are used [including] the Missouri Negro dialect."

The slave power deemed education of slaves a threat and forbade literacy. We trust that readers will look beyond grammar and syntax to understand and appreciate the beauty and passion of Malindy's unconquerable human spirit.

Stuart Symington, Jr.
Anne W. Symington

Authors' Acknowledgments

I acknowledge my beloved family as the inspiration for this book. This work came out of the desire to empower and encourage my family to be brave always and to view obstacles as opportunities to grow and learn spiritually on this journey of life. I hope this history of our enslaved great-grandparents may help our family to stand strong and tall in a world where racism is still very much alive.

I acknowledge my family for their contributions and courage in this society that has made it extra hard for them to survive because of their race. I encourage them to continue to use their freedom to make a profound difference through service to others, and to live life with the passion and purpose our ancestors had in extremely difficult times.

I also acknowledge my grandmother, Mrs. Ellen Buckner, for her vivid memory and insistence on passing the oral history of the family to me. She, through her voice, made this book possible.

My dear son, Eugene, has left us. I thank him for all the years that he believed in me and this work. He was my great encouragement. Also, much gratitude is due to my loving husband, Oliver, who also is no longer with us, for his patience with my absence in thoughts and obsession with this work. I greatly appreciate, with much thanks, the Stuart Symington, Jr., family for their ongoing concern and continuing interest in my family's story and in *Malindy's Freedom*.

Lastly, I wish to thank my sister, Theresa Delsoin, who agreed to be my co-author. Her cooperation and commitment, in conducting extensive research, writing, editing, and typing, has supported this work to completion. Her years of work and support have been a real joy and blessing.

In the research process, we encountered many kind people who gave us their generous support. We acknowledge the library staffs in the Florida, Illinois, and Missouri public library systems; the State Archives of Missouri and Illinois; the Missouri Historical Society; and the many outstanding authors who have written books on slavery, the Cherokees, the Civil War, and Missouri history.

Love to all,

Mildred Johnson

I acknowledge my sister, Mildred Johnson, for her persistence in fulfilling our grandmother's dream that the story of her life as a slave be told to many. I thank my sister for giving me the opportunity to work on this book and for her faith in my ability to be a co-author. It has been an arduous and long journey for me, traveling in the past with my ancestors as they stood bravely in captivity in the United States of America. It was a painful yet meaningful journey, for to know one's past is to know one's self. Thanks for this journey, my sister.

I acknowledge my friends and family for sharing me with the past. I sincerely thank Bennett Josephson, my yoga master and mentor, for his support as the journey became more difficult in its final stage.

Love, Respect, and Peace,

Theresa Delsoin

One time, I was praying in Cherokee,

and somebody said,

"How come you're praying for the trees?"

I said,

"Cause they're alive.

Without trees we couldn't make it.

We wouldn't have no shade and feel this clean air."

And I said,

"That's why I always

pray for creatures and the trees,

'cause God made us."

And somebody said,

"Well, He didn't make the tree." I said,

"Don't make a mistake,

He did make the tree.

He made life, water and trees."

Edna Chekelelee, from *LIVING STORIES OF THE CHEROKEE,*

edited by Barbara R. Duncan. Copyright © 1998 by the University of North Carolina Press.

Chapter One

THE WAY OF THE CHEROKEES

L ife's journey started for Malindy Wilson around 1820, when she was born into a Western Cherokee Tribe of the Cherokee Nation, a free people then living in the slave state of Kentucky. The exact date and location of her birth are unknown. Even her birth name is lost. Her great-granddaughters honor her beauty and grace with the name Rose Dawn. The Cherokees honored Mother Earth and used names drawn from nature in profound appreciation for all the gifts of the Creator. Two days after her birth, Rose Dawn was passed over a fire four times by a shaman who asked a blessing for the child. Seven days after her birth, the shaman took her to the river and offered her to the Creator. He prayed for her long and healthy life and then thrust her into the water seven times. An older woman of her mother's clan gave Rose Dawn a name that reflected her beauty, as other children's names might reflect some physical or personality trait. A child might keep that name for life or, after some great personal achievement, take another. In Rose Dawn's case, her name would be changed, but her clan of the Cherokee Nation would not change it. A white man would give her the name by which she was known for most of her life.

By the time Rose Dawn was born, the Cherokee Nation had gone through many social and cultural changes since their first contact with Hernando de Soto, the Spanish explorer, in 1540. Nevertheless, in some of the Western Cherokee groups much of the traditional culture persisted intact. The Cherokees remained a proud and brave people. Rose Dawn's childhood in the Cherokee Nation was joyous. Like her ancestors, she was raised and trained in the traditional ways of the Cherokees. The Cherokee family unit was strong; everyone understood clearly his or her role in the social structure.

There was no male chauvinism among the Cherokees. Indeed, they had a maternal society. The women had more power than nineteenth-century white American women: Cherokee women owned the land in the Cherokee Nation, and inheritance was determined through the mother's side of the family. The Cherokees were organized into seven clans (family groups) according to the ancestry of the mother. Usually, a woman lived with her husband, their children, and any of her brothers who were unmarried. The father felt close to his children but was not regarded as a blood relative. The father did not train his children; their maternal uncles did. The father, however, did everything he could to provide for and protect the clan. Rose Dawn learned much from the females of the clan. The boys of the clan were under the tutelage of their uncles, their mother's brothers. Rose Dawn's mother, along with the other females of the clan, did most of the farming, took care of the animals, prepared the clothing, and cared for the home and the children.

Cherokee women had great influence and power and were known as "ghighua" (beloved women). Before the nineteenth century, the traditional Cherokee women were also warriors. The most noted Cherokee "beloved woman" was Nan Yeke, or Nancy Ward, a brave warrior and tribal leader of the late seventeenth century, who tried to warn her people against signing away their land rights to the invading white culture.

Every morning, Rose Dawn's family would rise with an "oh-see-yoh" (hello) to the sun and a "wah-don" (thank you) to the Creator. At an early age, Cherokee boys and girls learned to perform tasks assigned to them. Rose Dawn learned how to do as the women did. She made cloth from the hemp plant. She helped raise indigo. She dyed cloth black with walnut bark and purple with maple bark. With a mixture of hickory bark and maple, she made yellow dye. As she worked with her mother and her female relatives, the boys were hunting, fishing, learning trades, and clearing the land.

While Rose Dawn was a growing child, her tribe enjoyed abundance. She never experienced scarcity. The Cherokees had a highly nutritious diet. It included plenty of corn, oats, potatoes, peas, pumpkins, melons, meats, fish, nuts, berries, herbs, and sunflowers. The Cherokees grew tobacco as well, but corn was the primary crop. One variety was ground into cornmeal, baked and topped with grease or oil from pounded nuts. A common dish was kanuchi, a rich broth made by boiling crushed hickory nuts in water. This was a special food mixed with corn and rice. Throughout the village, the pleasant aroma of soup or stew came from constantly bubbling kettles that hung over the hot coals of campfires. It was the tribe's method of using up the leftovers. A particular favorite was a mixture of game or fowl, usually squirrel, rabbit, or turkey, with corn, beans, and tomatoes. White settlers called it Brunswick stew.

As a rule, the Cherokee diet was better balanced than the whites' diet, despite the fact that whites regarded themselves as the more civilized people. The Cherokee diet helped to lessen the incidence of deficiency diseases. Cherokee children seldom suffered from scurvy, from which many white settlers suffered terribly. Spruce tea was the best remedy for scurvy.

By the early 1800s, the Kentucky Cherokees lived mainly in log cabins. The houses of the clan were normally located on a river or creek bank, amid woodlands. The children loved the wooded areas, where they played games and searched for the fairies and little people that the elders described in Cherokee legends and folklore.

Ceremony and ritual formed a significant and important part of Cherokee culture. The Cherokees held six major ceremonies each year, following the course of the Earth's growth and resting periods. The most important ceremony, the Green Corn Dance, took place at harvest time and celebrated harmony and renewal. At this time, all crimes of the year, except murder, were forgiven by the tribe. The tribe celebrated on the "stomp grounds," sites for religious stomp dances. It was a joyous time; people of all ages sang songs and performed rhythmic movements that created a sense of peacefulness. To them, the movement was a prayer. With intense passion, they danced before a sacred fire, lit from an ember, that never went out.

Special dances were held before hunting or any expedition. For example, the Buffalo Hunt Dance and Bear Dance were performed by both men and women to show respect for the animals the hunters would kill. At the Green Corn Ceremony and on other festive occasions, they roasted green corn. There was always barbecue meat and the staple food, hominy.

The Cherokees had a colorful oral history tradition. Storytellers played a vital role in passing on Cherokee culture to succeeding generations. By the time children were seven years old they would already know the history of the Cherokees, what their responsibilities were, and what was expected of them.

The Cherokees were highly artistic, known for the beauty of their drawings, baskets, and ceramics, along with pipes and tools made from wood and stone. For basket weaving, they used honeysuckle vine, cane, and hemp. The baskets were painted with dyes from various roots and plants.

Prior to the arrival of whites, the tribe had suffered no major epidemics. The shaman was the doctor, greatly trusted. However, when the various European diseases killed half of the Cherokee Nation, Cherokees could no longer rely only on the skills of their shamans. The Cherokees had no natural or acquired immunity to European diseases, such as smallpox. They knew of no treatments for them.

By the nineteenth century, because of all the new diseases from which they had begun to suffer, many tribal members began seeking medical treatment from the white doctors. The Cherokees believed, logically enough, that it took a white doctor to cure the European diseases. But the Cherokees also continued to respect the traditional medicine that remained effective for many illnesses, and they completely trusted the shaman's services. The shaman knew herbs well. For example, the root of the nettle was used on open sores. A tea brewed from witch hazel bark cured fevers. Tobacco juice was looked upon as powerful medicine.

Cherokees believed that spiritual aid promoted healing. The shaman, the spiritual leader, knew all the proper prayers and chants and the correct method of administering medicines to the sick. Purification of the body, mind, and spirit was considered a key factor in overall well-being. The Cherokees were extremely clean. In all seasons, they bathed together frequently in the rivers and creeks. The clan used springs and sweat lodges to heal the body from diseases. This was also their form of preventive medicine. Rose Dawn was influenced by the concept of purification, which she would carry throughout her life.

For centuries before the Europeans came to the Americas, Cherokees and all Native American tribes had a spiritual belief system passed down from generation to generation. The Europeans brought the Bible to America and tried to Christianize the Native Americans. But different Christian denominations quarreled bitterly about the truth and interpreted the Bible differently. On the other hand, all Native Americans, including the Cherokees, believed in the Great Spirit, the Creator, with a code to protect all things. There was no confusion on that point of reference. Among Native Americans, there was no such thing as an atheist.

As Rose Dawn grew, she enjoyed playing games with the other children of her clan. There was always laughter and chatter among the women of her mother's clan. She listened as the elders told the oral history of the Cherokee Nation, about their triumphs and perils, their wars, and the great warriors and leaders of Cherokee history.

At five years old, all Cherokee children underwent intense training in bravery to prepare them for obstacles in life. Rose Dawn had to learn how to survive for days without food, water, or shelter. The lessons taught other clan virtues, especially generosity. Legends of great generosity were told to the children, of how kindly their ancestors had treated the Yanks, as the whites were called. The early Iroquois, the Cherokees' ancestors, had opened their arms to the whites and taught them how to live on the land of the New World. The framers of the U.S. Constitution looked to provisions of the unwritten constitution of the Iroquois Confederacy as a model.

Rose Dawn was unaware of the social and political issues that were tearing the Cherokee nation apart: the land hunger of white Americans, the effects on the Cherokees of their attempted assimilation into white culture, the general destruction of the traditional Cherokee culture, and the development of a slave-owning class among the Cherokees themselves.

For many years, the whites had been acquiring Cherokee lands by both legal means and warfare. When the whites learned that Cherokee women owned the land in the Cherokee Nation, intermarriage with Cherokee women began to occur. After marriage, a woman no longer lived with her clan. Thereafter, women and their children emulated the ways of the Europeans, and the white husband controlled the land. Such interracial marriages were a major contribution to the destruction of the Cherokee culture.

The United States government recognized the Cherokees as one of the Five Civilized Tribes, along with the Creeks, Chickasaws, Choctaws, and Seminoles. But warfare ensued nevertheless, resulting in treaties, solemnly signed and delivered by U.S. government officials, that were not worth the paper they were written on. The betrayals were devastating. As white intruders pushed them off the land, it became increasingly difficult for the Cherokees to protect their territory from both the settlers and other Native American tribes. The process exhausted the Cherokees. They perceived white men as greedy and crafty. As a result, the Cherokees became extremely distrustful of negotiations with the whites.

The Cherokees regarded the Europeans as stingy folk and compared them to the cougar. The Cherokees say that a cougar will kill two deer at once, more than it can possibly eat. Yet the cougar will lie between the two carcasses, too greedy to share the surplus. The Cherokees believed that they were the true human beings while the whites were of an uncivilized, destructive nature.

The Cherokees referred to themselves as "ani-yun' wiya'," which means "the real people," as compared to the "tsa'lagi," which comes from a word for "people living in a cave."

Before de Soto's arrival, the Cherokees used the land only for their needs. They protected the earth and had great respect and reverence for all living things. Change occurred when white traders moved into the southern Appalachian region in the 1600s. Many Cherokees adopted the Europeans' material culture and comforts. These Cherokees increased their hunting to trade with the Europeans for manufactured goods, metals, tools, glass, cloth, firearms, and rum. The alliance with white traders changed Cherokee culture drastically; people no longer farmed or hunted just for survival, but for trade. Subsistence fell to commerce. As greed for material goods entered the culture, traders and hunters became the respected leaders, replacing the shaman at the apex of Cherokee society.

Consequently, many Cherokees lost respect for nature. In the eighteenth century, to trade with the British, they killed as many deer as they could. The number of deerskins that the Cherokees sold in a year increased from 50,000 to around 1 million by 1735. Deer were merely a source of leather in Europe but meant survival to traditional Cherokees.

Numerous Cherokees continued to assimilate, hoping to achieve peace with the whites. They knew the land, mastered European technology, and flourished across the Cherokee Nation. However, despite the existence of a traditional legal code, the adoption of a constitutional government, a written language, and other tangible evidence of a productive people by European standards, the Cherokees became more subjugated as they assimilated and were subjected to relentless demands for their lands.

The assimilation process was fostered by the American Board of Commissioners for Foreign Missions. The missions taught the Cherokees the fundamentals of the European practices of commercial agriculture, domestic art, English, reading, writing, and Christianity. The Eastern Cherokees led the assimilation movement, which included marriage to whites. By contrast, interracial marriages were not allowed by some Western Cherokee groups. The Eastern Cherokees became successful farmers; they owned large herds of cattle and acres of crops in Georgia, Virginia, the Carolinas, and Alabama. The Western Cherokees, and most likely Rose Dawn's clan in Kentucky, managed to avoid the rapid assimilation process. They clung to their traditional customs, fiercely resisted white culture and the sale of Cherokee lands, and only traded with white folk for what they needed to improve their lives. It appeared to these Western Cherokees that many of their own people had gone over to the enemy and had forgotten their ancestors' view of the white settlers and the numerous times they had betrayed them.

The lessons about generosity that Rose Dawn received included stories about how the ancestors and some of the clans of her own time also helped the African slaves. In the early days of African slavery in America, Native Americans extended their generosity to many escaped slaves. In the mountainous areas of the Cherokee Nation, in Kentucky and Tennessee and across the Native American territory, these escaped slaves lived under the protection of the Cherokees and other tribes.

During the 1800s, white settlers often paid Native Americans to hunt down runaway slaves. Some Africans who were captured by Native Americans were not turned over to the whites. Instead, they were given refuge by their captors, whose mountainous territories discouraged all but the most avid slave catchers. Occasionally, slave catchers were killed by runaway slaves in the mountains.

Rose Dawn saw some runaway blacks near her village. However, she had no idea what they were doing there until she heard the stories. She also visited villages where she saw Negro slaves working in the fields.

She had no understanding of the institution of slavery because her clan did not own slaves. But other clans, mostly Eastern Cherokees, did own slaves, and the legal code of the Cherokee Nation recognized slavery. Slavery had arisen among the Cherokees as the result of the whites' land hunger and the Cherokees' efforts to assimilate into the European culture.

Some Eastern Cherokees of mixed-blood ancestry had become slaveholders, by inheritance from white male forebears who had married Cherokee women in the seventeenth and eighteenth centuries, in order to obtain their land. These Cherokees justified slavery on economic grounds by saying that in order to obtain wealth like their white neighbors, they needed Negro slaves to handle their large herds of cattle, hogs, and sheep and to grow their large crops of every staple, including cotton, tobacco, and wheat. Such Cherokees had numerous apple and peach orchards and made butter and cheese.

In 1820 the National Committee and Council of the Cherokee Nation passed a law that prohibited the purchase of goods from a slave. This law provided that anything purchased from a slave that proved to be stolen property had to be restored to the rightful owner. The law also forbade marriage by both whites and Native Americans to slaves for the sole purpose of procreation. Slaves were prohibited from owning property. However, the Cherokees had no laws that dealt with insubordination and rebellion. Slaveholders of mostly mixed blood controlled the Cherokee government and most of the wealth, cabins, smokehouses, stables, and corn cribs.

The institution of slavery divided the Cherokees. Class stratification and a value system that conflicted with traditional Cherokee ideals caused confusion and factionalism in the Cherokee Nation. Western bands of the Cherokee Nation were outraged by the Cherokee slaveholders. Despite the dissension in the Nation, Rose Dawn's parents and relatives taught her to respect all people as equal, whether red, black, or white.

The Cherokees faced a bewildering dilemma. Slaves were property and a form of wealth, but traditional Cherokee economics avoided both the accumulation of property and the attainment of wealth. Traditional Cherokee views ridiculed the production of anything in excess of basic needs. The communal and democratic social structure of the Cherokees was the antithesis of the dictatorship under a plantation slavery system. Using slave labor required the imposition of centralized control and police power in the Cherokee Nation. This was in total opposition to the traditional Cherokee government, based on individual freedom with enforcement of behavioral rules regarded as a family matter. Prior to their extensive contact with whites, the Cherokees acknowledged only human beings and possessed no sense of racial identity. Cherokee enslavement of Africans, however, inevitably produced a feeling of racial superiority among the Cherokee masters.

While the Cherokees compromised their traditional values by adopting slavery, they also tempered the whites' peculiar institution. They eliminated or softened many of the worst aspects of plantation slavery. In most cases, the Cherokees did not treat slaves as harshly as the white slaveholders did. Cherokee planters intentionally avoided the rigidity and cruelty often displayed by white slaveholders. The Cherokee Nation, unlike its white counterpart, allowed slaves to have social organizations and to participate in social, religious, and educational activities. It has been recorded that runaway slave Henry Bibb said, "If I must be a slave I had, by far, rather be a slave to an Indian than to a white man."

The Cherokees who adopted plantation slavery felt that marrying blacks was not the right thing to do. The National Council, however, gave dispensation for unions between Cherokees and free blacks. In 1824, Captain Shoe Boots, a Cherokee slaveholder, petitioned the National Council to recognize the legitimacy and citizenship of his three children by a black slave. The Council granted Captain Shoe Boots's request on condition that "Captain Shoe Boots cease begetting any more children by his slave woman."

White settlers feared that Native Americans and African slaves would conspire to overthrow white rule, so they went to great lengths to prevent such conspiracies. They sought to drive a wedge between Native Americans and African slaves. Ironically, many whites felt that the Native Americans were much like them, except for skin color and so-called "uncivilized behavior." However, the whites' efforts to keep Africans separate from and hostile to the Native Americans failed. The two groups successfully resisted the misconceptions fostered about each other by the whites. Both groups recognized that they had a lot in common, including cultural similarities. Both groups emphasized living harmoniously with nature and maintaining its purity. Both attached

great importance to kinship in their social structures. Their economics were based on subsistence farming.

The Africans' and Cherokees' spiritual relationship to their environment reflected similar attitudes toward the physical world. The
spiritual merged with everyday activities in the community, such as getting
up in the morning, hunting, embarking on a journey, and, especially,
curing illnesses. No division separated the physical and the spiritual.
They were one. Africans linked mountains and hills, caves, and holes
with spirits and divinities. The Cherokees viewed streams and rivers as
roads to the underworld, and deep pools in the river and in the high
mountains as the haunts of Uktena, a great serpent with supernatural
powers. So, too, some Africans from Dahomey, which now is Benin,
believed in a snake, Damballa, as the main god, the Creator. In the
myths of both the Africans and Cherokees, animal representation was
a major force. According to the Christian whites, all of these belief systems were of a savage nature. However, to the Africans and Cherokees
these systems were real and lay at the core of their existence and survival.

Many African folkways prohibited the killing of sacred snakes. The
lizard symbol portrayed wisdom. Similarly, in the Cherokee myths,
the Great Buzzard created the mountains and animals and plants.
They formed distinctive groupings, and each group respectfully drew
its livelihood from nature. To the Cherokees, it was an obligation to
honor and not mistreat Mother Earth. Furthermore, to them nature
had a distinct purpose other than being exploited for profit.

In exploiting nature for profit, whites wreaked havoc on the environment. To the Africans and Cherokees, the whites were clearly confused about their relationship with nature. The whites believed that
nature was there to serve them and not vice versa. They had not grown
spiritually enough to realize the concept of oneness of human, nature,
and spirit. The belief systems of both the African slaves and the
Cherokees discouraged the misuse of nature, and their subsistence
economics did not demand it.

In 1827, Rose Dawn's clan were prosperous and productive. The
clan traveled to other states and territories to sell their products. The
clan were still a free people and citizens in their independent territory. For years they had passed throughout parts of the Louisiana
Territory and along the southwest border of Kentucky. They traded
with the French, Spanish, and Americans in that region. The

Shawnee, Osage, and Delaware tribes also lived fairly peacefully with the Cherokees in the territory.

This was the year that Rose Dawn's clan planned a journey into Missouri to sell as much as possible in one trip. There were always dangers in going into another territory. But slavery was not on the minds of the clan, for Cherokees were free to travel anywhere. They had no idea what destiny had in store for one of them in the slave state of Missouri. How could slavery ever affect a Cherokee? But the "peculiar institution" that existed in Missouri and in their own Cherokee Nation was somehow engraved into the destiny of Rose Dawn, a free Cherokee child.

"Indifference creates evil,

Hatred is evil itself,

Indifference is what allows evil to be strong,

What gives it power."

—*Elie Wiesel, Holocaust survivor*

Chapter Two

ROSE DAWN IS ENSLAVED

It was a beautiful day in the summer of 1827. At sunrise, Rose Dawn's clan prepared for their journey to Missouri to sell their products. As the men gathered the horses and wagons, the women prepared the inventory of merchandise. They all looked forward with great enthusiasm to a successful journey. Little Rose Dawn was excited about the trip, her first to the slave state of Missouri. "Rose Dawn, Rose Dawn, you must hurry now," called her mother. "They will be leaving soon." Rose Dawn was busy playing around the horses and had forgotten her assigned chores.

Many times, her mother had told her stories about the beauty of Missouri and its different trees. The land of Missouri was rich in natural resources. It was truly a blessed land of rare beauty. The diversity of the landscape was breathtaking. There were meadows, glades, mounds, woods, savannas, hills, valleys, ponds, and rivers. Missouri was composed of enormous sprawling prairies and vast forests, in which existed an abundant variety of plants and animals.

For centuries, the Native American tribes who inhabited the territory had protected the environment and conserved its wealth of vegetation and most of its animal species. In the nineteenth century, things

changed significantly. Its wealth of resources made Missouri a magnet
for thousands of European and American settlers who were looking for
a better life. They came to Missouri to hunt, to cut timber, to farm,
and to mine. They built roads, cities, and industries. Unlike the orig-
inal inhabitants, the Native Americans, the Europeans desired wealth.
They created an unhealthy situation both for the environment and for
those human beings who were not of the white race. Paradoxically, the
most endangered species was fellow human beings: the Native
Americans and the Africans, or Negroes, as slaves were then called.
Many stories were told to the children about the white men's destruction of Mother Earth. Now, Rose Dawn's opportunity had come to witness what her tribe had told her of Missouri.

The day of their departure for Missouri, the clan ate a meal of
cornmeal mush and stew. Then, the women hurried to prepare additional food for the trip. Rose Dawn helped the women to pack dried
fruits, nuts, meats, cornbread, and hominy in abundance, enough for
the clan and any guests. Then, she joined her father and uncles as they
rounded up the horses for the scouts and wagons. This little girl loved
horses. Often, she cleaned their beautiful coats. The adult males of the
clan allowed her access to the horses because she had an unusual understanding and command of them. As she talked to the horses, the men
loaded the wagons with all of their wares: baskets and earthen pots,
tools, blankets, moccasins, pipes, animal skins, herbs, and cloth made
from hemp.

All was in readiness. The men of the clan ceremonially smoked
their pipes of tobacco as a special offering of gratitude to the Creator.
Then, the whole clan joined in praising the Great Spirit for the abundance they enjoyed and asked for protection on their journey.

For some reason, Rose Dawn's mother and grandmother did not
join the clan expedition. Rose Dawn's mother said a special prayer for
her daughter: "Oh, Great Spirit, please protect my little one." Rose
Dawn's mother gazed watchfully as the caravan prepared to depart.
"Come here, Rose Dawn," she called to her daughter. The playful child
ran into her mother's arms. Her mother held her tightly. To Rose
Dawn, her mother looked even more beautiful than usual. Her long
black hair was pulled back, and she wore an exquisite beaded dress.

The thought of the adventure to come made Rose Dawn beam with
excitement and joy. Her mother looked at her sternly, "Now my

daughter, please behave and stay out of harm's way." Rose Dawn, her deep black eyes sparkling, responded, "I'll be good." She ran to the wagon and hopped into it with the other children and the elders. Everyone else was on foot or on horseback.

As Rose Dawn's mother began to walk back to her cabin, she turned and locked eyes with her precious daughter for the last time.

It took the clan many days to travel across the hills, valleys, and plains to get to Missouri. At night, the clan stopped to build a camp-fire, eat, and sleep. They prepared hot meals in earthen pots. As they traveled, a few scouts went ahead into the territory to get the news, and the others provided protection for the group. When the scouts returned to the clan, the stories flowed, with all at full attention.

When the clan finally crossed the Kentucky border and passed over the Mississippi River into Missouri, Rose Dawn enjoyed looking at all of the hundreds of trees in different shades of dazzling green. The branches from one tree entwined into the next in a harmonious embrace—she marveled at the beauty. The variety of canopy trees was astonishing: There were black walnut, hackberry, hickory, red oak, shagbark, and red mulberry on the mid-slopes, while on the uplands were the oak, white oak, and chinquapin oak. Missouri was a beautiful state. But, unfortunately, Rose Dawn would soon see its ugly side. The land was soiled with a horrific business: slavery.

As they moved along the road, Rose Dawn was caught up in the magnificence of Mother Earth. She had always had a reverence for trees. In her village, she used to climb trees. Often, as she sat in the boughs of a tree, blissfully daydreaming, her aunts interrupted her daydreams and made her climb down. Rose Dawn believed that the Creator made tree boughs especially for humans to meet the tree in a divine union.

This high-spirited, good-looking, bronze-skinned girl of seven had no idea what lay ahead. She was fascinated by the journey and full of excitement. As the clan went from one farm to the next, the white settlers waved and smiled, friendship on their faces. What was on their faces was not necessarily what was in many of their hearts. Nevertheless, they still bought much of the clan's merchandise.

Working northward, the clan stopped at a large farm in Franklin County. As Rose Dawn sat waiting impatiently in the wagon, she watched white children playing and laughing. The adults of the clan had given her strict orders to stay there with the other children and not to leave the wagon while the men and women sold their goods. The white children ran up close to the wagon. Rose Dawn wanted to play outside with them. A little white girl encouraged her to leave the wagon by showing her a rag doll. "Come and play with my doll," the girl said to her. The temptation was great as the girl waved the doll in Rose Dawn's face. Rose Dawn did not speak English. However, she understood clearly what the child meant. In part, Rose Dawn's nature was rebellious. She ignored the directives from her elders and she made a child's decision, with no understanding of the consequences, to go with the white children. The clan had never had a problem with any child on a trip before. They naturally assumed that all the children would stay put in the wagon. The children usually obeyed the elders' orders, especially in hostile territory. However, Rose Dawn was far too assertive and defiant to stay put. She always had a strong propensity to take risks. Intrigued by the strange-looking rag doll, Rose Dawn went off with the white children into a nearby wooded area to play. The clan adults did not see her frolicking away, because the children were not near the wagons.

Rose Dawn had no problem playing with the children despite the language differences. They all played and laughed through the woods near a red barn. It was fun playing with the white children, and much like playing with children in the Cherokee Nation. Unfortunately, while Rose Dawn played, her clan left the farm without her. It had been a long day. Everyone was tired and hungry. They were grateful to the settlers for their purchases, but they yearned to get back to the Cherokee Nation.

Strangely, no one noticed Rose Dawn's absence for several days. After the clan crossed the Mississippi River back into Kentucky, they stopped for a rest. Her father discovered that Rose Dawn was not with them. How could this have happened to one of the children? He was upset and saddened, yet knew that he was responsible for losing the child. The clan decided to find her. However, going back into Missouri was not something they all wanted to do. Instead, they sent a few scouts back to Missouri to find her. Cherokees always protected their own, especially the women and children. Losing a child was incomprehensible. How could this be explained to Rose Dawn's mother? The scouts had no luck with their search for her. At this point, Rose Dawn became a lost little Cherokee child.

When the white children discovered that Rose Dawn's family had left her, they panicked, fearing their father's wrath. "What will Poppa do to us? We are in big trouble now," said the little girl's brother. In strange surroundings with her family gone, Rose Dawn was fearful. However, she felt sure the clan would come back for her. She had no idea of the difficulties and risks that her clan had to take to find her.

The sun was setting, and the Negro slaves in the fields were coming in from a hard day's work. The white children were scared out of their wits. Quickly, they had to figure out how to handle the situation. With the rag doll that had entrapped Rose Dawn now under her own arm, the little white girl's face was strawberry red with fear. She was truly scared of the beating from her father that undoubtedly lay ahead. "Let's put her in the barn," she said. Immediately, she and her brother took Rose Dawn to the barn. The boy told her, "You stay right here in this stall; no one will see you." It was full of hay and smelled of manure. There were horses there for company. Rose Dawn loved horses and had no problem with the odor. After the brother and sister had tucked their new friend into her hiding place, they rushed home for supper. They pledged to each other not to tell their secret about Rose Dawn to anyone. When they entered the dining room for supper, their father asked, "Why are you youngins late, and what did you do today?" The little rascals looked at each other and in unison said, "Playing" and "Nothing much, Poppa, jest our chores." Their mother spoke, "Children, eat your food now." They both took a deep breath and sighed in relief.

At the same time, Rose Dawn was hungry in the stall of the barn. She was hungry enough to eat the hay in the stall. Her Cherokee bravery training came in handy. She was conditioned to tolerate going without food. Nevertheless, she tormented herself by thinking of her mother's good soups. While she was still lost in memory of those savory soups, her wish came running to the barn, and before her stood her friends with food in their hands. They were excited; they enjoyed the idea of having a shared secret and a new friend. After dinner that night, they had managed to get extra food from the black slave cook in the cookhouse. The cook was very suspicious of their actions. "You chillen is always up to sumf'n. Here, take dis food and git out er my way. Whatever you is up to now, it come out soon or later," she said. She gave them one of her hard, long looks, and they ran out with the food. Unknowingly, Momma Sue had given food to them for a child who would become a part of her own destiny.

A number of days passed by. Rose Dawn longed to be with her family. She waited for rescue, sad and patient, in the barn. For days, she heard the voices of the slaves singing in the fields, the sounds of cows and horses. Cherokee children were trained to rely on natural instincts. She figured that she had been in the barn for six days. During all this time, the white children secretly brought her food and played quietly with her in the stall. Between them, there were no conflicts or differences. There was no racial tension; they were simply children being human and sharing together.

During the day in the summer months, it was hot and muggy in the barn. Missouri's heat was dangerous. Yet, Rose Dawn endured her time in her hideaway. There was a good-sized crack in the side of the barn. Through it, in the evenings, she could see the tired faces of the slaves as they dragged themselves slowly toward their cabins. The aroma of cooking food that wafted from the cabins was unfamiliar but smelled good.

Rose Dawn's heart cried out for the warmth and affection of her tribe. She had visions of her mother's eyes as her mother released her from her arms. Even at that early age, Rose Dawn understood the concept of fate. In Cherokee culture, the Creator is the planner of destiny with minor input from humans. Therefore, she accepted her situation and prayed for deliverance and protection. Her little friends had told her not to cry, for someone was always around the area or in the barn, and would hear her.

At last, one morning, Rose Dawn's heart suddenly overflowed from all its anguish, fear, and thousands of hidden tears. Now, for the first time, she was a lost child who felt tremendous sadness and homesickness. She wailed for minutes at a time. Her fervent sobs penetrated through the cracks of the barn wall to the outside, where the farmer happened to be standing. This man was the "massa" of the farm. The sounds startled him. As Rose Dawn huddled behind the hay, she heard heavy footsteps coming toward the stall. "Who's there?" the farmer yelled, "I say, who's in there?" Rose Dawn stopped crying as she pushed her small body into the corner of the stall.

Sitting with her head on her lap and her legs bent, Rose Dawn heard a deep breath over her head. She looked up. There stood a giant of a white man with a startled pale face. "What in the hell is this? A Injun gal in my barn! Where did you come from, and who put you in my barn?" Rose Dawn didn't understand much of what he said to her. However, she was familiar with the white man's term "Injun." With her usual assertive manner, she responded in her native tongue that translated into English as, "I am not an Injun gal. I am Cherokee. Please take me to my people." The farmer did not understand a word she uttered. To him what she said didn't matter anyway. He was the "massa" of his domain, and that was all that counted to him. He disappeared in a rage and returned with his naughty children and his wife. There was another woman with him who resembled the Cherokee people somewhat.

The farmer and his family were all excited. Rose Dawn heard a torrent of loud, angry, and fearful voices. The farmer's two children were crying, holding tight to their mother's waist. The children were scared out of their pants because a severe whipping was on its way. At an early age, they knew much about beatings. This was the way the master disciplined his children and his slaves. When he whipped his slaves they were scarred physically and emotionally for life. The master had his belt in his hand. Rose Dawn didn't understand a single word, but she sensed the emotions of anger, fear, and pure hopelessness.

Although Rose Dawn was excited herself, she remained passive, a watcher, as the turmoil increased along with the master's anger. The slave woman stood nonchalant. The master's anger was nothing new to her. She had witnessed his rage and violence against the slaves many times and had become conditioned to his behavior.

This was all new to Rose Dawn. Her mind flashed back to memories of the peace at home with her tribe. At home problems were resolved differently, with far less strife. Rose Dawn was shocked to see a father ready to whip his children. Whipping children was not permitted in the Cherokee Nation. The Cherokees considered whipping an insult to the person. In her clan, nothing was ever done to an individual that would take away his dignity and respect. There were other forms of discipline that did not destroy a person's self-esteem.

From the behavior of the farmer, Rose Dawn knew that she was in great danger. She could not have imagined, however, how hard her life would become and the great suffering that lay ahead. That day, the farmer made a decision that was in total violation of the treaty between the United States government and the Cherokee Nation. He decided to keep the little Cherokee girl as a slave instead of reporting her to the Missouri Office of Indian Affairs as a missing person. This enslavement of Rose Dawn simply reflected the attitude of many whites, an attitude prevalent across Missouri at that time. There was a notion that rights belonged only to whites, not to blacks or Indians, and that the law's protections did not extend to nonwhite people.

The farmer looked at Momma Sue and then at Rose Dawn. Momma Sue could read the master's mind. She knew he was up to no good. She understood that most whites in Missouri did not respect the rights of the Native Americans. To this farmer, the lost Cherokee girl was an opportunity. He would have a new hand on the farm to add to his slave list. She would also grow up to breed him more slaves. The farmer depended on slave labor. He did not view Rose Dawn as a free citizen from another nation. Without an ounce of guilt or shame, he gave a directive that would change this child's whole life.

The mulatto slave woman maintained her composure as the sordid scene played out. She appeared to be a kind and loving woman who never took her eyes from Rose Dawn. The little girl was beset with fear. She shivered to her bones in the stall. The master looked at Momma Sue.

"I put her in your care now," he said.

"She needs a name," Momma Sue said.

"We'll call her Malindy," said Massa. "We'll tell everybody she's your granddaughter, understand?"

"More lies on my poor tired tongue," Momma Sue said under her breath. She understood clearly that she better not ever speak the truth about the true identity of this child.

In one day, Rose Dawn lost her Cherokee name and got a new caretaker, home, and way of life. Momma Sue held out her hand to the child and said, "Come, now you go wid me, chile." As they walked to Momma Sue's cabin, other slaves watched them curiously. Sympathetically, in words and by pointing her finger, Momma Sue attempted to explain to Rose Dawn that she had a new name. "Chile, you's Malindy now." Malindy angrily shook her head to say, "No! No!" scattering tears with each shake. Grief filled Momma Sue's heart. She patted and hugged the little girl as they continued to the steps of the cabin.

For Malindy, the door of the cabin became symbolic of a safe shelter along the path of a long and harsh journey. As she entered the cabin, she cried even harder. Robust Momma Sue grabbed Malindy up into her arms and placed her on her huge lap. She looked down into Malindy's deep black eyes and said, "Don' cry, chile; Momma Sue gwine to take good care of you. Don' worry yo' lil' head 'bout nuffin. When you gits old like me, you gwine to be full of worry. Let me do de worryin' en you do some eatin' now." Malindy continued to cry out like a howling wolf. Momma Sue moved to the pot in the fireplace and said, "Hush, chile, now we eat supper." While Malindy filled her mouth with food, she thought of how scared she felt before she first entered the cabin. Now, the little cabin was a breeze of fresh air, a relief for her. She was happy to be away from that mean man. Malindy knew that she was in the care of this sweet-looking Indian woman and not the master. She had no idea of the relationship between the farmer and Momma Sue. Though Malindy had heard Momma Sue say passively, "Yes sah, Massa," Malindy had no clue about the oppressed condition of slavery summed up in the simple phrase "Yes sah, Massa."

Momma Sue lived in the cabin with her family. It was a far cry from the way the master and his family lived on the farm. The master's family was well off and lived in a big wooden frame house. The slaves lived in roughly built, single-room, hewn-log cabins between twelve and eighteen feet square. The cabins had chimneys, dirt floors, hearths, and small window frames with no glass. They were cold and drafty in the winter and a fire hazard. A table, washbasin, spinning wheel, some pots, earthenware dishes, and a few knives were all the furniture and accessories inside. The cabin was crammed with children and adults; half a dozen children and their parents squatted in such quarters. Some poor whites also lived in similar log cabins with their slaves. They divided the cramped living space of the cabin with the white family on one side and the black slaves on the other side.

When Malindy walked into Momma Sue's cabin, the first thing she noticed was the fireplace with a few pots hanging across the top. Everything about this new environment spoke of scarcity. The subsistence of the slaves was less than meager. It was nothing like Malindy's clan's homes in Kentucky, where there was always plenty. In spite of this difference, Malindy was still grateful to the Creator as she embraced her surrogate grandmother, the new jolly lady in her life.

From the very beginning, Malindy yearned for her family and the freedom of movement she had experienced with her clan. As she

Slaves like Momma Sue spent much time at the stove in the cookhouse.

HALFTONE OF A PAINTING BY BERTHA ROCKWELL, 1906. FROM *OLE ANN AND OTHER STORIES*, MHS LIBRARY.

observed her new home and family, she was aware of the differences. She was neither black nor white. She was red, a Cherokee. Nevertheless, she understood that they all were human and created by the same Creator. The black slaves knew she was not a Negro but dared not speak of it for fear of heavy reprisals from the master.

Soon, the other slaves accepted her completely, for they were all in the same boat called slavery. Malindy realized that life was one great struggle every day for the black slaves. Momma Sue's family worked the fields in the day and slept on straw mats on the dirt floor at night with burlap covers. Over their meager meals, they spoke of their dreams and of freedom. They desired more food, better housing, education, and wages for their labor. With their dreams, they also carried shame because of the master's power over them. A grave sense of powerlessness always underlay their very existence. For her part, Malindy dreamed every night of reunion with her parents and clan in Kentucky.

During the first year, Malindy stayed close to Momma Sue in the cookhouse next to the master's big house. Momma Sue prepared ham, bacon, eggs, biscuits, grits, molasses, jams, and coffee for the master's family for breakfast. Everything on the master's table manifested some slave's hard work. Yet, for the slaves, Momma Sue prepared small portions of corn mush, sometimes with fried salt pork and hoecake, a biscuit bread cooked on top of the stove in a skillet. The slaves lived on a diet low in nutrients. This was hard on Malindy. Her people did not use white flour, and she missed a variety of foods, such as meats, fish, roots, and herbs from the tribal storehouse. She longed for the soups and stews prepared by her mother.

Echoing in her thoughts, she heard her father's voice talking about the glory of the Creator and the need to protect the blessed Mother Earth. She visualized the ceremonies of the tribe. The stomp dance was her favorite. Now, she was no longer a free bird in the forest and on the prairie. Yet she knew one thing for sure: She understood that her spirit was free. She also saw her enslaved surrogate grandmother's free spirit as she guided Malindy on her new journey of submission to whites and the annihilation of her remembered Cherokee culture. Momma Sue knew who she really was within herself. She was not a slave at heart, and somehow she would transmit this concept to Malindy without words.

For seven years, Malindy had lived fully as a free human being in a loving and generous community. From freedom in the Cherokee Nation of proud people to slavery on a farm with a debased black slave population and a cruel master was a gigantic leap. Teaching someone who had enjoyed freedom to become a slave was an arduous task that Momma Sue did not enjoy. Nevertheless, with much regret, she persevered and taught Malindy to survive in the atrocious system of slavery.

To Momma Sue's way of thinking, the only way to survive was to submit to the whites. That was how some of her own ancestors had survived. Although she never accepted slavery as a just practice, she became a so-called good nigger. The master had told her, "Make that gal a good slave, just like you, and she'll be all right." Momma Sue looked at Malindy and saw that it would be a hard job. As she treated Malindy with love and warmth, she mourned inwardly for her. The master had a future of pure devastation mapped out for her.

The months seemed to pass rapidly. Malindy's mind drifted in and out of visions of her Cherokee folk as her heart grew fonder of Momma Sue. By now, Malindy had learned enough English to communicate and comprehend what others said, especially about the master. Naturally, her accent was different from both the whites' and the blacks'. She still knew Cherokee.

Every now and then, Malindy would ask Momma Sue, "How come my people don't come and get me?" Momma Sue remembered the master's harsh directive. She responded, "Gal, you jis' stop dat kin' of foolish talk 'roun' here. Ol' massa gwine to whup us all if you keep on talkin' dat stuff 'bout goin' home."

At sunrise, Momma Sue woke the family up while she softly sang her song:

Yes, we be free,

Yes, we be free,

Yes, we be free,

When the Lord shall appear.

Some days the melody in Momma Sue's low voice was angelic and joyous. However, it often had a cloistered weariness flowing out of an abyss, a bleeding heart, and a broken spirit. As she cooked breakfast for her family, Momma Sue transcended her depression with thoughts of glorious deliverance and freedom. The food was scanty;

nevertheless, she made sure that Malindy had enough to eat every day. Malindy was never treated like an intruder or outsider in Momma Sue's cabin. Momma Sue knew that she owned nothing, yet she had an abundance of love and compassion in her heart. She tried to console and soothe Malindy.

When she helped dress Malindy in the shabby clothing the master furnished to the slaves, Momma Sue remembered the beautiful beaded garments and moccasins Malindy wore that first day in the barn. Malindy was growing into a beautiful young lady, yet she was more tattered looking in her burlap dress than the rag doll that got her into this situation.

With every breath, Momma Sue still dreaded the task of training Malindy to be a good slave. How could she get this wild, free, beautiful, and spirited child to serve the master and mistress with total obedience? Malindy's ego had to be eradicated. She must be totally disassociated from her past identity. Momma Sue knew that it would be a difficult job; Malindy was the personification of rebellion. She did not yet fully comprehend the consequences of disobedience to the master.

In 1831, Malindy was approximately eleven years old. Missouri had one of its beautiful spring days. The sky was a powdery blue; birds were singing on the branches of the huge green trees. The branches moved to the melody of the wind. The prairie cordgrass, big bluestem, and Indian grass were lush. The New England aster, rough leaf goldenrod, and Michigan lily decorated the land. Malindy loved the beautiful landscape and felt peaceful as she danced merrily with the four-toed salamander and wood frogs in the bell flowers and blue violets.

Malindy enjoyed herself, playing in the warm sunshine. It was her job to care for the small white children on the farm. They would roam over the hills and through the woods, gazing at the wonders of nature in bloom. She was a preteen, yet she had already learned how to care for the white children. Momma Sue's directives and training prepared her for these responsibilities. Malindy understood the expectations of the mistress and master and was alert to the danger of childish whims such as the one that had separated her from her own family. The master's children, who had enticed and then befriended her when she became lost from her clan, were no longer her friends. They became her masters. Malindy cleaned up their messes and ate their crumbs and wore their old clothes. The game was new: Malindy was simply there to provide them complete service on a daily basis.

In 1831, Malindy could not read or write. But slavery could never quench her thirst for knowledge. On several occasions, the mistress caught her taking glimpses at her little master's book. Every time, the mistress snatched the book from her and told her that reading was not for her. The master forbade it.

Malindy knew nothing of the rationale behind her not being allowed to learn how to read a book. The first seven years of her life with the Cherokee had been full of generosity and learning. She could not fathom what was happening to her. Sometimes, she asked Momma Sue, "Why can't we read like de white folk?" Always, Momma Sue had the same response: "Don' you bother wid dat, chile. Jis' do yo' work. You don' need dat white man's learnin'. Look what it done to dem." Then she would laugh and say, "You want to be like dem folks? Lord, I pray not!" She understood Malindy's sorrow, but she felt if somehow she could get her to accept the situation, the pain would be less.

Momma Sue had never told Malindy that she was a slave. She did not have it in her heart to tell this child of her horrible fate. In time, she felt that Malindy would realize her true status on the master's farm. Malindy did not have the look of servitude in her eyes, nor was her posture like the other slaves'. She didn't call on God as they did constantly. She figured that God meant the same as the Creator. Momma Sue said "God" with the enthusiasm and reverence that Malindy heard from her Cherokee parents when they prayed to the Creator. Momma Sue was a very spiritual person, like Malindy's parents. In spite of her plight, Momma Sue had faith and hope for freedom. Her faith in God and her belief that there was some goodness in people gave her strength to get through the day.

Curiously, the master persisted in educating his slaves about God and Christianity. Malindy had now learned enough English to make distinctions in intonation and context. Especially when the master or the white preacher talked about God, it was a far cry from the tone in Momma Sue's voice when she spoke of her God. To Momma Sue, God was her savior, creator, and protector. The master had a different take on the Bible. Along with most masters he exposed his slaves to many self-serving Bible passages: "He that knoweth his master's will and doth it not shall be beaten with many stripes" (Luke 12:47); "Brethren let every man wherein he be called abide therein in God" (1 Cor. 7:24); "If ye be willing and obedient, ye shall eat the good of the land" (Isa. 1:19).

Some white preachers read from Isaiah, "But, if ye refuse and rebel, ye shall be devoured with the sword, for the mouth of the Lord has spoken it" (Isa. 1:20). As the slaves stood in a circle listening to the master or preacher, they generally were not impressed because the whites preached to the slaves only about being good and obedient and working hard for their masters. Often the slaves were told that they didn't have souls and that "niggers" didn't go to heaven.

Understandably, the slaves endured much emotional pain. Malindy saw it in the faces of a debased people born into slavery. This was reason enough for her not to want any part of the master's God. The hypocrisy was crystal clear. Therefore, every day she looked to the Creator for strength. For her, the gospel had become too mixed with the ideology of slavery. Many slaves could see no beauty in it and felt no respect for it. However, on some farms and plantations, blacks were trained to be preachers. Some of them brought a different perspective to the teaching of the gospel for the slaves. They could see their situation in the stories of Abraham, Moses, Joseph and his brothers, and the oppression of the children of Israel. The bondage in Egypt and the life of Moses reminded them of their servitude.

No matter what the master taught from the Bible about the justification of bondage, Malindy knew that she was born free. The black slaves understood well that their ancestors had been stolen from Africa, where they were free. Some were the descendants of African queens and kings.

As Malindy witnessed the discrimination and inequality on the farm, her mind filled with unanswered questions. She was a lonely girl because of her different speech and appearance. Her days were full of wishes, especially to see her mother and father. Sometimes she imagined that she was bathing in the river with her Cherokee clan, playing with the children and swimming with the fish. Often when she performed her many tasks, she had quiet and peaceful thoughts of her past. These thoughts helped her to maintain her sanity. At the end of the day, a child herself, she had to help the smaller white children with their baths, put them to bed, and tidy the room. Each evening, exhausted, she walked to the slave cabin to eat, sleep, and help

Momma Sue clean the place. Sometimes, at night, the slaves laughed, told jokes, sang songs, and told stories. In strict secrecy, they talked about events overheard from conversations between whites or from free black men.

One evening at suppertime, a big ruckus broke out about a slave named Nat Turner. Momma Sue said that the white folks on the farms were in an uproar and scared out of their skins. She went on and on talking about Nat Turner. "Dey's a Negro killin' white folks in Virginny. Dey says dis Nat Turner is a preacher. Don' seem right for a preacher to be killin' white folks. Some white folks is low down, true, jis' ain't no cause to kill 'em."

On the farm, the situation became tense. Momma Sue noticed how the master and mistress watched her every move, especially as she cooked the food. There was much talk across Missouri about slaves poisoning the masters' food. Momma Sue told her family, "Ol' Massa's mean as ever. But I believes in God en I won't kill nobody or de Debbil." Momma Sue had served the master's family with complete loyalty. She didn't understand why they turned on her. As she spoke to her family, they saw her disappointment and hurt as her voice trembled with sorrow. Malindy listed to Momma Sue as she sat in the corner on the cold dirt floor of the cabin and said, "Dem folks ain't got no heart at all." Momma Sue turned to Malindy and said, "Now, girl, you be extra nice, hear me. We gwine ter git thoo dis."

The mistress assigned more tasks to Malindy that were harder and involved more direct contact with the master and mistress. A cold winter came on, and Malindy had to scrub the cold floors of the Big House and the cookhouse on her knees. Every time Momma Sue saw Malindy with her hands almost raw from the strong lye soap, it broke her heart. Momma Sue had seen slavery kill her mother and grandmother at early ages, and she knew the marks it had made on her own worn body. She and the mistress were about the same age, middle-aged women. Momma Sue looked twenty years older. Her hands were hard as steel with rough skin. The hard life had taken its toll.

Momma Sue was mulatto. She was never proud of her mixed blood. Perhaps it was because whites let it be known that they viewed slaves like livestock or hunting dogs. A purebred dog was better than a mixed-breed, mongrel dog. The Missouri slave census for 1850 listed slaves like livestock, by age, sex, and race. Their names were not listed.

Malindy was pure Cherokee, and everything about her heritage was deeply embedded in her character. Rebellion could have been her middle name. Her nature, sparked by the cruelty that she had already witnessed on the farm, had her blood boiling over. She was ready to defend herself. Her attitude only increased the hard times for her. Momma Sue would hear Malindy mumbling angrily in Cherokee. She watched in fear and prayed that her wild child would not explode at the master or mistress.

"The sale may happen at any moment and is one of the greatest miseries hanging over the head of a slave. His life is spent in fear of it. The slave may forget his hunger, bad food, hard work, lashes, but he finds no relief of the ever-threatening evil of separation."

—*a former slave*

Chapter Three

MALINDY BECOMES A
HOUSE SLAVE AND IS SOLD

A s the years passed, Momma Sue foresaw the mistress's new role for Malindy. She had grown into
a tall, statuesque, leggy miss. She was probably
fifteen years old. Up to this time, her chores,
compared to those of the Negro slave children,
seemed to be hardly anything. However, Malindy
never forgot how the mistress had made her scrub
floors with harsh lye soap that burned the skin on
her hands. She did finally forgive the mistress when she taught her how
to knit, because learning to knit was fun. It was one of the few things
the mistress was willing to teach her. Knitting reminded her of the
women in her clan weaving, making blankets, and creating baskets.

One day, a major change came about for Malindy. No longer would
she be allowed to stand idly in the morning gazing out of the windows
for a few minutes as she thought of her tribe. "Malindy, Malindy, where
are you, gal?" repeated the Missus. Malindy acted like she didn't hear
her. She hated the name Malindy, for she still remembered her
Cherokee name. Momma Sue looked at Malindy and said, "You knows

you hears de Missus. You git over to de house right now. Take dis cook-ie now, don' let Missus see it, put it in yo' pocket fo' later." Quickly, Malindy ran to the mistress in the front hall of the house. The mistress was stylishly attired in a cotton dress made of fabric imported from Europe. Slaves in the South had picked the cotton before it was sent to Europe to become fabric for the dress. The mistress was in her glory. Beside her stood her daughter who was about the same age as Malindy. She, too, was all dressed up in fashionable clothes, and she wore a big condescending smile.

The mistress picked up two plain calico dresses from the elegant mahogany table and gave them to Malindy. She looked at Malindy firmly and said, "You will work now only in the cookhouse, and you'll be my daughter's maid." Malindy, under her breath in Cherokee, said, "Now she has a human rag doll at her beck and call." The mother and daughter looked at each other. "Gal, did you say something?" the mis-tress said, angry that Malindy had spoken Cherokee in her presence. Malindy had done this many times before, and it intimidated the mis-tress because it made her experience incomprehension and powerless-ness. Angrily, the mistress looked at Malindy and said, "Gal, you'll learn how to be a good cook and servant, hear me? And don't give me any more of the mumbo jumbo."

The mistress placed Malindy under the supervision of an experi-enced Negro slave woman in the cookhouse. Malindy knew this woman well. When Malindy was younger, she was the woman who always pulled her out of the trees. The master and mistress called this woman "Auntie." Malindy noticed that many adult female slaves were called Auntie. One day she asked Momma Sue, "Why does all the women and men have de same name? Massa, he always call dem aun-tie and uncle." She never received an answer. The older slave men were indeed called "uncle." The younger men were called "bucks" or "boys," and girls were referred to as "gals." The overseer called every-one "coon" or "nigger."

Malindy's new teacher was very bossy. Her blue-black skin glowed, and she never stopped talking for a moment. Somehow, this pleased Malindy greatly. Everyone talked about Auntie's good cooking. Malindy had begun to feel her growing pains, and this new adventure was an opportunity to learn something new that appealed to her. She had mostly had her own way with Momma Sue. Now, she had to really obey and work. No one played with Auntie. The black children were terrified by her, and even the white children watched their step around her. She was someone to be reckoned with on the farm.

Auntie looked at Malindy and said, "Now gal, Auntie gwine to teach you everything I know, hear? Jis' don' give me no trouble, hear? When you's wid me, you do what I says. When missus comin', you do like she says." Then she whispered into Malindy's ear, "I knows you's an Injun. You keep dose Injun ways out er my way." Auntie kept on talking. "Malindy, keep dis in yo' haid. I ain't yo' gramma, Momma Sue. I ain't gwine to take yo' wild ways. Remember, you mus' make it, fo' de day a-comin'.

Malindy responded, "What day a-comin'? Momma Sue, she all time talkin' 'bout de same thing, 'Day a-comin', Day a-comin'.'"

"Jedgment day a-comin', chile, jedgment day is on its way," responded Auntie, smiling broadly.

Malindy was grateful for the two strong black women who patiently taught her the art of survival. They were patient not only with themselves but with everyone else. Despite their oppressed lives, they claimed peace and integrity, wholeness. No one could split them apart. They endured with a secret belief that freedom would come someday.

For years now, Malindy had played, eaten, worked, and slept with Negro slaves. They had just about become her family. On the other hand, sometimes she felt that she was a member of the master's family, who did her part of the chores. Still, she held tightly to her Cherokee identity. No one had ever told her directly that she was a slave, and her whole plight was still not clear to her. The master could not risk his neighbors or the Department of Indian Affairs knowing his dirty secret.

When the slave children played with her, they sometimes poked fun at her because she was different from them, especially in the way she talked in broken English with a strong Cherokee accent. Malindy's Indian identity was secretly reinforced by the black elders, griots, on the farm. They told her not to forget where she came from. They told her to pass on her story to her children so her ancestors would live forever.

The slaves had befriended Malindy and helped her to live through a harsh transition. Malindy was truly grateful to them. She was a loving person; her strength shone through her eyes. Her concern for her black companions touched and impressed them.

Slaves longed for peace of mind and rest from their never-ending chores.

HALFTONE OF A PAINTING BY BERTHA ROCKWELL, 1906. FROM *OLE ANN AND OTHER STORIES*, MHS LIBRARY.

Malindy's pure spirit and strength of character protected her from the master and mistress. Sometimes, they were confused by how they let her get away with disobedience. When his wife complained about her behavior, the master would say, "That gal is strange, just a crazy Injun, pay her no mind." The master never whipped Malindy. But as she grew up, a whipping was a minor danger compared to some of the other dangers that faced teenage girls on the farm.

As a child on master's farm, Malindy had never felt unsafe in the natural environment. She loved to play in the woods near the farm. She needed no protection from the poisonous snakes, bears, wolves, and panthers that lurked in the forest. She thought of the animals as her friends.

As a teenager, Malindy had no protection from human predators. She was taller than most children her age, and she became more beautiful as she developed into a woman. But as her breasts grew fuller under her calico dress and her hips spread with womanhood, the male slaves and white overseers began to watch her with lust in their eyes.

Female slaves were frequently raped by the master, the overseers, and black male slaves. For centuries, the masters and overseers on farms and plantations had used female slaves for both sexual gratification and breeding purposes. The whites were aware that sexual abuse of female slaves was widespread. Yet, though slave rape was never condoned by public opinion, it had its defenders, and there was no law against it.

Malindy was still a virgin, for a number of reasons. In the slave quarters, there was a high standard of morality. Sexual activity among female slaves under the age of fifteen was uncommon. Malindy had great belief in herself and felt in control. The deep, intense look in her eyes challenged anyone to dare touch her. Her status as a Native American offered her some protection. The men did not want to tangle with a wild, crazy Injun like Malindy.

Momma Sue was experienced and knew how bad it could be for Malindy. Most black female slaves were sexually powerless in the slave society. They were unable to protect themselves from the physical assaults of either white or black males. On the other hand, black males were forbidden access to white females and when charged with raping a white female were either tried and executed or, as in Missouri, castrated and lynched by a mob with no trial by a court. Momma Sue prayed that no one would rape her child.

Malindy began to feel hopeless as she became more aware of her friends' rapes and the overseer's whip as it put twenty cutting lashes across a slave's back for so-called disobedience. One day, she witnessed a young black male slave beaten to death. Blood gushed out of his open wounds. Malindy was consumed with sorrow like that of the black slaves who worked in the fields. The songs they sang told the story. The intonation in their voices was one of sadness. Many were ill with crushed spirits and bodies. They faced the chronic threat of illnesses, such as cholera and typhoid fever, which brought death to many, both white and black. But, unlike the whites, the black slaves had to deal with not only nature's blows but also the continued injustice of slavery.

Every day, long before the white children prepared to go to school, Malindy ran to the cookhouse to help make breakfast. Every morning at 5:30 a.m., Auntie stood watching out for Malindy as she crossed the yard. Auntie was always happy to see Malindy as she played tough love with her. "Come on, chile, we got to git dis food ready. Don' want no trouble from ol' massa dis beautiful mawnin." Malindy worked closely with Auntie. The work in the cookhouse was hard. Malindy was burned many times as she learned culinary skills and the handling of the pots. Over time, she learned not to burn herself.

Malindy loved to iron, and her mistress praised her for her work on the children's clothes. While she ironed the beautiful clothes, she looked down at the old drab calico dress she wore every day. She dreamed of the day she could return to her clan and her beautiful tribal clothes. If she had to live on the farm and work as hard as she did, she felt she deserved better clothing. As she ironed, she thought of the stories about the mistress whipping slave girls who scorched the clothes while ironing. Malindy made sure that didn't happen to her. Malindy suddenly stopped trying to understand what seemed to her the insane behavior of the white folk. She took Momma Sue's advice and asked no more questions. There was really no rational answer. Momma Sue had trained her well to survive. "Gal, don' ask no questions, jis' do like you's tol', and you gwine to be all right." For a while, Malindy followed that advice. She became an excellent cook. Auntie left her on her own to run the cookhouse.

As Malindy became wiser and more observant, she became aware of Auntie's vast sorrow. At times, Auntie's lips would move with silent words. She paused and looked up imploringly. It was as though she were in a silent prayer or trance. She seemed to drift away, out of her old worn-out body, to escape the harsh reality of the moment. Day after day, Malindy saw Auntie's tears well up in her eyes. Her mournful humming was as continuous as her plight, slow and dragged out.

When the mistress or master entered the room, Auntie's sorrow turned into a big smile, a face full of bright white teeth. "How you be, massa? Got some good food today, yes sah, massa. I'm a-cookin' jis' what you like."

The master laughed and said, "You're a good gal, Auntie. Just make sure you teach Malindy to be a good gal and stay in her place."

"Yes, sah, massa, yes sah."

Malindy much resented the master, especially when he referred to Auntie as "gal." She was no girl and old enough to be his mother. Malindy loved Auntie and was ready to fight for her. Yet, she maintained her cool as the master condescendingly insulted them both. The moment the master left the cookhouse, Auntie's smile disappeared and her heavy round shoulders slumped. The kitchen filled with the gray mist of Auntie's depression as her light dimmed. Then, Auntie's agonized deep voice sang over and over, "I couldn't hear nobody pray."

All white men and women did not live like the prosperous farmers and plantation slaveholders' wives. Some were the poor whites, often referred to as "poor white trash." In a way, the poor whites still had the status of serfs, much as they had existed in feudal England under the king. They were uneducated, hungry, dirty, raggedy, and paid extremely low wages. It was said that the slaves had better clothes and food than this group. Most of them blamed the Negro slaves for their own low status. In slave states, the poor got poorer, the slaves remained in servitude, and the lords got richer through commercial farming.

Malindy overheard the stories about the situation in Missouri often as she served refreshments to the mistress and her friends. They talked about the "poor white trash," "darkies," "niggers," or "coons." Ironically, the folk whom they were speaking about in negative terms made it possible for them to live their relatively luxurious lifestyle. From their conversations, Malindy became aware of the true extent of the slaves' plight. Once, the mistress remarked that she and her husband had to sell some of their "darkies" due to the great expense of maintaining them. The slave families had increased too much to make it worth keeping them all.

"How much do you want for them?" asked another of the ladies.

"You know some of these niggers are worthless, lazy, and crazy," said another.

"Don't worry, all of our niggers are good niggers."

"We had a few who got out of hand. A few floggings with the over-seer's cowhide whip, and a little smoking taught them a lesson." The "smoking" was known as Virginia Play. Masters chastised slaves by whipping them and then tying them out in the smokehouse like a ham, to be smoked by a fire made of tobacco stems.

"'Old Virginny Play' puts the niggers in line quick."

"Have my husband look at a couple, we need more help," said Malindy's mistress.

It turned Malindy's stomach. Her heart thumped rapidly as she stood there, stoically pouring the tea. This was news to her. She did not understand, for no one had ever been sold on the farm to her knowledge. For a moment, she stood frozen in suspense.

"Gal, pour the tea. What's wrong with you?" said the mistress. One of the ladies looked strangely at Malindy.

"Where'd you get her?" she asked the mistress. "She sure is pretty with all that black, straight hair."

"Malindy is Momma Sue's granddaughter," the mistress lied. "She has some notion that she is a Cherokee Injun. I don't reckon I know where she got that notion 'cause she was born right in Momma Sue's cabin here. You know some of these niggers are simply born just plain crazy."

When the mistress had completed her lie, Malindy's eyes rolled and her blood steamed hot in her veins. Under her breath in Cherokee, she said, "Liar! Liar!" The mistress' guests looked at each other and laughed, for they knew that the mistress had just told a big "white" lie.

From that moment on, a lingering, dark aura enveloped Malindy's usual radiance. The sparkle in her bright eyes dimmed, and her smile disappeared completely. At last, she came to understand what every Negro slave felt almost from birth. "I am a slave, chattel, property, a non-human being in the white folks' eyes." The white family she had accepted as her family, where she simply played her role and performed her duties, was not her family. They could sell her at any time for money. She could be taken from Momma Sue, whom she loved, and be thrown away.

It was not in Malindy's nature to be trapped without resistance. She was given to fiery outbursts and displays of stubbornness as she did her chores. The mistress often complained to the master about Malindy's behavior, how she refused directives and would not respond to the name Malindy. She had become outright belligerent. It infuriated Malindy when she heard the blacks called "nigger" and other demeaning names.

One day, when the master's daughter called one of Malindy's friends a "nigger gal," she said, "You knows, she got a name like you, she ain't no nigger gal." The girl cried and ran and told her mother. The mistress was furious and told Momma Sue to get Malindy under control or the whip would do it for her. Momma Sue now feared more for Malindy's safety. When slaves were uncontrollable, they were beaten, killed, or sold on the auction block.

Momma Sue knew in her heart that Malindy would be taken away from her soon. Often, Momma Sue attempted to persuade Malindy to behave and be silent around the master. This did not work, and Malindy continued her insolence. Momma Sue did not argue with the mistress's conclusion that Malindy was untamed because of her "Injun" blood. Yet, she knew it had nothing to do with Indian blood, for she knew black slaves who behaved just like Malindy. Some of them died, some ran away, and some submitted to the master in the end. Momma Sue grieved at the prospect of losing her Malindy, whom she had grown to love as her own child.

Malindy would strut around like a peacock. She felt the Eagle Spirit inside her to be free. At such times, she did not fear anything, and the master and mistress could see it. When Malindy got back to the cabin, she enjoyed some solace. At night, the slaves would sit down before a fire and sing all kinds of songs. A few men would play, striking music on the banjos. The slaves were used to entertain the master's guests, so the master gave them discarded banjos and violins. They were great fiddlers who learned music by ear. Some of these evenings there was plenty of food. They made molasses candy and everybody would sit around and shape their candy, like a game. These festivities made it possible for the slaves to rejuvenate their spirits for the next day's hard tasks on the farm.

The slave cabin was a place for the family to come together and chat, eat, and unwind.
STEEL ENGRAVING, 1859. FROM *JOURNEY IN THE SEABOARD SLAVE STATES*, MHS LIBRARY.

⊢ MALINDY'S FREEDOM ⊣

Malindy was aware of Momma Sue's fears. Out of love and respect for her, Malindy worked tirelessly to subdue her rebellious nature. Momma Sue was relieved, recognizing her effort.

By the time winter came again, Malindy had begun to get a little more enjoyment out of life with the other slaves, regardless of the burden of bondage. One day, she strode across the yard to the Big House feeling pleased with herself. Now, she was a real young lady. The moment she was inside the house, she took a quick look at herself in the mirror. For the first time, she noticed there were dimples in her cheeks and her skin was clear and a reddish brown. Her hair was beautiful, coal black and glossy, with braids that stood high across her head. Malindy was behaving much like a sixteen year old. Suddenly, she was startled out of her thoughts as the master instructed her to return to her cabin and pack her few belongings. The haunting fear that had lurked in her heart became a reality. Malindy was frozen with fear. A question she dared not ask entered her thoughts.

Malindy ran back to the cabin. She had a lump in her throat; she was in a daze and not fully conscious of her movements. When she got to the door, she was there and not there. The screech of the opening door brought her out of her daze. What would she say to the family members inside? At that moment, Malindy realized how attached she had become to Momma Sue and the other slaves. She still wanted her people to come for her and dreamt of freedom. Nevertheless, she had bonded with this slave family, whom she loved dearly. That bond made parting more difficult for her. When she walked into the cabin, the slaves were unusually quiet. The silence was broken only by the hustle and bustle of other slaves who were packing already. Malindy's eyes met those of some of her friends. There was no need for words. The look in their eyes revealed the depths of sorrow in their hearts. After Malindy put her few things in a scarf, she turned to face Momma Sue, who was staring into space humming her favorite tune, "We be free, we be free."

This was another day of terror, sadness, bewilderment, and rage for Malindy. It was just as painful a day for Momma Sue. She truly loved this lost Cherokee child who was now almost a woman. They both stood stiffly as they gazed into each other's eyes. No words could begin to express what was in their hearts. Suddenly, Malindy fell to her knees and buried her head in her dear friend's skirts. Hot tears streamed down Malindy's cheeks. Momma Sue embraced her as she had that day ten years ago. Malindy would never forget that embrace, the familiar hand comforting her trembling body with a gentle pat. Malindy had only one consolation in her aching heart. Other slaves were leaving with her, young men and women who were her friends. The master received a good price for young slaves.

As Malindy was leaving the cabin to gather with the other slaves for the journey, her eyes again filled with tears. She braced herself and raised her head to the sky like a Cherokee warrior. Angrily, she said, "One day, my Creator will free me. My ancestors will avenge me." She walked slowly up to the Big House where the other slaves stood with their bundles at their sides. The tears had disappeared from her eyes. She was far too proud to let her oppressors see her emotions. All her fear vanished as she watched the master and mistress walking with a strange white man toward them. It was customary for the slaves to step forward and bow to approaching visitors. The other slaves bowed in submission to the white man. Malindy intentionally stood straight as an arrow and looked squarely into the man's eyes.

"What's wrong with that gal, lookin' at me like that?" he asked the master.

"That's Malindy, kind of crazy, but a hard worker and a darn good cook," the master responded. "She's all right."

The white man continued to look them over from head to toe. He looked pleased. Evidently, he thought he had gotten a bargain for his money. Malindy glanced at her mistress; there was a faint, stoic smile on her face. Malindy was only a piece of property to her, yet the mistress had a fondness for her. That was part of the ambiguity of slavery.

Momma Sue was in Auntie's arms crying as they watched the children climb into the new master's wagon. She cried out, "Baby, you got wings, you got wings, remember dat, my chile." Malindy looked tenderly at Momma Sue; she understood the message well. It meant that freedom was coming one day. Then she looked at the mistress and could sense the mistress's dilemma. Now, the mistress no longer was smiling. She looked sad. Indeed, she was troubled and confused much of the time. The poor mistress had almost a love-hate relationship with Malindy. Her bond with Malindy was as strange as slavery.

Their new master climbed into the driver's seat of the wagon. He yelled loudly, "Giddy up." As Malindy sadly watched the second home she ever knew fade slowly from sight, her heart was full of thoughts of vengeance. An inner voice told her to forgive her oppressors. Her response was, "Those folks destroy my life, I'll destroy their life. Judgment is going to come to them in the night." Then she drifted into a silent chant with memories of how her tribe prepared to deal with their enemies. She sat extremely still in the back of the wagon as she chanted a Cherokee verse to destroy life. In English, the translation is:

Listen! Now I have come to step over your soul. You are of the wolf clan. Your name is "a'yu ini." Your spittle, I have put at rest under the earth. I have come to cover you over with the black rock. I have come to cover you over with the black cloth. I have come to cover you with the black sack. I have come to cover you with the black slabs never to reappear. Toward the black coffin of the upland in the Darkening Land, your path shall stretch out. With the black coffin and with black slabs, I have come to cover you. Now your soul has faded away. It has become blue. When the darkness comes, your spirit shall grow less and dwindle away, never to reappear. Listen! . . .

As the new master's wagon bumped along the road, she felt the presence of her ancestors. Her thoughts of revenge drifted away as she slept in the cool mist.

"As I would not be a slave, so I would not be a master. This expresses my idea of democracy. Whatever differs from this, to the extent of the difference, is no democracy."

—Abraham Lincoln

Chapter Four

LIFE IN THE BIG HOUSE

I t was a cold winter morning. The sky was a soft blue, and the Missouri green pines saluted the heavens. Malindy was chilled to the bone and too distraught to enjoy the exquisite beauty of nature. As the new master drove the wagon along the road to his farm, Malindy held on tight to a little boy who had been sleeping in her arms. Tears were streaming from his big, frightened, eight-year-old eyes. This was his first separation from his mother. "Hush now," Malindy told him as she kept a watchful eye on the master. "Don' let Massa see you cry. You got to be strong." The hot, angry look that Malindy gave the master could have cut right through a block of ice. "We're here," called out the master to the slaves, his new property. The wagon stopped at the new Big House. As Malindy walked by the horses, she looked into one of the horse's eyes. The horse's lonely eyes watched Malindy's every move, seeming to understand her anguish. The horse was also the master's property.

The farm was huge, with many acres of fields. It had a big, beautiful, frame family home and slave cabins. The master told everyone to go into the Big House. When the five slaves and Malindy set foot in the house, they were simply in awe. The house was grand with the odor of pure wealth. The black house servants wore uniforms. Malindy and the other slaves with her had never seen such grandeur and elegance.

The mistress came into the room with the overseer and looked them over from head to toe like a butcher looks at a hog or cow before buying it and cutting it up to sell to a customer. Malindy hated every moment of the inspection; she knew that she was merchandise to them, nothing more, nothing less. This debasement she would endure for years. She understood that freedom could come only through an act of justice or death. She forgot about herself and stood tall, straight and at full attention. She wanted to be an example for her mournful younger companions. The mistress was not concerned about their feelings. She smiled and nodded to her husband. She was quite pleased with his acquisition of these slaves, the young, strong, innocent girls and boys.

However, she dared not look into their eyes and see the agony of separation, and the visions of their mothers and families as they were torn from their arms. The screams and moans of their families lingered in their thoughts as they held back their tears. Of course, none of this was relevant to the mistress. For years, she had justified her mistreatment of others to achieve wealth. Their feelings did not matter.

The new mistress looked at Malindy sternly and said, "Girl, what is your name?" Malindy had decided to be as pleasant as possible. In a soft and humble voice, she responded, "Mistress, my name is Malindy."

"Malindy, you will come with me," the mistress said. She told the overseer to take the other slaves to the slave quarters, as they were assigned to work in the fields. Malindy followed the mistress to the kitchen. They sat down at a large, square wooden table with six chairs around it. "I hear you are a good cook," said the mistress. Malindy had been well trained in cooking and baking light breads. The mistress introduced her to the cook, the mammy of the farm.

The mammy was a motherly figure with a strong authoritative demeanor. She could do anything and often do it better than anyone. Like most mammies in the slavery system, she was an expert in all domestic affairs and the head house servant. The master and mistress depended greatly on her. Malindy saw that Mammy was very dedicated to the white family, especially to the children. The master gave her complete charge of managing domestic affairs in the Big House. The mistress and master were always running to Mammy for advice and disturbing her in her slave cabin at night for something or the other. She was a surrogate mother, cook, waiting maid, wet nurse, and seamstress. Mammy was one hard-working slave. As Malindy observed Mammy's behavior, she had no aspirations to graduate to Mammy's status.

Mammy was happy to get a strong helper, and Malindy felt fortunate to be assigned to her. She sensed that Mammy would protect her as much as possible under the circumstances. Malindy well understood Mammy's role in the system of slavery because for ten years she had been under the tutelage of two strong black women who loved and protected her. She understood their peculiar dilemma as she understood her own.

Survival in slavery required many compromises that were not pretty. Often, the field slaves called Mammy a "house nigger." They viewed her as being "white-washed." Yet some came to her for favors, or to intervene on their behalf with the master to avoid punishment or sale. However, this seldom freed them from their doom.

Malindy saw Mammy in a different light. She was grateful for Mammy's courage, compassion, dignity, and self-respect. The well-being of her family was always first on Mammy's mind. Mammy felt that if she became a friend to the master and mistress, she could possibly protect her family from abuse and the auction block. Mammy's story was like Malindy's saga, entitled, "Survive, Survive!"

From the kitchen window, Malindy could see the fields. She was pleased to have been saved from the drudgery of the field hands. Adults and children worked in the huge fields. The field hands were poorly clad in shabby and insufficient apparel. Slave life was drab and so was their clothing, made from so-called Negro cloth: calicos, linsey-woolsey, duck, kersey, and jean. Mammy and the house servants were far better clothed and groomed than the field slaves. Malindy was so tired of the calico dress she had worn for years that she looked forward to something as simple as the uniform that was the badge of the "house nigger."

As the mistress introduced her to the other house servants, Malindy moved like an automaton to keep from showing her emotions. Loneliness, rage, fear, and helplessness assailed her. When she got to the servants' quarters, the room next to the kitchen, she was silently screaming for freedom. The room was sparsely and neatly furnished. It had two high beds and two trundle beds that could accommodate four servants. Malindy was grateful to see that she would not be alone in the room. She had never slept alone before. She was afraid of the master's or his male family members' sexual advances.

Malindy knew that if a white man desired her, her only protection from him would be death or divine intervention. She had made up her mind that she would choose death before she let a white man take her virginity. She prayed every day for safety, for there were no laws to protect her from a white man's lust. Moreover, white mistresses whose husbands used the slave sexually rarely had compassion or empathy for the slave. White women felt that white men held all the cards. White men were rulers who ran a black harem under the same roof as their white wives and daughters. These grand, hypocritical southern gentlemen trampled upon their wives' affection and hopes of living happily. Plenty of mulatto children were running around to remind wives of their husbands' infidelities. White mistresses readily named other men as the fathers of the mulatto children but never named their own male relatives as fathers; the mistresses would never accept them as their husband's children. Most slaves in the slave quarters knew whom the master slept with but dared not talk about it.

Survival raised the ugly image of Jezebel in the black slave quarters. Some black women did not resist the white man's sexual advances, choosing adultery in the hope that they would receive favor, freedom, and protection. Some endured rape out of fear of death and severe punishment. Yet, every time a female slave willingly accepted such advances without shame or remorse, she gave life to the degrading image of Jezebel that brought disgrace on her family.

Missourians engaged in the so-called fancy trade, the sale of light-skinned mulatto women for the exclusive purpose of prostitution and concubinage. The so-called fancy girls could be found in separate jails in St. Louis before they were put on the auction block. If they were disobedient, they were put in the slave pens like other black slaves. The mulatto women sold for $1,500, triple the usual price. Malindy could easily have been targeted for this trade. She was extremely beautiful. However, anyone could see that she was an Indian and not a mulatto. Momma Sue had warned her of the danger that her beauty posed for her. For her protection, she often wore her hair like a matron and very loose clothing. Beauty was not an asset in these circumstances.

Malindy's three roommates came into the room. Immediately, one said to her, "What you doin' heah, you ain't no nigger. You look jis' like a Injun to me. I bet Massa and Missus knows you's a Injun." Malindy responded, "Maybe dat's true. But you ain't no nigger nei-

Field hands performed the cruelest work, with the overseer's whip always threatening.
WOOD ENGRAVING, 1849.
FROM *THE NARRATIVE OF THE LIFE AND ADVENTURES OF HENRY BIBB, AN AMERICAN SLAVE*, MHS LIBRARY.

MALINDY'S FREEDOM

ther, you's African." Malindy did not trust her roommates enough to reveal her true identity. She moved them away from the subject and asked them how long they had been on the farm.

One of the girls said that she had been born on the farm and that she and her parents were once field hands. The master had sold her parents when she was about eleven years old, then made her into a house servant. She told of the harshness, pain, and struggle of life as a field hand. She had worked long hours in the fields. "We done de work de master felt was too hard or beneath white folk, so says my folk." Most whites thought that the strong African slaves were endowed by God with shining blackness and more sweat so they could work better in the hot sun.

In the master's fields, slaves cut down trees, cleared the fields, plowed the land, sowed the seed, planted corn, planted fruit trees, cultivated the gardens, raised hemp, pulled out potatoes, gathered peas, cured tobacco, cared for the livestock, hauled fodder, killed the hogs, and salted the meat. Slaves built the slave quarters. When they returned to their cabins every night, slaves had to do their own gardening, cooking, sewing, and cleaning. "Gal, Massa done work us to de bones!" one of the girls said. "Oh, it was somethin' tur'ble, gal, for us chillen." The girl sang Malindy the rueful slave song:

We raise de wheat,

Dey gib us de corn;

We bake de bread,

Dey gib us de crum;

We sif de meat,

Dey give us de skin;

And dat's de way,

Dey takes us in.

The old slaves told Malindy their stories, too. "I had to do field work. Even us kids had to pick a hunnet en fifty pounds of cotton a day or we got a whuppin'. Durin' de cotton hoein' time, de overseer, he wanted all of us dat's de bigges' ones, to stay right in line en chop along. We had to keep up wid one another. En if we didn't, we jis' got de bullwhup. De overseer would ride up en hit us over de back if we didn' do our job right." The overseer was a real monster who kept the blacks in line.

Malindy remembered her first day at the Big House. The mean-looking overseer was there with the mistress. The role of the overseer was as policeman and enforcer. He stayed constantly in the fields while the field hands were at work. He searched the cabins periodically for weapons or stolen goods. He guarded the corn crib, smokehouse, and stable. From one day to the next, he implanted personal inferiority in the slaves' consciousness by debasing them with physical and verbal abuse. He kept them in their place and enforced the notion that bondage was their natural status, because their African ancestry tainted them. Their black color and blood were badges of degradation.

The slaves could not be out of their cabins after the "hornblow," usually at eight o'clock in the winter and nine o'clock in the summer. At night, the overseer or the master toured the cabins to make sure no slaves were missing. A slave was not allowed to leave the farm without a written pass stating his destination and time to return to the farm. In most cases, the slave was not allowed to sell anything without a permit. Slaves could not have liquor in the cabins. Quarrels, fights, and the use of abusive language were not allowed; such behavior was only for the whites.

Malindy and her roommates understood that the rules were harsh, demeaning, and unfair and that they had to play the game for survival. One of her roommates warned her about the mistress, "Gal, you stay out de overseah's way en don' be fool' by de missus's smile. She slap you like she swat a fly." She looked intently at Malindy and said, "Yes, indeedy, you sho' looks like a Injun to me. Massa en Missus knows you's not s'posed to be here. Dey is real low-down folk."

This roommate's obvious joy in life amazed Malindy. In spite of all the hardship, her roommate was able to laugh and joke. She was an amazing example of an indomitable spirit. As Malindy listened to her, she wondered what her own life would become on the master's farm. She refused to call it her home for she well knew that nothing there belonged to her. It was all the master's property.

The weeks passed, and Malindy quickly found out that being a house servant was far from a haven. Nevertheless, the house slaves were a little better off materially than the field slaves. The house slaves received cast-off clothing from the master's family. By giving some benefits to house slaves, the master encouraged the field hands to resent and distrust the house slaves, so they would not combine against him.

When the field hands were coming out of the fields at sunset, the house slaves still had long hours of work ahead. They hauled the water, fanned the flies, spun the yarn, milked the cows, and swept the floors. They were butlers and maids. They were even used as foot warmers.

The master and mistress had many parties and dinners. Malindy and the others had to work as long as the guests were there. They served meals to people who called them "wenches," "niggers," "coons," "sambos," "darkies," and "mammies." They stood awaiting the white folk's every beck and call. The mistress seemed to have one single thought, "Oh, that I had a million slaves or more, to catch the rain drops as they pour."

Malindy and the other house slaves worked silently, making no response to mental or physical abuse. However the mistress treated Malindy, she held fast to her Cherokee roots and her belief that freedom was on its way. Every night Malindy and her friends went to bed weary. They talked in a low whisper as they poked fun at the white folk and discussed their own visions of freedom.

Despite their invisible shackles, Malindy and her friends fashioned a life beyond slavery for themselves. They had an amazing capacity to forge much out of nothing. Malindy encouraged the others to fight to hold their spirits intact to get them through their ordeal. When white men totally broke the spirit of slaves, they became empty shells of human flesh and bones, like zombies. Malindy saw some men and women like this. They were traumatized; their speech was muffled, lacking clarity or any sense of self. It was as if the master had snatched their souls and locked them away in a cold vault.

Malindy promised herself that she would stay alive and would never become part of the "walking dead." Every day, she prayed to the Creator for these men and women and wished for a revival of the spirit in their lives. Malindy believed that the Creator saw her not as a slave, but as a divine creation. In contrast, the master saw his slaves as beasts of burden, childlike creatures that had to be taken care of by the superior white race.

While she was cooking for the master's family, Malindy had no doubt about the cruelty of slavery in Missouri. She also had concerns about her tribe. From overheard conversations in the Big House about the "Injun problem" she learned that her own people were in harm's way. The nation was soiled with the blood of many Africans and Indians. Their agony penetrated the earth and rose again each day to touch Malindy's sensitive heart. Their pain was her pain. However, her will overcame the pain.

Foremost in Malindy's mind was survival. Conscientiously, she strove to accommodate the master's family and learn their way of life. Her magnetic personality drew the other slaves to her. Unlike some of the house servants, she was not "uppity" toward the field hands. She realized that a slave was a slave—whether in the house or in the field made no difference. Malindy made friends and spent time visiting in the slave quarters. Her favorite time was wash day, when the women talked and caught up on the news.

In Missouri, wash day on the farms and plantations was usually Saturday. For hours, slave women washed piles of clothes for master's family, talked, and sang songs. Occasionally, Malindy and the older women would slip off to hold their own prayer meetings, usually in the woods. A strong mutual bond held the women together. They exchanged glances with one another in the fields and in the Big House and understood the nonverbal messages the glances transmitted. At the end of every meeting, they walked around shaking hands singing, "Fare you well my sisters, I am going home." Malindy and her friends enjoyed themselves deliberately to show the master that their bondage had not vanquished the God-given natural right of joy.

One day the mistress asked Malindy, "Why are you folks so dern happy, just a-grinning and smiling all the time?" The mistress did not understand or like the idea that a downtrodden slave could be deliriously happy. Malindy responded as if her Cherokee ancestors spoke through her, "De sky is blue, de stars dey shine; de moon glows at night, missus. Wid all of dat, why not be happy?" Malindy stood up straight and proud. The mistress looked at her, perplexed, and rushed out of the kitchen. During this time, Mammy was also in the kitchen observing Malindy. When she saw the mistress's face turn red with anger, she became concerned for Malindy.

"Gal, now I tol' you to watch yo' smart mouf. Some day, it sho' nuff git you in big trouble. Massa don' like no smart niggers 'roun' here, nor no wise ones neither. You jis' keep dat up, gal, en Missus a-gwine to sell you fo' sho'," said Mammy with a voice so deep and trembling with fear that it sent a chill up Malindy's spine. Mammy knew that Malindy appeared far too smart for the mistress's satisfaction; Malindy's wisdom confused the bewildered mistress.

Instinctively, Malindy sensed that she did not cause the mistress's embarrassment. The mistress was embarrassed by her own shameful life in the master's confusing slave kingdom. Malindy looked at the mistress sadly and compassionately, because her own greed would not allow her to try to cure the malignancy in her home. The mistress won no victory. The idea of white supremacy had limited her own humanity and injured the divinity within her. Was there any solace for her or peace as a slaveholder? Malindy continued to smile; a golden glow seemed to surround her. She whispered to her ancestors to stand with her. Their voices whispered back, "Weave, my child, weave your way."

At Christmastime Malindy wove gifts for her friends with Mammy's help. The spirit of generosity remained with her from her Cherokee culture. The Negroes had befriended her with their generous love, caring, and sharing. She looked forward to the few days of holiday celebration with her friends. Usually, the slaves were given four days off from some of the work. They normally did not have good thoughts about their work, except during Christmastime, corn husking, hog killing, and harvest. At these times, there was always plenty of food and fellowship. The master gave each slave a small gift, usually socks and a scarf. The main reward at these festivities was the variety of good food to be eaten.

One day Malindy asked Mammy, "How do Massa and Missus know dat God made us to be dey slaves? Did God come to dem en tell dem dis or did dey fly up in de sky and talk to God?" Mammy looked at Malindy with no hope for her rescue from master's wrath. She shook her head and said, "Dere you goes agin, wif all dem questions. You jis' don' understan', gal. My mammy was a slave, her mammy was a slave, en her mammy coulda been an African queen. Now I's a slave, no African, no queen. Dat's what I knows, en I knowed you was a Injun de minute you walk in my kitchen. Now you is a slave, jis' like me. I know you ain't never gwine to make a Big House mammy like me. Yo' blood's too hot. I sees it in yo' eyes ever' day when you look at de missus en de massa. I knows I's free in my Lord's eyes. I knows my Lord ain't a-gwine to hurt me or you neither. De bullwhip is in de han' of de Debbil. You 'member dat en stop de askin', gal, jis' do yo' wuk."

Mammy loved Malindy as a daughter, as she loved all the other young slaves. She could not show her real feelings for them in the Big House, yet they knew her heart. She also understood that Malindy's questions were legitimate. Far better than Malindy, she realized the danger in asking such questions. If the master overheard Malindy's conversation, grave consequences would follow. Malindy would be considered insolent. She would surely be punished in some way. Discreetly, Mammy posed questions to Malindy that provided her with the necessary tools to discover herself and to build the needed courage to get through the day.

Mammy and Malindy continued the same ritual every evening in the master's kitchen while preparing his dinners and his parties. Somehow all of Malindy's intense questions faded into the twilight of indifference. As Malindy daydreamed about freedom, Mammy softened her pain with song in the white man's kitchen:

If you want to bake a hoecake,

To bake it good and done,

Stop it on a nigger's heel,

And hold it to de run.

My mammy baked a hoecake,

As big as Alabama,

She threw it 'gainst

A nigger's stomach

And hold it dere all day.

Mammy's songs always took Malindy's thoughts away from the kitchen to another place. She thought of the slaves in the cabins cooking hoecake and fatback for supper as they sat close to the fireplace to stay warm. She looked out the kitchen window to the slave quarters. It was pitch black outside; a dark mist shadowed the moon. The great fires in the cabin fireplaces lit the cabin windows. She visualized her friends talking and laughing cheerfully around the fire. There was old Pops sitting in the corner smoking a pipe; there were children sitting in a circle fireside.

People were genuine in the cabins. There was good society. There was no master or mistress watching your every move until you slept; there was no pretense. Malindy wanted to run to the people in the cabins and share with them the food she had prepared, as she felt their comfort, kindness, and authenticity. Instead, she stood there next to Mammy, an automaton to serve the master's every need. Malindy felt frozen in space and time as the austere monotony clouded her brain. One of Mammy's questions haunted her, "Gal, what do you know?" Malindy acknowledged that she knew little or nothing. But one thing she knew for sure. Malindy wanted to escape from her predicament, and not wait on ungrateful white folk for free.

At dinnertime, she poured Massa's and Missus's coffee into fine bone china cups. As she moved closer to master, he said, "Yes, indeed, Malindy, you are a dern good cook and servant. You must be about seventeen. You look it. Yes sir, you'll make a wife for some strong young buck." He laughed and looked at the mistress, who also had a scheme in her smile. "I know our gal will bring us some fine little pickaninnies." Malindy stood there, undisturbed, a stoical expression on her face. Having a husband and children had not entered her mind. She only thought of getting away from the master somehow and reuniting with her people.

That night, Malindy lay weary in her bed. She whispered to her roommate, who slept on the trundle next to her bed. "Wake up, I want to talk, I can't sleep. De massa said I's gwine to bring him some fine pickaninnies."

"You's in trouble now," her roommate responded. "Massa gwine to git you a husban' to fill yo' stomach up wid poor little niggers to serve him. He gwine to be comin' after all of us soon." Malindy shivered as she imagined having children born into slavery.

After that evening, Malindy noticed that the master watched her more, and the black men on the farm began to approach her with romantic intentions for courtship. Definitely, she could not imagine anyone on the master's farm to whom she would give the time of day. She had heard that the master routinely bought slaves and assigned them to marriage for breeding purposes. It was known that he was always looking to improve the quality of what he called his "stock."

Mammy knew about the master's plans for the young female servants. She had produced twelve children of her own in the system. She had lost her husbands and children on the auction block. She had experienced the misery of it all. The older slaves knew the story well:

> Some niggers dies, but more is born, 'cause the slave master sees to that. He breeds niggers as quick as he can, 'cause that is money for him. No one had no say who he have for a wife. But the nigger husbands wasn't the only ones that keeps up having children cause the master and drivers takes all the nigger gals they wants. The children is brown, and I seed one clear white one, but they slaves just the same.

In Missouri and the other slave states, the female slaves were used as reproduction machines. If a woman was a good breeder and cooperative in the process, her owner was proud of her. If not, he sold her, or worse. The psychological and physical pressures on the female slave were unimaginable. Now the master wanted to put this load on Malindy. The pressure was escalating for Malindy to marry. Malindy feared that some young man that she didn't fancy would become her spouse. She feared that there would be no love or romance or even the sanctity of a real marriage. If she married a slave, there was always the threat of permanent separation. Malindy dreaded the whole idea. She had no protection alone, and a slave husband had no authority or power to keep her safe. Her security was subject to whims and unpredictable factors controlled by the master based on his needs. If the master sold her mate, he would expect her to get another husband to have more children.

The sword hung over Malindy's head for months. She and her friends spent their free time absorbed in conversation about her prospective fate.

In her Cherokee culture, it was an honor to marry and have children. The family was the core of the Cherokee society, as it was in the African culture. She struggled with the concept that a female's natural duty is to marry and have a family. She asked her friends, "Do you want chillen?" "We bring chillen in the world to be slaves? No! No!" one said.

The women easily comprehended the alternatives to childbearing and were well schooled by the older women. Some women used abortion as a way out. It was said that certain herbs, such as tansy and rue, the roots and seeds of the cotton plant, pennyroyal, cedar berries, camphor, and gum spirits, were useful for that purpose. Some females tried to escape, risking whippings and death.

There were also incidents of infanticide. In 1831, a Missouri slave woman was accused of poisoning and smothering her infant. Tragic cases were reported in other slave states. In one of Missouri's border states, Tennessee, a mother in Nashville who had been sold and separated from three small daughters had gathered them together, slit their throats, and killed herself as she lay next to them.

In Missouri, William Wells Brown, a slave, had two friends who were forced to remarry when the master sold their husbands. Another slave in Missouri refused to have any more children. When her master forced her to marry again, she made sure she married a man whom she knew had a disease and could not become a father.

Malindy heard such sordid stories and saw what happened to the poor children and parents on the farm. As she walked around the farm, she saw the condition of the children as they played merrily in their dirty, ragged clothing. She revisited her separation from Momma Sue, along with the other children who were snatched from their blood mothers and fathers. She prayed for deliverance.

On Sundays, the slave children's parents stood in line at the corncrib and smokehouse to pick up their weekly allowance of food. As the slaves waited for a peck of corn and three pounds of pork or fatback handed out to them by slave helpers and the overseer, some heads were bowed low. Others looked to the sky with pleading eyes to God. Some silently groaned to themselves. Some gave thanks for the fact that they had endured. The food ration was not enough, nor was it very nutritious.

Malindy realized that the same fate threatened her. As she passed the waiting slaves, she made eye contact with them. She cried passionately in her heart, "These poor men can't protect themselves or their families. Tomorrow, every one may be on another farm with a new wife and children. Creator, please hear me and don't let this be my fate. I want to love and respect my husband. I want to protect my children from this terrible world."

She had become reconciled and made peace with herself about the issues of motherhood and marriage. That day, the enslaved parents unknowingly gave her a precious gift. She was able to see their love for their children. Thereafter, her visits in the slave quarters only reinforced her determination that she could deal with her natural duties as a woman and do so on her own terms. Despite the fear of separation, she saw the parents live in the moment as they loved and cared for their children with no parental right of decision-making power for their future. Massa had not killed the love in their hearts or their compassion.

Malindy empathized with the slave children. Slavery had robbed her of much of her own childhood. She recognized that some of the children would survive as she had. Some would dream and fight for freedom in their own way. She reckoned that as long as her dream of freedom stayed alive, there was hope. She told the slave children to dream and to become unconquerable through faith. Malindy's visits to the children in the slave quarters renewed her own spirits and made her happy.

One day, Mammy said jokingly to Malindy, "Do you go to prayer meetin'? Maybe it can git you ready for de husban' Massa gwine to git you, chile."

Malindy laughed, "I ain't a-gwine to be no wench, no Jezebel, or one of dem fancy gals. En fo' sho' not a good, hard-workin' Mammy like you en be all smilin' en good to Missus en Massa all de res' of my life." Malindy did not intend to insult Mammy, for she loved and respected her; Malindy was just being honest. "Mammy, I's gwine to be a wife wid my own husban' and chillen." Mammy did not doubt a word that came from Malindy's mouth. The truth moved through Malindy. Mammy had heard Malindy speak her truth to the mistress and never get punished for it. Her truth had an uncanny power. Mammy understood Malindy's willpower and strength. The mistress saw her as weird and strange. Malindy knew what she wanted in a husband, and somehow she determined to find him.

That evening Malindy's normal emotional turbulence had subsided into a euphoric melody of calm. Her sixth sense told her that a part of her dream was on its way to her. In fact, at that very moment, her future husband was driving his buggy toward the master's farm. Malindy served supper that night happily, with a smirk on her lips. Her non-verbal communication said, "Yes sir, indeed, you will never select or buy a husband for Malindy or sell any children the Creator gives me away from me. Never! Never!"

"How we are astonished . . . when we reflect that to the race of Negroes, at present our slaves and the objects of our extreme contempt, we owe our arts, sciences, and even the use of speech, and we recollect that, in the midst of those nations who call themselves the friends of liberty and humanity, the most barbarous of slaveries is justified and that it is even a problem whether the understanding of Negroes be of the same species with that of white men."

—*Count Constantin de Volney*

Chapter Five

MALINDY MEETS OLD FREE CHARLIE WILSON

O n a summer day in 1837, everyone on the farm was busy preparing for an annual special event. Mammy had told Malindy that in early summer the master and mistress would have a picnic on the farm for their friends and the slaves. Malindy and Mammy had to cook enough food to feed many people. The slaves also provided the entertainment at the picnic with song and dance. This was a great festivity, for which all the slaves got dressed up in their church clothes. Sometimes, some freedmen would pass through looking for work or selling their products, such as herbs. Malindy knew of this and wished that one would come to the party. As long as she had lived in Missouri, she had never seen a black free person.

Missouri law did not recognize marriages between freedmen and slaves. The masters feared that freedmen would put "freedom non-sense" into the slaves' heads. Sometimes, however, masters allowed such a marriage. Slave marriage was not recognized as legal by the state of

On rare occasions the slaves were allowed to mingle with the whites and enjoy good food and music.
Wood engraving, 1849.
From *The Narrative of the Life and Adventures of Henry Bibb, an American Slave*, MHS Library.

⊣ MALINDY'S FREEDOM ⊢

Missouri anyway. Malindy knew all of this. She intended to have a freedman select her for a wife. This could be her ticket to love, freedom, respect, and real happiness with a man of her choice.

Malindy was moving through the picnic area with Mammy, who was bossing every slave around. Malindy laughed at how the slaves always jumped at Mammy's growl. The grinning fiddler was playing his violin with great vigor and skill. The slaves were stomping their feet in time with the music and clapping their hands. Malindy and Mammy were both singing as they prepared the tables for the event. The fiddler and the banjo players lifted Malindy's spirits. She stood at Mammy's side preparing the food as the mistress looked on.

"Now, Malindy, you get one of those fine bucks interested in you," said the mistress. Fearing that Malindy would crack back with a smart remark, Mammy responded quickly: "Yes, ma'm, dey all de time a-comin' in de kitchen tryin' to see dis pooty gal. We gwine to git her a good, hard-workin' buck soon. Don' you worry, ma'm, Malindy gwine to have plenty of fine lil' chillen, jis' you see." Mammy was smiling with her teeth to the mistress, but her eyes signaled to Malindy to keep her mouth shut on this matter. Malindy wanted to give the mistress a piece of her mind, but this time she decided to listen to her dear, protective mentor, her clever and manipulative Mammy.

Beguiled by Mammy, the deluded mistress believed every word she said. Mammy continued to delight her. "Oh, yes, we's gwine to have a hitchin'-up real soon." Malindy rolled her eyes at both of them and gritted her teeth like an angry lioness. The mistress stared at Malindy and said, "Malindy, now you hurry and git that done, or me and Massa will help you."

At this point, Malindy's bronze complexion had turned almost a deep red as her fury surpassed any of her thoughts of survival. Still, she complied with Mammy's command and remained silent. Malindy's will was strong, but she was wise enough to control it. She recognized that Mammy was protecting her as she often protected the young slaves who sometimes forgot the consequences of assertiveness. Opinions were exclusively for white folk, not for slaves. Many times, Mammy used her influence to protect opinionated slaves from unjust punishment. On the other hand, they both realized clearly that in the matter of Massa's breeding needs, Malindy would not be spared. No one could protect a slave from sale or from the master's breeding machine.

Every day, the master talked about his need for more hands for his future expansion. He speculated on his growth potential as he counted his unborn pickaninnies. At the party, he would surely show off all of his little darkies with great pride and a sense of accomplishment, as if he were the creator of each one. This day the master's slaves and beautiful mares would be on display, both with the same status: the master's property.

Malindy fully understood Massa's scheme and promised herself that she would not let him interfere with her joy at the party, even though he looked at her as his pickaninny machine. When she completed her work in the kitchen, she asked Mammy if she needed any herbs from the woods behind the house. Malindy could identify the different herbs in the woods. Often, she picked them for Mammy. However, today she just wanted an excuse to go into the woods. The woods were her retreat, her sanctuary. There she found peace as she offered gratitude and a prayer to the Creator. Fervently, she prayed that the Creator would provide her with the right mate. As she strolled through the woods, she was soothed by the sounds of the birds and the crickets. As she gathered the herbs, she continued to pray to her Creator.

In the woods, Malindy was truly in her element. The radiant sun pierced through the leaves of the black, white, shingle chinquapin, and red oak, as well as the black gum, elm, and white ash trees. All of nature revived her spirit after the ordeal she had experienced earlier in the mistress's kitchen. Her anxiety and rage were replaced by serenity as she collected the herbs: snakeroot, goat's rue, horse gentian, and culver's root. The magnificence of the woods so mesmerized her that she almost forgot the party.

Quickly, Malindy composed herself and ran back to the house. She gave Mammy the herbs. Mammy said, "Gal, you try to fool me wid yo' woods stuff. I knows you do dat Injun stuff out dere, wid all yo' talk about some Creator." Malindy smiled at Mammy tenderly. She appreciated a woman who could read her mind and see her soul. "Git out of my kitchen, go en put on dat pooty dress I made you," Mammy said. Malindy ran to her room, put her long black braids across her head like a crown and put on a dress made from some leftover beautiful blue cloth that the mistress had given to Mammy. Quite excited, Malindy passed the mirror in the foyer of the big house. Her image reminded her of her Cherokee mother. If only she had a beautiful handmade beaded dress and makeup! For a brief moment she felt somewhat sad; yet somehow she knew that this was a special day for her.

An atmosphere of joviality pervaded the picnic. The men were barbecuing, and the women were buzzing with conversation as they set food on the tables for the guests. The sun shone bright; the sky was as clear as the whites of Malindy's eyes, beaming with excitement. All the food looked inviting and delicious. The musicians were tuning their instruments. It seemed that time had stopped for a moment, that slavery was no more.

It was, of course, just an illusion as far as the slaves were concerned. In life, what appears to be real is not always for real. It was a day when their pain was covered with extra layers of deception that everything was just fine on master's farm. The diligent and well-behaved slaves served the master's family and their guests, as usual. The whites sat there with Massa's home-brewed rum and mint juleps as they observed the happy slaves dancing and singing their heads off. The slaves enjoyed the moment as they concealed the fear of the future that lay suspended for a time as they planned to fill their stomachs with as much food as humanly possible. Tomorrow, they would be back to their diets of fatback and hominy.

As Malindy worked, she observed every little thing. She had never experienced anything like this affair before and was not too sure about how to act among so many people. Soon these thoughts drifted away when she saw the guests arriving in wagons. They swarmed to the picnic tables like ants looking for honey. Malindy's job was to place the food on the tables and welcome the guests.

This was not always a pleasant task, for she remembered some of the guests from the mistress's previous parties. These guests had constantly insulted the male slaves, calling them "Sambo" and poking fun at them. On the other hand, there were some guests she liked and could tolerate in her heart despite their ownership of slaves. These guests had always been kind to her and treated the slaves like human beings.

Malindy greeted Massa's minister, who blessed the food with a prayer. He rejoiced, "Thank you, Father, for this food today and our wonderful hosts, and for all these fine darkies who cooked this wonderful food. May they multiply and bring more prosperity to this land." (What he meant was more prosperity for the whites.) As he and the white folk rejoiced, the slaves lamented in their souls. The docile adult slaves and their children looked on pitifully as the guests and the master's family filled their plates with food. One male slave cracked a joke to the musicians, "When dem white folks gwine to let us niggers eat?" They all laughed while some little slave children played and sang a song that ridiculed the white folk:

My old missus promised me,

Before she dies, she would set me free,

Now she's dead and gone to hell,

I hope the devil will burn her well.

Mammy and Malindy heard the children. Mammy said, "Min' yo' manners, chillen, or Massa whup you for sure. Don' let me hear dat song agin."

After an hour, the slaves were allowed to eat the cold leftovers. The white folks were full of food and liquor as they watched the black minstrels. The performers' dances and songs filled the air with glee. One guest told the master, "You got some awfully happy darkies."

Malindy had just fixed her plate and walked over to the table with one of her friends. One of the young male slaves called out to her, "Come heah, Malindy, bring dat food over heah, gal, wid yo' pooty little se'f." Malindy simply smiled at him politely with no interest whatsoever. He was definitely not the man for her.

Something caught her eye. It was a clean, black buggy drawn by a beautiful clean horse with a glossy brown coat. She had seen many whites in buggies like this. This day, however, the driver was a tall man with a light donut complexion and shoulder-length, straight black hair. He appeared to be about twenty years older than Malindy, which would have made him thirty-seven years old. Every ounce of her being was drawn to him as he parked his buggy near the slave quarters. As she looked on in complete awe, she heard a slave say, "Dat's our man, Ol' Free Charlie." This man had great presence and style that Malindy had never seen in a man in Missouri.

Malindy stood there with her plate in her hand. Her mouth was open as she trembled in her shoes. She did not know what was happening. At first, a strange feeling overwhelmed her. But she recovered promptly. There was no doubt. This was it! She just had to meet this Old Free Charlie. As she watched with curiosity the slaves rushing over to greet him, Mammy looked at her and said, "Gal, sit down en shut yo' mouf, hear! You look like you sees a ghost."

"Dat's one good lookin' man, dat Ol' Free Charlie."

"Yes, indeedy. Don' worry about a thing, chile, he be comin' over here real soon. I sees him jis' a-lookin' at you wid dat come yonder look."

Malindy sat with friends. They laughed and joked about the young black men while waiting to be asked for a dance. Malindy reckoned that when the men would pass her table to flirt with her friends, they would introduce Charlie to her.

From the moment they made eye contact, their every move and breath were directed at each other. When the music started, everyone danced merrily. The white guests who had some of the master's brew under their belts forgot themselves for a moment and danced alongside the slaves. Charlie glanced at Malindy as she sat there all polite and proper. Mammy had warned her to be reserved and not too anxious. The older women and men at her table gave her sound advice about courtship.

Finally, Charlie approached her table. He politely greeted the elders first. With a soft, yet strong and gentle voice, he said, "Hello, I am

Charlie Wilson. I hear that you are Malindy. What a pretty name. Miss Malindy, may I have this dance?"

Malindy was startled by the way he expressed himself. No one had addressed her as "Miss" before, and it startled her for a second. Malindy could do only her Cherokee dances. She was embarrassed because she had no idea how to dance like the others.

"I can't dance like dat," she said. Charlie persuaded her to try and said that he would teach her.

"In a few minutes, I'll have you dancing up a storm," he said.

Mammy kept her eyes closely on them. She whispered to one of the women at the table, "Look like my Malindy got her man."

Charlie reached for her hand. It was not a soft hand, but one that had seen more than its share of hard work. It didn't matter to him, for her regal beauty and spirituality reminded him of his own Native American heritage. He told her, "We'll do a very easy step until you feel the pleasure of dancing." As he held her in his arms, a special feeling swept over her. This moment was something to cherish and remember. This was a feeling that she had never experienced in her life, a pure rapturous moment. The heat radiated from both the sun and their two bodies as they danced. That day, the opinion of both Malindy's and Charlie's friends was that "they gwine to be a smitten goin' between these two people."

Malindy noticed that Charlie did not speak like the slaves. His diction sounded more like the master's. The white folk called him Old Free Charlie. He was Irish, Indian, and African, a freedman who had manumission papers that allowed him to move about freely. He made his living as an itinerant vendor of herbal remedies. His Irish father had given him the right to an education and had given him his freedom. He knew about the abolitionist movement and the Underground Railroad. Unknown to the whites, he was a freedom messenger for the enslaved blacks. He wrote and read well; he was articulate and shared with the illiterate slave people information concerning events that could lead to freedom. Every time he met with them, his message was to cultivate courage. He inspired them to seek and know the truth and told them to keep the faith because freedom was on its way.

Malindy sensed both his strong confidence and his rebellious nature. He and she were much alike. Charlie knew she was Native

American. The slaves had told him in great secrecy, for they trusted him with the information and verified Malindy's true identity to him.

Charlie asked her, "What are you doing here on this farm as a slave?" Malindy did not respond, for everyone was watching her, especially master, who acted as if he could read lips sometimes. She dared not chance the truth, for if she did the overseer's paddle or bullwhip would reach her hide.

Speaking under her breath, she said, "Massa watchin' me now; someday I'll tell you my story."

"It's all right, I understand, Malindy. I'm free, but as long as my people are slaves, I have my cross to carry as a black man." In his eyes was a glint of sadness as they walked over to the buggy. It was time for him to leave. Under his supply of herbs was tucked a tightly closed tobacco tin containing his precious manumission papers. He kept his papers hidden, because if he lost them, he could easily lose his freedom. Quickly, he retrieved the tin and showed the papers to Malindy. She was excited, for the Creator had delivered to her a real freedman.

This was a day for Malindy to remember. Old Free Charlie's embrace would remain eternally in her heart. As he headed his buggy toward his next destination, he embraced Malindy warmly with his eyes. He promised her that he would return just to see her again. Malindy kept her eyes on him and savored his every word. The sun's heat had disappeared with the sunset, to be followed by a breezy evening. Malindy's head still felt warm as she thought of Old Free Charlie. She visualized him riding under the protection of the bright moon and glittering stars.

In bed that night, she thought of Charlie's precarious position as a freedman. The master was always afraid that someone would escape through the Underground Railroad. The master and mistress were suspicious of freedom. Over the years, they came to believe that they had no problem with Old Free Charlie. They bought herbs from him. They had no clue that he was also a freedom messenger. They did keep their eyes on him, but he was far too clever for them, and the slaves never betrayed him. Massa and many slaveholders thought that they and their neighbors were targets living over gunpowder. The black slaves whom they depended on to provide their every need were the explosives.

Regardless of his manumission papers, Charlie often was met with fear and hostility from whites. Like all freedmen, he was like a released prisoner on parole. Antagonism from whites constantly threatened his security and disturbed his peace of mind. During this period, one slave state after another insisted on the removal of freedmen from the state. Charlie could easily have been kidnapped and sold back into slavery.

As an herbalist, Charlie was a skilled worker. Most freedmen had a reputation as hard workers. In Missouri, with their own money, freedmen built churches and schools, founded improvement organizations, and fought for the freedom of their enslaved brethren.

On the roads, Charlie got most of his trouble from the poor whites. Most freedmen could read and write. This infuriated the illiterate poor white trash because most of them lacked the motivation to learn to read and write and saw themselves as victims of the slave system. They had to compete for employment with both educated black freedmen and slaves. Unfortunately, they did not comprehend that their real enemy was the slaveholder, not the slave.

White slaveholders rightly feared freedmen, for many freedmen fought fiercely for the deliverance of their people. Frederick Douglass said that some freedmen loaned their manumission papers to runaways to help them escape. The runaways mailed the papers back to the freedmen from a free state. In many cases freedmen risked their own freedom, giving of themselves in acts of kindness. These black women and men were heroes. Like Charlie, they realized that they were only quasi-free in America, under many unfavorable conditions. Yet, they were far better off than their enslaved brethren, who faced the bullwhip each day.

Charlie had to travel often to Illinois, a free state, to get work. Freedmen were not allowed to work with either poor whites or slaves in Missouri. In Missouri, Charlie could only sell his herbs and do his secret work for freedom with the slaves. It was a hard environment in which to survive.

The weeks passed rapidly as Malindy thought mostly of Charlie. In her mind's eye, she could see the sparks in his eyes. She relived the exhilarated feeling she had experienced from being with him. But, at the same time, Malindy became more burdened by the master's cruelty. She saw him withhold food from "rebellious slaves," hang slaves by their thumbs to beat them with the bullwhip, shut slaves up in the "nigger box," castrate, mutilate, and chain slaves for running away.

She got sick of seeing blood and torn skin and the overseer's vicious smile as he whipped the master's slaves. She saw Massa sell loyal and

Slave owners used force to keep slaves subservient.
Wood engraving, 1849.
From *The Narrative of the Life and Adventures of Henry Bibb, an American Slave*, MHS Library.

⊰ MALINDY'S FREEDOM ⊱

obedient slaves whom he had promised never to sell. He broke his promise because money was more important to him than a promise to a slave—integrity did not exist in this jungle of untamed humans. Malindy despised all the evil around her. Loyalty and obedience did not protect a slave from sale or any abuse. Punishment was built into the system of slavery to keep a slave a slave, no matter how attentive or obedient he or she was on the farm. The master always found an excuse to use force.

Like all the slaves, Malindy was dancing to Massa's tune, and it exhausted her every day. Every atrocity she saw depleted her energy. She looked forward to Charlie's return. The thought lifted her out of the pit of depression and gave her hope. And Charlie did return. Every time he came home to Missouri, he rushed to see Malindy.

When Charlie came to the farm, he helped his slave friends with hog killing, sawing firewood, building slave cabins, and shoeing the horses. Charlie joined in to help his friends so as to be close to Malindy. His industry pleased her. She did not want a lazy man around her. She never saw lazy black folk, but she did see far too many lazy white folk. When the master referred to some black slaves as lazy, she thought he was out of his mind. Black folk provided him with his every need. She and Charlie were two of those folk.

Everyone on the farm took a liking to Charlie. Massa saw Charlie as a prospective husband with some earned income that could support Malindy. Missus and Massa paid him for his herbs, but not for the work that he did on the farm. Charlie and Malindy had little time to be together. However, they enjoyed each moment as Charlie told Malindy of his travels. There was no physical intimacy, for she had promised that she would remain chaste until marriage.

After a few months, Charlie decided to ask the master for Malindy's hand. Massa still had no idea that Charlie was a freedom messenger and that he spoke against slavery to the slaves. Massa gladly agreed to let them marry. He ignored the Missouri law that did not recognize marriage between a slave and a freedman. Massa allowed this union from purely selfish motives: to get some slave children from Malindy and support for her from Charlie.

The news that Malindy and Charlie were getting ready to "jump the broom" spread across the farm like wildfire. Much planning preceded the wedding. Malindy was a real prize. Massa knew that his investment would pay off when she produced some babies. Malindy had forgotten all the serious talk months ago with her friends about the pitfalls of motherhood and marriage. She could think of no reason for not getting married now. She understood that she had to marry one day, and now she had the opportunity to share her life with the man whom she loved passionately. She was radiantly happy as her friends embraced her and wished her well. Charlie had to leave for Illinois to work and make money. They promised to marry in the spring of 1838.

As the days drifted by, Malindy had visions of her wedding day and wondered what she was going to wear. Recently, the mistress had taken a liking to her, because she was an excellent cook, and because the mistress felt that an Indian was closer to whites than a Negro slave. Malindy proudly acknowledged her heritage, yet she perceived the blacks as the family that cared for her. At no time did she flatter herself that she was superior because she was a house servant or a Cherokee. She saw herself as a human being—and saw everyone in that light.

Missus was excited as she rushed into the kitchen one day and said, "Don't worry about your dress; I just finished it with a white hat and white flowers and a long veil. This is your gift from me and Massa."

Malindy was surprised and grateful to the mistress for the gift. "Why is she doing this?" Malindy wondered. Malindy thanked the mistress and dismissed all suspicion, accepting the gift at face value. Smiling, the mistress patted Malindy on the cheek. The smile was overcast with a shadow of sadness, for she knew that her motive for giving the gift was not genuine; it was another investment in her property. She was, however, pleased that she had made such a beautiful dress for one of her girls.

"Now, Malindy, put it up and we'll look forward to the day. I am so happy for you. Just imagine, I have the best cook in the county and soon there will be the best herbalist for my medicines right in my slave quarters. Soon, I'll have some more darling little darkies."

Missus talked and talked about her prospective benefits from Malindy's union. Malindy was so thrilled with the dress that she ignored the mistress's remarks.

In her mind, Malindy said, "I played the white man's game and got my wedding dress. Yes sah, Massa, yes ma'am, Missus. Obey, Malindy, and you will survive." Malindy knew that rewards for obedience were only a maybe. Missus and Massa could change on her like a snake changes its skin. She had no trust in them. This was a heavy burden to carry each day.

The great day arrived for Malindy's wedding. It was a beautiful, warm, spring day, in the period of renewal and rebirth. Colorful flowers and plants were in bloom in the garden where the ceremony was held for the handsome couple. A slave preacher or the master usually performed the unofficial ceremony or "hitchin'." All the slaves were there along with the master's family. All eyes were on Malindy, with her long black hair hanging to her waist. This day she risked the exposure of her Cherokee black hair that for years she had worn in braids or a matronly knot.

Malindy felt her mother's spirit and her ancestors around her. Momma Sue was somewhere looking on, for her little Indian girl was about to jump over the broom into another chapter of life. The memories of her Cherokee mother and Momma Sue helped her. Everyone who had touched her life was in her heart that day. An invisible spiritual cord connected her to them forever. This day, she had woven an event that would take her to the next step of her journey. As the rays of the sun surrounded her head like a diamond crown made just for Rose Dawn, she, the Cherokee princess, beamed and glowed.

Malindy and Charlie stood facing each other, love and tenderness in their eyes. Charlie loved this woman and wished to erase some of her loneliness and fear. He wanted to earn enough money to bring her freedom from her master some day. There he stood, a freedman, in front of the master, who owned his wife-to-be. Massa stepped forward with the Holy Bible. After a few words about Adam and Eve and the slaves' commitment to the master to produce and to profit the land, he quoted the marriage vows to them. Massa had implicit, though not legal, authority to pronounce them husband and wife under the eyes of God. Massa used the same authority to separate families when he decided to sell slaves.

Charlie and Malindy kissed each other, joined hands, and jumped over the broom. Everyone shook their hands as they wished them a long and happy marriage. In reality, longevity in a slave marriage was not guaranteed. It all depended on the master. However, on a day like this, the slaves put such matters out of their minds. They rejoiced with the couple. This day master supplied plenty of good food, and Mammy baked a wedding cake. Mammy had never seen such a grand wedding for a slave.

The music, song, and dance faded away in the diminishing sunlight. The couple retired to master's new home for Malindy. Malindy could no longer live in the big house. The master provided her with a slave cabin on the slave lot. Charlie had worked on it. He put a wooden floor down and brought from Illinois utensils, pots, pans, dishes, dry foodstuffs, and cloth. Charlie wished he could give her more some day, a big house like the mistress had. The knowledge that he could never achieve that goal made him feel less than a man. Malindy praised him and was grateful for everything, and Charlie began to feel like more of a husband.

The log cabin had a loft, used to store "put down" foods, dried fruits, and herbs. Charlie made a strong ladder for his wife to use. The cabin also had a bed, fireplace, table, and some chairs Charlie made. He was a good carpenter. Mammy had made her a beautiful blanket from old britches.

Slaves enjoyed the merriment of weddings, pushing aside thoughts of possible separation from loved ones in the future.
WOOD ENGRAVING FROM *HARPER'S WEEKLY*, 1861. MHS LIBRARY.

⊣ MALINDY'S FREEDOM ⊢

As evening approached, Malindy had no fear of Charlie. He was very much a part of her. Mammy had told her what to expect on her wedding night. She trusted her husband completely. That night two spirits ignited into one powerful force. Creation was in the process, for that very night Malindy conceived her first child.

Massa had given Malindy the day off. When she awoke that morning, she decided to fix breakfast for herself and her husband at the fireplace. Charlie was still asleep. With admiring eyes, she looked at her Old Free Charlie and prepared to cook the hoecake, eggs, and bacon he had brought her. It would be the first food she had ever cooked that didn't come from master. She was proud of her husband. But she regretted the fact that he could not live with her on master's farm as a freedman. Soon, he would have to leave her in order to earn a living. Tears filled her eyes as she ran out of the cabin and into her haven, the woods. She was thankful and had to give the Creator a thank you. On this day, her slavery was not uppermost in her mind. Her body felt strange. She sensed that she was already with child. Hurriedly, greatly excited, she ran back to the cabin to feed her husband.

The great age difference between Charlie and Malindy didn't matter to them. They only cared about their love for each other and shared the hope of a future of freedom. As Charlie ate his breakfast, he was somewhat sad. His thoughts dwelled on the last words master had spoken to him privately on his wedding day: "Malindy may be your wife now, but remember she is still my property; your children will belong to me also. Boy, make sure you don't forget that, you know how you educated freedmen try to be uppity sometimes. To me, you're still a nigger. Don't put no foolish notions in Malindy's head about freedom."

Massa had done a good job of putting Charlie in his so-called place. Charlie had no control over the situation. In Massa's eyes the best thing Charlie was good for was to help Massa with the upkeep of Malindy and to provide him with some pickaninnies. To the master, Charlie was to simply a stud for his breeding factory. Charlie vowed to himself not to tell Malindy what master said. He looked across the table at Malindy and said, "My pretty girl, I'll be with you always. Don't worry; never stop dreaming of freedom, for it is coming, believe me."

Now Malindy had the privacy of her own cabin. She and her husband talked about many things. Malindy told Charlie of the great agony caused her by her separation first from her family in the Cherokee Nation and then from Momma Sue. The two separations took a heavy toll on her. Charlie told her more about himself. He was part Native American also. His mother was part Indian and part African. Since his home was in Missouri, he probably was part Osage, Shawnee, or even Cherokee.

From his Indian and African roots, Charlie had learned much about herbs and cures. He had supplies of devil's claw, prickly pears, nettles, jimsonweed, witch hazel, sweet gum, sassafras, flowering dogwood, and many other herbs used for stimulant expectorants, antiseptics, purgatives, and cures for fevers, diabetes, and female complaints. The families of white farmers were happy to see his buggy coming down the road. He had a reputation of being a healer with a buggy full of cure-alls. He taught his customers to use garlic, onions, and leek for croup, pneumonia, and chest colds; goldenrod for colds and toothaches; hawthorn as a tonic for nerves; Indian hemp for rheumatism, dropsy, asthma, and whooping cough; Indian turnip for bowel problems, fevers, and malaria; mint for blood purification for colds; senna and snakeroot for many complaints; and corn for the kidney and bladder.

In the austere, dim cabin, Charlie taught his wife the art of healing and planting herbs. She looked up to him as he read her the Bible. Old Free Charlie was perceived as an extremely mystical person, especially by the black slaves who came from a culture of shamans and medicine men, often referred to by whites as witch doctors. He told his wife, "My enslaved mother told me to help my brethren; she told me I should never feel higher than my poor enslaved brothers and sisters. Malindy, we are different in many ways from the slaves here. They have never known freedom as we have known it. We must remain strong for ourselves and them. Never, never forget your great tribe, your Cherokee folk. I never forget that I am Irish. The white man would like me to forget that and reminds me over and over that I am a nigger and only a nigger."

As Charlie continued to talk with his wife, he remembered the tragic news he had heard about her people. He hated to tell her, but she longed for information about her tribe. He feared the devastating news would tear her apart. Charlie knew from his talks with members of the Cherokee Nation that betrayal by whites and by some of their own had torn the Nation apart. Fighting Indians did not deter the whites; they did whatever it took to take over the rich Cherokee territories. The whites' motto was, "Give me liberty or give me death, but in any case, give me Kentucky." They took Kentucky and Malindy's clan's village—and much more.

In 1838 and 1839, the U.S. government removed the Cherokees from the foothills of the Smoky Mountains to Indian Territory (now Oklahoma) in the West. Of 18,000 Cherokees, 4,000 perished on the Trail of Tears. Charlie finally told Malindy what had happened. She cried and trembled; her thoughts were with her clan, for she imagined that they fought for their land. They might have been killed in the struggle. All of the years she had spent alone with visions of her peaceful Cherokee village had sustained her life. Now, no village remained; her people had been robbed, perhaps enslaved, by the whites' greed for their land. The sad story was not in her imagination. It was real.

By the winter of 1838 Malindy's stomach was big with her baby. She missed her husband, even though when Charlie learned that she was pregnant, he had decided to stay in Missouri as much as possible. There were rumors about how some freedmen had wives in every state. This was true in some cases. Malindy trusted Charlie and did not worry about the rumors. She believed in her husband. He had made their cabin very comfortable for her, and she appreciated it. When he came home, he always brought her things for the cabin, and he made all the needed repairs. She felt fortunate as she looked around the slave quarters. She shared food with those who had far less than her household.

Now, Malindy had no home to return to among her own people. She had no idea where her folk were. Were they hiding in the hills of Kentucky or Tennessee with Uktena, who would protect them from harm? Her mind roamed over all possible scenarios. The situation numbed her for days, during which she ceased to feel the movements of her unborn child.

The impact on Malindy of her slavery, all the bad news about the Cherokee Nation, and her solitary cabin was intense. Often when Charlie was away on his trips, she became depressed and strove to hold on. After her hard day's work at the Big House, she could barely drag herself to her cabin. Before Malindy went to bed, she would sit in front of the fireplace, peering into the fire. She remembered the elders of her tribe by the big fires in Kentucky. The warmth she felt from the fire was like an embrace from all of her ancestors. A voice came to her through the flames, "One day, you'll be free. Don't worry, Rose Dawn, we are free." Malindy saw the shadows surround her as she drifted into sleep. In her dreams, she was free and released from the shackles on her soul.

Malindy was moving closer to childbirth. Day to day, she felt the baby's kick. She thought of her Charlie and hoped he would return before the baby was born. He promised her he would be there. However, on the treacherous roads, anything could happen to a freedman that could prevent his return. Mammy watched over her and warned her to be careful. Mammy was aging, and Malindy had to do all the heavy work in the kitchen. Soon, she would be fully in charge of the kitchen because Mammy was going to join the other elders to care for the slave children in the nursery.

One day, the master said to Malindy, "Where's Old Free Charlie? Haven't seen him around. Don't matter, he's all right with me. He got your belly big quick, yes sir, he did. Soon, I'll have me a new little nigger."

Malindy cringed and initially wished master the worst. Then, however, she focused on what Charlie had taught her about forgiveness. Charlie was a real Christian who believed strongly in the Bible and forgiveness. Malindy lived in the beliefs of the Cherokees. She loved all people. However, if someone was destructive to her, in her mind that person needed to be destroyed immediately. Charlie worked with her, but for a long time she refused to accept the religion of the evil white man who tore her life to pieces every day.

That day, Old Free Charlie was crossing the border from Illinois to Missouri, headed home. It was not a pleasant experience for him. Volunteer patrol groups of Missouri citizens on horseback were out on the roads looking for runaway slaves. On the road, he often had to act like a very humble and dumb Negro in order to persuade the patrols to let him pass. Somehow, he found a way to avoid a confrontation with the vigilantes by focusing his thoughts on Malindy as he drove his buggy homeward. "I'm coming, Malindy, your Charlie is coming," he would say over and over in his mind. Often on the lonely roads he talked to his horse about Malindy.

That night as Malindy lay in bed praying for Charlie's safety, she heard footsteps on the cabin porch. Then a knock. "Malindy, it's me," said Charlie. Malindy moved slowly toward the door. Charlie had sawn a heavy board for her to put across the door and lock herself in. She opened the door and saw Charlie there with two sacks of goodies for her.

"Girl, look at you. I have only been gone for two months, and look at your stomach. That boy will be jumping out soon." Malindy smiled as her husband took her into his arms.

"Now, Mr. Charlie, how do you know I got a boy? Only de Creator knows dat," said Malindy.

Jokingly, Charlie responded, "I am the great doctor of Missouri; ask Massa, yes indeed, we got us a boy."

Malindy couldn't wait for the news as she poured Charlie some hot coffee.

"Charlie, I jis' knowed you was a-comin'. I could hear you chatter to yo' hoss. It was like you was right here. I says to myself, 'I better keep dis hot coffee on, for my Charlie gwine to be here tonight.' Charlie looked at his mystical wife with all her talk about visions. He believed every word, yet he laughed because she was so intense about it. As he laughed, Malindy frowned.

"What's wrong?" he asked. "Malindy, what is it?"

Malindy did not say a word; she simply pointed to the floor. Her water had broken.

"Baby comin', Charlie. Go and git Mammy quick," she responded.

Charlie ran to the big house. Mammy was in the kitchen talking with the mistress. "Mammy, Malindy needs you. The baby is coming."

Mammy got some cloths from the mistress, called one of the midwives from the slave quarters, and went to Malindy's side. Malindy was prepared for this great event. She had collected some "daiga nige unaste tsi," yellow root used by her tribe in childbirth. She told Mammy to blow the powdered yellow root onto the top of her head, her breast, and the palm of each hand. Mammy understood clearly and did what she was told. This was the Cherokee way.

Malindy was propped up in a sitting position, and she drank a mixture of the powdered yellow root and water and repeated words in Cherokee to help the baby jump down. Charlie marveled at how she remembered what to say and do.

"Malindy, stop that talk. The missus may come," Mammy said. Malindy paid no attention. She was in a trance, joined with her ancestors, as she repeated the words over and over. The ancestors stood vigilantly, as a new member of the clan was about to enter the world.

Charlie refused to leave his wife's side as their child traveled through the birth canal into the world. The baby boy jumped down just crying. Malindy was handed her firstborn by Mammy. Malindy and Charlie looked at each other happily.

Then the mistress walked through the door, a big smile on her face, to see the baby. She picked the boy up from Malindy's arms and looked at the parents. "He sure looks like you both. A real fine little buck."

Malindy and Charlie both gave her a cold look. Nevertheless, the reality was that their firstborn was the master's property. The mistress said nothing about his ownership. She didn't have to; the look she gave the baby said it all. Charlie took his son back and put him into his mother's arms. He looked at the mistress firmly and said, "Yes, indeed, we do have ourselves a fine son. We name him Sammie."

For the rest of that night, Charlie watched over his child and wife attentively. Now, his ambition became stronger to get money to free his family. That night he had many thoughts of hate for whites and prayed for forgiveness. Where could he take his family? Maybe he could go west to where Malindy's folk might be in Oklahoma. It was hard to think about. The important thing was that he and Malindy had a new child in their family.

Malindy's people also had growth on the way. The Cherokee tribe became whole again. On July 12, 1839, the Eastern and Western Cherokees formally merged as one body politic, the Cherokee Nation. The Nation was established in the northeast corner of the Indian Territory. In September 1839, the Nation adopted a written constitution.

True to Cherokee tradition, members of the tribe who had betrayed them in the past were assassinated. Like her clan, Malindy deeply desired revenge. She prayed each day to overcome her desire. Charlie understood his wife's bitterness; he carried a similar cross. He went over in his mind all the obstacles he must overcome to release his family from bondage. He realized that money was not the answer because master could still refuse to accept Charlie's offer to pay to free them. He vowed to implant in his son a sense of self-worth and courage to survive the harshness of slavery.

Malindy looked at her husband's worried face and said, "Charlie, take Sammie en pass him over de fire four times; in seven days, take him to de creek en offer him to de Creator. Then we pray for freedom. Don' worry too much. The Creator done give us a wonderful gif'." She worked hard to console her husband as she said, "My Charlie, go to sleep. In sleep, we's free."

Go Down, Moses

When Israel wept in Egypt land, let my people go,
Oppressed so hard they could not stand, let my people go.

Way down in Egypt land
Tell ol' Pharaoh, let my people go.

O, let us all from bondage flee, let my people go;
And let us all in Christ be free, let my people go.

Way down in Egypt land,
Tell ol' Pharaoh, let my people go.

———◆———

Steal away to Jesus

Steal away, steal away, steal away to Jesus!
Steal away, steal away home, I hain't got long to stay here.
My Lord, He calls me; He calls me by the thunder;
The Trumpet sounds within my soul:
I hain't got long to stay here.
Steal away, steal away, steal away to Jesus!
Steal away, steal away home,
I hain't got long to stay here.

Chapter Six

PRAYER MEETINGS AT THE GRAPE ARBOR

Malindy and Charlie stood strong together. They still lived in Gray Summit, Franklin County, Missouri. Charlie worked hard to bring comforts to his family. They felt his love and care. Malindy's master was pleased with her. She and Charlie had another son together, another "buck" to work in the master's fields. They named him George. Malindy labored day and night in Missus's kitchen. She did her tasks well and loved and cared for her sons.

Often, Malindy thought of the wind, and how wonderful it would be to move about so freely. She looked at her sons lovingly and said, "One day, you gwine to be jis' like de wind dat moves North, South, West, and East. It go where it want to go. It's strong en powerful. It's free. My sons, you's a-gwine to be free like de wind some day. You be like Poppa; travel en see things en learn."

As Malindy whispered encouragement to her sons, the North and South were becoming more divided over the issue of slavery, and

Missouri was becoming more of a police state. Many Northerners believed that the slaveholders, the "slave power," threatened to engulf all the states and destroy democracy. The Southerners sought to use the federal government to protect and promote their interests. The slaveholders moved to suppress the democratic rights of free speech, free assembly, free press, and free elections. Some white folks believed that the slave power in America would eventually reduce even free whites, especially poor white laborers, to slavery.

While Missouri proudly wore the banner of slave power, Malindy and Charlie took refuge in each other. In the privacy of their cabin, they energized each other with love, prayer, and shared hopes. The life of the spirit was their main tool for survival. They were spiritual warriors who fought to preserve their identities and sense of self-worth. They did not drown themselves in self-pity. Rather, through herb ceremonies, prayer, forgiveness, and forbearance, they cleansed the core of their lives from the taint of slavery.

Charlie was a man who knew his purpose in life. He wanted to ransom his family from slavery. But as the nation's political division over slavery progressed toward its violent conclusion, it became increasingly difficult for him to acquire the thousands of dollars needed to purchase their freedom. At least he could bring books back to the cabin and teach his wife and children how to read, especially the Bible.

On the road, Charlie remained committed to his freedom work. Malindy saw the passion in his eyes when he talked about it. She never doubted that her husband was engaged in a sacred task. She feared for his safety if caught, but he had the gift of a seer. He could sense danger ahead of time, and this helped to protect him as he moved about in the circle of his enslaved folk.

Malindy never succumbed to her fears for Charlie. She shared his vision and mission and prayed for him when he was away from home. She was convinced that Charlie's compassion for his people would shield him from the enemy. A recurring image came into her mind: "Charlie, you are like the tree. Your roots are firm in the earth, as you look to the sky. You are my tree and my strength."

Most of the slave children spent the day in the slave nursery, but Malindy kept her sons in the kitchen with her. This was a favor the master allowed her. She constantly feared that because of all the uproar, her sons would be torn from her side. She moved about her daily work cautiously, a prayer often on her lips. By now, Malindy had learned to pray the way Charlie taught her. She said the Lord's Prayer.

Massa grumbled to Malindy. "Those free niggers have the support of a bunch of nigger-loving white folk from the North and right here in Missouri. We need to hang those traitors by their toes. When Charlie comes back, you remind him you belong to me. He better watch his step on my farm."

It was an awful time. The master and his neighbors were almost crazy with fear. Across the county, it was a common practice for slave-holders to train the slave children to spy on their parents. With buttered biscuits and sweet cakes, the mistresses induced black children to inform on parents who were suspected of sabotage, plots to escape, or insurrection. Recruiting children to spy on their parents was a device to substitute loyalty to the master for loyalty within the black slave family. Rumor had it that some masters even put parrots in the cookhouses and fields to act as spies.

While Charlie was on the road, Malindy needed someone to talk to. She longed for Mammy's comfort. She rushed to the slave nursery to see Mammy and relieve her pent-up feelings.

"Jis' look at me. I's tired en ol' already. Massa, he never let up. Now, he done put poison in our chillen's heads, to be agin us. I's gwine to die b'fo' I let him do dat to my sons." Tears poured from Malindy's eyes as her rage tumbled out in words.

Mammy was weary. She knew that Malindy had the potential to kill both the master and the mistress. Malindy's heart had never become as good, obedient, and tolerant as Mammy's.

"Don' you worry yo' pooty li'l head 'bout our youngins," Mammy reassured her. "White folks is scared of dey own shadows now. All dey sins is catchin' up wid' 'em. Dey knows freedom is jis' 'roun' de corner for us. No more Mammy, Uncle, Auntie, buck, en nigger to take care of dey sorry, lazy behinds." Finally, Mammy calmed Malindy down. Laughing heartily, Mammy said, "Sweetie, kin you jis' see de ol' Massa wid a plow en a bucket of water? Missus in de kitchen wid de big black pots? If her han's look like mine, she'd jis' die! Ha! Ha! Yes, sir, justice is a-comin' 'roun', en de debbil knows it. Our chillen ain't a-gwine to tell dem white folk nothin'. Dey too scared o' me! Dey knows I git 'em good."

All the children respected Mammy's might. Malindy understood exactly what she meant. Mammy's wrath was like the devil coming out of the pit of Hell. Malindy laughed herself, and the sadness was swept from her face as she looked into her dear old friend's loving eyes.

"Whah's Ol' Free Charlie?" Mammy asked. "He's a-gwine to blow Massa right outten his britches if he mess wid you or yo' chillen. Don' you worry 'bout all dat freedom work. Charlie, he smart like a fox. He be'n talkin' to us 'bout freedom for years. Massa never git wind of it. Ol' Free Charlie outwit de white folks all de time. We jis' loves dat man of yours fo' his work at de grape arbor. God's wid him, chile; jis' look, he's still alive en free."

"Mammy, I don' worry none 'bout his work," Malindy said. "I knows one day he may grab Massa. I jis' worries 'bout dat when he's here." This was always Malindy's greatest fear, for she knew that if Charlie so much as touched Massa, Massa would surely kill him and the law would do nothing.

Mammy continued to praise Charlie. "Yes, Lord, yo' Charlie got a heart of gold en de stren'th of a bull. Ol' Free Charlie, he gwine to be fine. Now you go wid yo' chillen en cook dem fine white folks' dinner." There was a tone of sarcasm in her voice. "De poison is on its way to dem. Jedgment Day's a-comin'," Mammy said. Malindy's spirit was rekindled as Mammy held her in her comforting arms.

Charlie knew all there was to know about the grape arbor. He told Malindy the story. Early in the 1800s, Ballwin, Missouri, was surrounded by a wilderness. There was a meeting place in the town square with a large grape arbor to the side. A farmers' market was held in the square. Slave traders from Jefferson City and St. Louis stopped to do business there. The market was an all-day affair. To stay cool, the slaves gathered in the shade of the grape arbor. Here they prayed to God for help, because they knew that at any moment they could be sold or traded away from their loved ones.

A feeling of fellowship grew among the slaves as they took part in these market-day prayers. Few slaves had Bibles. Most could not read or write. But freedmen like Charlie and even some whites helped slaves learn to read. Those who learned to read kept it a secret from their masters. Courageously, these slaves started a weekly prayer meeting that met secretly by night under the grape arbor. This was a bold step, because the masters had vigilantes riding at night to keep watch on the slaves and prevent them from traveling without permission.

When the vigilantes reported to the slave owners that the slaves were meeting at night in the grape arbor by the town square, a great uproar arose. Some of the masters trusted their slaves to go to the meetings on Wednesday nights to pray, but many forbade their slaves to attend the meetings. Many slaves disregarded their masters' orders and sneaked to the meetings, and the vigilantes were authorized to whip the slaves to death or to hang them for disobedience.

The threats did not deter the slaves from coming to the meetings. They enjoyed the fellowship and prayer. They learned to protect themselves from the vigilantes, becoming more courageous and fighting back. They set up barbed wire around the trees where the vigilantes had to enter the arbor. They prayed and sang Christian hymns and black spirituals. The news about the meetings quickly spread to slaves all over the countryside. More slaves came secretly to the meetings—more trouble lay ahead.

One of the slaves who served as a deacon at the meetings was a big, burly fellow. His master had told him: "The next time that you are caught at the grape arbor meeting, you will pay dearly. I have given an order that you be beaten to death. One way or another, you niggers will be stopped."

Despite the threat, the deacon continued to go to the meetings, in faith that God would protect him. One Hell's night, a vigilante surprised the group in the meeting and rode into the prayer ground on his horse. The vigilante trapped the deacon as he tried to get away and attacked him. The vigilante whipped the deacon to the ground, where he was trampled by the vigilante's horse. As the vigilante fiercely lashed the slave with his bullwhip, the slave's survival instinct overcame his fear. Refusing to yield up his life to the white vigilante, he grabbed the whip and snatched the vigilante from his horse. Wrapping the whip around the vigilante's neck, the slave garroted him.

This incident began a terrible time for all the members of the faith. All the slaves were questioned and threatened for a long time. No one admitted to knowing anything. The slaves stood together, protecting their fellow slave. This was a true test of their fellowship. They were adamant in their loyalty to one another.

The vigilante's horse was found several days later, still saddled, grazing in a field. The body of the vigilante was never found. It was said that he had a wife and family, with a sweetheart on the side. The rumor was that he had run off with his mistress. Of course, it seemed strange that he would leave his saddled horse behind. Then, everything was hushed up. The masters didn't want the slaves to know of the vigilante's supposed indiscretions. The vigilante was a highly respected individual in the community. It was an honor to kill disobedient "niggers," but to have a mistress was dishonorable.

Some whites showed kindness, good deeds that weighed against the general injustice. One day in 1832, Judge Higgins, the town judge, was passing through the town square. He was startled to hear a thirteen-year-old slave girl praying to God for a place where the slaves could worship without fear of being killed by the slaveholders. The judge was so touched by what he heard that he went into his office and issued an order that all the slaves had the right to construct a building to worship in on the town square grounds.

Of course, his order infuriated the masters and the vigilantes. They disliked the idea that white men did not have the right to stop "niggers," their own property, from praying on the square. They watched resentfully as the slaves built a log cabin and organized a church. The slaves still had no peace. The vigilantes caught some church members outside the town square grounds and beat them by order of some masters. A sign was posted on the property, reading Niggers Beware of Death by Hanging. The slaves continued to pray, organize, and sing. They worked to grow in faith and serve their Lord.

Ruthless white mobs destroyed two log cabin churches by fire, but the slaves refused to give up. One deacon was hanged by a mob and left hanging for three days before the church members were allowed to cut him down. They buried him as they sang,

> O, I couldn't hear nobody pray,
>
> O, Lord, I couldn't hear nobody pray,
>
> O, way down yonder by myself,
>
> And I couldn't hear nobody pray,
>
> On ma knees, wid ma burden,
>
> I couldn't hear nobody pray.

By 1837, the grape arbor fellowship had raised enough money to buy the lots on which their church stood. The courageous church

First Baptist Church in Ballwin. This building was erected soon after the Civil War
and remained in use until a new building was erected in 1961.
PHOTO COURTESY OF THE AUTHORS.

Parishioners at the 121st anniversary of First Baptist Church in Ballwin.
PHOTO COURTESY OF THE AUTHORS.

trustees, Perry Champion and Roy Anderson, were denied the right to purchase the lots for their estimated value of $37.50. In 1852, with the support of their white friends Frederick and Mary Shelp, the deacons legally purchased two lots for the sum of $52.00. The fellowship built a new church, one that could seat a hundred people. These brave people carried the torch for freedom and created the future. Their church fellowship still exists today as the First Missionary Baptist Church of Ballwin.

The slave masters underestimated the slaves when they introduced them to Christianity. The African culture of fellowship along with the slaves' belief in a savior, Jesus Christ, and the fact they had their own church, provided the slaves with a refuge. In fellowship and prayer, they could revive their spirits and cleanse away the daily suffering and defilement of slavery, if only for a moment. In church, they ceased to be victims. Ironically, the depravity of the slaves' masters impelled the slaves to open their hearts to the masters' religion, allowing them to achieve self-respect.

Slaves became creators of their own destiny as they prayed, and at times they plotted insurrection and escape to freedom. They were determined to have their own sites for worship that included aspects of African culture and excluded the slaveholders' cant and propaganda. The slaves sang a hymn reflecting how they felt about the hypocrisy of the whites' church:

Ole Satan thought he had a mighty arm.

He missed my soul and caught my sins.

Cry amen, cry amen, cry amen to God.

He took my sins upon his back,

Went muttering and grumbling down to Hell.

Cry amen, cry amen, cry amen to God.

Ole Satan's church is here below.

Up to God's free church I hope to go.

Cry amen, cry amen, cry amen to God.

Occasionally, abolitionists came to speak in the churches. As the abolitionists continued to beat the drum for freedom in Missouri, the slaves were torn between hope and fear. Malindy loved her children, yet she resented the fact that each time she gave birth she provided another slave for the master and consigned another human being to a life of fear. When these negative thoughts crept into her mind, Malindy remembered her mother. As a Cherokee child living at home, Malindy had learned harmony, sharing, cooperation, and reverence for all life. She vowed to her ancestors that she would instill those qualities in her children. She told her sons always to be brave and to respect all life.

At this point Malindy had four children, with another on the way. Sammie, her firstborn, was old enough to start helping in the Big House. George was still too young to be of any real use. Ellen, Malindy's first girl, was born in 1844. Lara, her second daughter, was born a year later.

Sammie was the big brother. He worked hard. Malindy often watched him struggle to carry buckets of water or logs for Massa's fire up to the house, while George tagged along behind him. Malindy kept Ellen and the baby, Lara, in the kitchen with her. George, who often managed to get into trouble, was sent to help Mammy in the slave nursery.

It disturbed the mistress to see Ellen and Lara in the kitchen. She said to Massa, "Who does Malindy think she is, with those children in my kitchen? I have tolerated her nonsense far too long. She has to keep those pickaninnies in the nursery. Where is that husband of hers?"

Massa responded, "Don't you go bothering Malindy about Old Free Charlie. That nigger is all right with me. He got Malindy four babies and he provides for them. He saves me money and makes me money. Got me two fine bucks and two beautiful gals. Yes, Charlie is my kind of nigger."

The mistress did not have her way this time, so she grew more resentful of Malindy by the day. Malindy felt the tension from the mistress and said only what was necessary to her. Years ago, she had been warned that the mistress was like a poisonous snake and could never be trusted by the slaves.

The seasons passed quickly as the children grew older. When Charlie was away on the road, Malindy was often sad and missed her husband. Charlie continued to bring home food, clothing, and other items for his family. When Charlie opened the cabin door, the cloud of despair would vanish, to be replaced by excitement and a girlish blush on Malindy's face.

Malindy and Charlie were exceptionally good parents. They both had an affinity for the woods, and they took the children there to play and learn about the wild plants. They spent time observing the wonders of creation. These were happy moments, as the family's spirits became one with the trees and wildlife. To Malindy, this was the essence of

Slave families could grow crops, raise chickens, and hunt to supplement their meager food rations.
WOOD ENGRAVING BY W. L. SHEPPARD FROM *HARPER'S WEEKLY*, 1870. MHS LIBRARY.

being truly civilized and human. In the Big House, in her opinion, she saw neither humanity nor civility.

Malindy and Charlie did not whip their children for disobedient behavior, as some other slaves did. The children saw enough beatings and cruelty directed at the slaves by Massa. As parents, Malindy and Charlie always treated their children with dignity and respect. Other methods of correction were used that were not cruel; the children might have to do more work, especially work that they did not like.

Charlie did not want Malindy to stand in line on Sundays at the corncrib and smokehouse for the slave rations, a peck of corn and a few pounds of fatback. Sometimes the pork had maggots in it. So Charlie provided the basics. The family thrived on the bounty of Malindy's garden and leftovers from the cookhouse. Ellen worked with her mother in the garden, planting cabbage, collards, turnips, mustard, and kale. The boys learned to trap squirrels and other animals, and they raised a few chickens. Charlie taught the children how to fish.

Malindy and Charlie were happy that the children were healthy and clean. They delighted in seeing them play games. The children played happily at marbles, hide and seek, hide the switch, stickball, and jump rope.

Malindy held on to her Cherokee values and passed them to her children. She and Charlie told the children stories of their ancestors. Ellen was always intrigued by the stories and wanted more. Her eyes beamed with excitement as her mother taught her to cook and can fruits and vegetables. The children were taught self-control, discipline, forbearance, respect, and honor.

Malindy and Charlie cherished no illusions about the whites ever freeing the blacks. Malindy realized that Massa and his neighbors wanted slavery to last forever. She hated her situation and missed her tribe, yet she accepted the fact that her difficult life was due to her own disobedience to her clan. She understood that order underlies the universe and that behavior has consequences. Malindy also believed that, in due course, her circumstances would change. One could always depend on change. While waiting for that time, Malindy eased her mental suffering by concentrating on her children's well-being. She rose to the challenge to live, outwitting the master who tried to crush her spirit. She suppressed her rage, but it never disappeared.

Charlie told Malindy that some men, black and white, proposed to solve the problem of slavery by shipping slaves to Africa, from where

*No matter how tired they were, at the end of the day slave
women were able to spend time with their own families.*
HALFTONE OF A PAINTING BY BERTHA ROCKWELL, 1906.
FROM *OLE ANN AND OTHER STORIES*, MHS LIBRARY.

some of their ancestors had come. The repatriation solution frightened the slaves. Most of them did not view going to Africa as a beneficial alternative. They feared the unknown. It was worse than being sold south. For Malindy, the prospect of being sent to Africa, a continent she had never seen, meant not freedom, but exile. America was Malindy's country, not Africa. Charlie felt the same way. He thought that the racist society he and his children were born into might not accept them for centuries to come. But for him, too, this was his country, and he was not leaving.

As the years passed, Malindy continued to miss the comfort and companionship of her husband. Sammie and George, eleven and ten years old, each carried a man's load in the fields as well as working in the Big House. During the day, Lara went to the nursery with Mammy. Ellen and her new brother, Henry, stayed in the kitchen with Malindy. Trying to please the mistress in all the work she expected Malindy to do, day and night, left Malindy little time to care for her own family's needs. This took a toll on her; she was tired all the time. She and her five children were worn out at the end of the day. As she tugged them along to Massa's cabin, her home, she prayed for God's mercy. In the evenings she managed to play with her children and do some of her own work. In every way she could, she showed her children that they were worthy and special.

Mammy was still on the farm. Malindy could safely relieve her anger in Mammy's sympathetic ear.

"One day, when I goes up to dat kitchen, de Missus a-gwine to git her due," Malindy told Mammy. "I knows how to git de cougars. Dey ain't a-gwine to have no more breff to order me en' my chillen aroun'." With each word, resentment and contempt ignited in Malindy's brain. During these rash moments, Charlie's voice came to her in a faint whisper, "Malindy, I love you. God loves you. Hold on, Malindy, hold on. You will be free." Malindy was always calmed by her visions of her husband.

Charlie worried about Malindy's high-strung nature. He did not want to lose her and all his children. If she gave in to her anger, she might win a battle, but her family would be broken up in retaliation. Often, he wished that Malindy and George had the demeanor of Sammie, calm and obedient.

George was manic. He was aggressive and did not understand the concept of "stay in your place, boy." He played with Massa's sons and always won the games. He refused to let them win because they felt entitled to win. George was a fierce competitor, and in his encounters with the young white masters he often forgot that he was a slave. George looked just like Malindy and had her spirit, fiery to the core.

Charlie was brave, but he had learned to use diplomacy rather than direct assault to outmaneuver white people. Charlie tried to teach both of his sons to learn when to take action and when to refrain. "George has the Cherokee blood strong, like some of those Indians out west who are still fighting the white man. I reckon our George will not take much off of Massa," Charlie said to Malindy. Ellen adored her big brothers, Sammie and George. She loved George's brave spirit.

Ellen was her mother's helper and her father's little angel. She looked after the two youngest children. Instinctively, from the time she was five years old, she was motherly and protective. Like George, she was also extremely sensitive and had many questions. But it seemed that George always asked the questions that were in her head.

"Poppa, you's free, why ain't we free like you?" George asked. "Please take me wid you de next time." This question saddened Charlie. He was free, but not free enough to put his family in his buggy and drive them around the countryside. Charlie looked at his son and said, "You will be free, George, just be obedient and help Momma. Don't get into any trouble with anyone. Massa will kill you in a minute. You and Sammie have to protect the family when I'm away." Deep in his soul, Charlie realized that George was going to go his own way, and that his only protection from death at Massa's hand was the hand of God.

Malindy and her family lived on Massa's farm for some fifteen years, fifteen long years of invisibility to the white folks in the Big House. She worked her hands to the bone to keep whites in comfort. She got no rewards to speak of for all her work. In the Big House, no one cared whether she was happy. No one opened the door for her or even noticed that she was a human being with feelings and emotions. She was an entity who served them, that was all. She was a strong woman, performing multitudinous tasks for no pay but a sorrowing heart.

Malindy vowed that one day the truth about that gloomy place would be told to her descendants. Every day, she told Ellen her memories and feelings about her perilous journey. Malindy felt that Ellen would be the one to tell her story—the story of her loss and gain, how she had lost her own Cherokee people, her family, and her freedom and how she had joined in love with her husband and his people to build a family and win freedom someday.

As time passed, Malindy continued to be solaced by her thoughts of Charlie. His steadiness and kindness balanced her warrior nature and kept her alive. Otherwise the tyrants who owned her could have killed her easily, either when she lost her temper or as she became older and worn out. She was not a quitter, but she was tired. The slaveholder carried the whip of subjugation. He held the power of life and death over her body. But he did not own her soul. Malindy refused to become a shell with no will.

Regardless of the demands on her family, Malindy still managed to tune her spirit to connect with the Creator. Self-discipline, patience, and love took her across treacherous valleys. Like Charlie, she was a seer. She had a peculiar gift of knowing things without a shadow of doubt. Malindy turned her oppressors over to God. She refused to let injustice consume her. In spite of her enslaved condition, she resuscitated herself and endured. Her well of strength was as deep as the rivers.

The Whip

"The lash is ten feet long, made of small strips of buckskin, tanned so as to be dry and hard, and plaited carefully and closely together, of a thickness, in the largest part of a man's little finger. At the farthest end of this thong is attached a cracker, nine inches in length, made of strong sewing silk, twisted and knotted, until it feels as firm as hardest twine. Once felt on the bare flesh, the burning sting of the whip could never be forgotten."

—James Ball, a slave in South Carolina

Chapter Seven

SLAVE MOTHERHOOD:
MALINDY FEELS THE LASH

E ven though their circumstances became more difficult in the early 1850s, Malindy and Charlie constantly defied the white man's concept of them. Courageously, they created a bond and a sense of family for their children that transcended their lives as slaves. As the slaveholders' attitudes became more rigid, Malindy and Charlie became stronger.

During all this time, slavery still thrived in Missouri. The slavocracy looked forward to continued prosperity from the labor of the slaves. Slaveholders continued to see slavery as an economic necessity, effective resource management, a moral right, and their lawful entitlement. Malindy's master and other slaveholders across Missouri regarded their slaves as their most valuable livestock. Masters wanted to keep slaves in healthy working and breeding condition, but, at the same time, they controlled their slaves by brutality. Malindy's master called her an "Injun" but treated her as a black slave.

Most slaveholders did not allow their slaves to read or write. In 1847, the Missouri General Assembly had prohibited teaching slaves to read and write, in order to prevent them from reading abolitionist tracts that might incite insurrection. Slaves were also forbidden to assemble at religious services where the preacher was black, unless some officer of the court was there as an observer. Unlawful assembly and seditious speeches were forbidden. Possession of a weapon was punishable by thirty-nine lashes. Freedmen and freedwomen were forbidden to immigrate to Missouri.

Charlie's work with the grape arbor religious fellowship became more perilous. Defying danger, the brotherhood of brave freedmen and slaves grew in learning and lived in faith, while Missouri's white churches continued to support slavery. For Charlie, the danger of travel around Missouri and into Illinois increased as the slaveholders felt their position threatened. The border and roads were full of vigilantes carrying rope and driving carts with coffins in them. Thus the vigilantes advertised their goal, to hang and bury "niggers" or "nigger lovers" (abolitionists). However, the coffins were intended primarily as intimidation. Vigilantes did not waste coffins on lynched blacks. Charlie kept his eyes and ears open as he swam through the white-capped ocean of danger and oppression.

Malindy feared Massa's desire to fatten his pocketbook. She knew that her family had monetary value. The master could have sold her and her children for close to four thousand dollars. He also could have chosen to hire out his slaves to another master at a substantial fee—but still far less than the wages paid to white laborers.

Malindy became more apprehensive every day. Sammie and George were prime targets for sale or hire. George was already viewed as an unruly troublemaker. So-called "bad" or "trouble-making niggers" were the first to be sold south to the Dixie Belt. Malindy tried to warn George: "George, you do like Massa say. We don' want no trouble. He gwine to put you right on a steamboat down yonder, far away from us. Trust me, son, we gwine to be free some day."

"When's dat day a-comin? Don' seem like it's on its way none. You see Massa crack his whip 'cross de back of de folk 'roun' here. He ever touch me, I's gwine to kill dat redneck for sh'o. You'll see." George's eyes flamed rage.

Malindy knew that her son meant every word he said. How could she reason with him when, in his short life, he had already witnessed so much suffering, and when he himself was a captive? George had never been allowed to go even two miles away from Massa's farm. Seeing his friends hired out and sold by Massa added fuel to George's rage.

George found it difficult to comply with his mother's wishes. Unbeknownst to her, he ventured out to the road from the farm. He challenged Massa's rule, saying to himself, "Today, I'm going to see what's out there." As George was reassuring himself that everything would be just fine, the overseer rode up right behind him, drawing out his whip to give him a lesson. George heard the horse. He turned around quickly, saying, "I uz jis' lookin' fo' my Poppa. He s'posed to be here today."

"You git on back to your cabin," the overseer barked. "You better not let me see you out here again."

George took a deep breath and promised himself, "Some day, I'm going to be so far gone on the road to freedom that no white man will ever stop me."

Malindy heard about the incident by way of a stern warning from Massa. She was exasperated with George, but she sympathized deeply with him. She shared his thirst for freedom and understood his passion. Malindy believed that one day her restless child would find a way out of slavery on his own. In his thoughts was a desire to undo the master. He did not care about the grave consequences. George, at his tender age, could be hanged without trial. Slave violence against a slaveholder resulted in vigilante justice so swift and deadly that it made prosecuting the slave moot. No need to try a dead body. The whites' fear of slave violence was even greater than their fear of abolitionists and slave stealers.

As her sons became teenagers, they copied the ways their parents evaded Massa's rules. This put the whole family in harm's way. Sammie and George wanted to be freedom fighters, free like Charlie to work for the people. They devised a way to teach some of the children to read, secretly. It was all hush-hush in the slave quarters.

Massa had finally heard about Old Free Charlie's freedom work from one of his white friends. Massa questioned the slaves about it. The slaves never betrayed Charlie. They played dumb when Massa asked them about Charlie, leaving Massa with only his suspicions. The slaves pretended that they did not know anything about freedom fighters or white folk that "loved niggers." It was all news to them.

The slaves said, "Massa says niggers is real dumb. Yes sah, we's gwine to be real dumb about our friend, Ol' Free Charlie." They had a bond with Charlie that no white man could break. They understood that a slip of their tongue could easily cause Charlie to dangle from a tree.

George had his mother's fire, but it was Malindy who first suffered Massa's ire. One day, the mistress became angry with Malindy for taking a break to feed her new baby, Henry. The mistress felt that Malindy gave the baby far too much attention and that the baby belonged in the slave nursery with the other small children. The mistress came into the kitchen and berated Malindy for not performing her duties quickly enough, especially the family's ironing. It was not done the way she liked. She accused Malindy of slamming the iron down too hard, so that it made too much noise. Then, the mistress snatched baby Henry from Malindy's breast and tossed him in the crib near the ironing board.

The mistress turned on Malindy, slapped her ferociously across the face, and said, "Nigger, you do as I say or you and your little nigger will be on the auction block. Leave that baby alone and do your work."

"Do my work?" Malindy retorted. "Dat's all I done since I's been here wid you and yo' lazy chillen." As she spoke, all the years of anger and hatred filled her weary mind like hot lava erupting from a volcano. A vision of her ancestors in their war paint flashed before her eyes. The mistress could not bear the intensity of Malindy's piercing, dark-eyed stare. The mistress was afraid and turned quickly to leave the kitchen. Enraged, Malindy leaped at her mistress's braid and then grabbed her with both hands around the neck. The mistress's pale white face turned red as a pokeweed stem as she gasped for breath.

Poor little Ellen stood there, in the midst of the fight, terrified. She tried to stop baby Henry from hollering. She had to keep her little brother from crying himself to death. She had to stop her mother from killing a white woman. The thought of her mother hanging dead from a tree was too much for Ellen to bear. She had to do something. When Ellen looked into her mother's face, she could see that Malindy was determined. The mistress would be dead soon if Malindy did not release her grip. Ellen started to jump up and down hysterically.

"Momma, Momma," Ellen shouted. "Please, don' kill Missus." Malindy released her hands from around Missus's neck and then a fracas of scratching, hair pulling, and throwing things exploded.

Suddenly, with no other human being present, a supernatural force removed Malindy's hands from the mistress's braid. The mistress ran out of the kitchen. Malindy felt her own heart still racing.

For a moment, she had completely lost control and leaped into madness. Now, she hardly realized what had happened. She was brought back to reality when she heard the mistress screaming from the laundry room: "My husband will take care of you when he gets home tonight. You're going to be punished for what you did to me, you crazy Injun." This was the first time the mistress had ever acknowledged Malindy's true identity. Ellen knew about her mother's Indian roots. However, Malindy had told the children never to discuss the subject with others.

Malindy stood straight and tall, with baby Henry in her arms. Ellen comforted her. She was so relieved that her mother had not killed the mistress. The terror of losing her mother to the hangman's noose had cut into Ellen's soul. Malindy had no regrets for what she had said and done to the mistress. She told Ellen that she would do it again, if anyone ever touched her children. Malindy had no doubt that serious consequences lay ahead for her. She came from a warrior race, and she knew that victory and defeat, life and death, come in their time to all. Whatever the price was, she was ready to pay it.

For well over twenty years as a slave, Malindy had never come face to face with Massa's bullwhip. That evening, a whipping would certainly come her way. She had seen the brutality of the overseer and Massa as they tore backs to pieces. The slaves remembered their floggings. The whip's scars were engraved on their backs forever. Malindy refused to be consumed with fearful thoughts, or to make decisions based on fear. Fear begged her to plead for mercy. She refused to listen to her fear and moved on to complete her work for Massa, while preparing herself for the onslaught of violence upon her person.

The sun shone bright that day, glancing off incandescent clouds in a violet sky. Trees and fields seemed washed clean and glowing after Malindy's brawl with the mistress. The anger that Malindy had suppressed for so many years had finally erupted and flowed out of her, leaving her shriven and purified. At last, she had broken the chains of fear and was true to her nature. She laughed to herself, for although she had almost killed the mistress, that silly woman still trusted Malindy to cook her dinner. It would be an easy thing to poison the food. Some Missouri slave cooks did poison their masters. Malindy knew which herbs to use, and she had the boldness to use them. However, Malindy would never have poisoned white folk, because it was not the Cherokee way to fight an enemy. She did not judge those who used poison, however; she understood what drove them to it.

The underlying cause of tension between Malindy and the mistress was the excessive work the mistress laid on Malindy's children, especially Ellen. The mistress ordered Ellen to scrub the kitchen floor on her knees with a bucket of hot water and strong homemade lye soap. Malindy felt that the job was too hard for little Ellen. Malindy remembered how, when she was young, that task had destroyed her own hands and marked up her own knees.

The mistress had a different idea. She had decided that it was time for Ellen to become introduced to her duties, to learn the harsh drudgery of a slave's life, without her mother's protection. The mistress realized that Malindy would never be a mammy, nor would she train her daughter to be a mammy. Malindy ignored the mistress's orders for Ellen. She kept Ellen by her side. Every time Missus threw out her demands to Ellen, Malindy gave the mistress the silent treatment. Ellen refused to move an inch without her mother's permission. The mistress recognized that Malindy's silence was her resistance to subjugation. Malindy refused to submit and refused to let Ellen scrub the floors. Ellen heard her say, "You wants my chile to clean yo' dirty floors while yo' chillen read en play. When my chile look at yo' chillens' books, you grab 'em from her en shame her." Of course, Malindy did not say these words out loud to the mistress. Releasing her anger and confirming to herself that she was in the right, Malindy spoke them in a low voice, just loud enough for Ellen to hear.

When Massa's children read stories to Ellen secretly, they got in big trouble with their parents. Malindy wanted her children to have an education. They deserved books just like the white children. Ellen knew how to read a little, but the mistress did not know that. Charlie had brought a few old books for the children and taught them to read. But Massa's children went to school, and there was no school for slave children. Malindy was burdened by these disparities. As she labored to improve the life of Massa's family, her own children had less than second best.

As Malindy stood there, a powerless slave, seething with frustration, her thoughts turned to her own people, the Cherokee Nation. If she were still with her tribe, her children would have the right to go to school. Charlie had told her that the Cherokees had organized two seminaries of higher learning in 1851. "When's all this unfairness coming to an end?" Malindy asked herself. Her body felt heavy with grief. She felt as if her feet were glued to Massa's floor. On this evening she dragged through her chores, and each movement became harder as she drifted in and out of memories of her life as a slave.

Waiting to be whipped, Malindy continued to make the light bread for supper. She thought of how bare and lonely her life was without her husband beside her. The love she had for her children and the comfort she felt from that love could not adequately take the place of her absent husband. She relied on his warmth and caring ways. In Charlie's presence, Malindy felt safe. Massa was not too keen on punishing anyone when Old Free Charlie was around the place.

Malindy had promised Charlie that she would not give in to misery without a battle to the very end. She fought against tears. She focused on the happy times when Charlie came, or when the children said something comical, sparking laughter around the fireplace. At the same time she had to acknowledge sadness, especially when Charlie had to leave them. She had to look at the long faces of her sons as they loaded the buggy with his working tools and clothes for a long stay in a free state. The worst moment was when they had to pack all the books, paper, and pencils in the buggy. They loved the books, but they could not keep them in Massa's cabin. Yes, indeed, it surely was Massa's cabin. Charlie never referred to the cabin or the farm as home. When he traveled toward the farm, he always said, "I'm on my way to Malindy and the children." The cabin was simply a stop on the road to emancipation. Charlie protected his family by heeding Massa's rules. By taking all educational items with him, he kept his family safe from Massa's wrath.

Every time Charlie departed for a journey, Massa rapped on the cabin door and ordered Malindy to open it. Then, Massa ransacked the cabin for possessions that slaves were forbidden to own. He tore through the cabin, with no respect, leaving everything in disarray, a huge mess for Malindy to clean up when the raid was over. Malindy felt defiled by these raids. They infuriated her, but she never said anything because she did not wish any harm to come to the children.

Ellen saw this demeaning scenario played out so many times that it left an indelible impression on her young mind. She carried its load on her spirit for years. She never forgot the fear she felt as Massa searched through the cabin, rambling on sarcastically to Malindy: "That Old

Free Charlie talks all his crazy talk about freedom from slavery. He's a big fool to think you'll be free one day. He can't help you now. Ha! Ha! You're better off living here. I'm taking better care of you than Old Free Charlie could ever do."

At this point in the diatribe, Malindy would remember the other slaves complaining about maggots in the meat that Massa's overseer provided. Malindy knew Massa was plumb crazy if he thought she was fool enough to prefer him to her husband. No one could turn Malindy against her husband, especially not Massa.

As Massa continued his rant about Charlie, Sammie and George would turn hot with anger. Yet they stood still with a frozen, stoic expression on their faces. Charlie had told them to protect their mother. In this situation, inaction was the proper protection. Sammie understood that only passivity could save the family. Therefore, he gave his brother a stern look that meant, "George, keep yo' rump still and yo' mouf shut." It was especially difficult for George to remain passive. However, he too understood the bloody consequences that would follow if he moved an inch toward Massa. At these times, when Malindy looked at her sons she knew exactly what was weltering in their brains.

Malindy and George shared similar thoughts: "It's time to bury Massa." As they gazed on Ellen, Lara, and baby Henry, they knew they could not risk it. They had to save the family at any cost, even if it meant giving up their pride and postponing revenge. Malindy and George turned a deaf ear to Massa's insults. They soothed their rage with thoughts of freedom.

Finally, the search would end. Massa, weary of destroying their household and peace, would leave the cabin. Then Malindy reacted, "Thank God, dat crazy man's done gone away. Now we jis' cleans up mo' of Massa's mess. My chillen, some day you won't have to clean Massa's mess no mo'." As she and the children put the cabin in order, they sang songs and made jokes. Once more, the slaveholder had failed to break their spirits.

The evening of her fight with the mistress, Malindy, attentive as ever, served supper to the master and the mistress. Malindy knew that the mistress had complained to her husband. She had her head down and did not look at Malindy. The mistress's wish was forthcoming, a bullwhip across Malindy's back. Slavery dehumanized the mistress, too, as she crawled voluntarily into the web of sadism.

It had been a long day, and finally Malindy's time in the Big House was over for the night. What had happened seemed necessary, unavoidable. She dismissed all negative thoughts. A surge of energy filled her being. Her body felt light and seemed to float.

Quickly, Malindy, Ellen, and Henry walked back to the cabin, picking up Lara from the nursery on the way. Not a word was spoken about the incident, but a rushing monologue filled Malindy's mind. "How dare the Missus treat my Henry like that, throw him in the crib like my baby's some rag doll. I'll never, never let her frighten him again and shock his innocent little soul. Whip me, kill me, you'll never treat my babies like that." Malindy's warrior nature emerged as she planned for the battle ahead of her.

As soon as she entered the cabin, Malindy moved every piece of heavy furniture that she could handle, putting them against the cabin door as a barricade. She had decided to protect herself from the master's wrath. She reckoned that, if she had to go, she was not going to submit without a struggle. As she sat at the table to eat supper with her children, she wished that Charlie were by her side. The dreadful reality was that Charlie was not there and would not be able to protect her at this critical time. This time, she had to stand alone. She prayed that Sammie and George would not come home when Massa came for her. Her main concern was that George would attack the Massa and get himself killed. If George were there, he would fight Massa with all his might.

While Malindy was in prayer, she heard many footsteps outside. Ellen peeped through the crack of the shutters. Massa and his two sons had arrived to perform their hideous task. These were the same boys who had often pulled at Malindy's dress when they were babies. Malindy had helped to nurture and raise them. Now, they were her tormentors. Massa yelled through the door, "You come right on out here and git what you deserve. You had it comin' a long time. Now it's here. You know I can't let you git away with hittin' the Missus."

Malindy had Henry in her arms. She did not move, but yelled back, "You want dis woman, come on en git her, 'cause dis woman ain't comin' to you to git what you en all yore Massas en Missuses deserves, a dern good whippin'. No sah, Massa, you got to come and git dis woman outen here."

"Don't make us break down the door," the Massa hollered.

"You awluz breaks in, Massa," Malindy cried. "I's ready fo' you, come en git me."

Massa was astounded. He shook his head in disbelief. His sons said, "We oughta kill that wild nigger right now." Then there was a great silence. Not a sound came from the cabin. Malindy and her children stayed dead still. Malindy prayed to the Creator for strength and courage and told Ellen to take care of the children. Ellen took baby Henry and put him in his crib. Lara hid in the corner near the fireplace. Massa kept yelling for Malindy to come out. Malindy tuned out Massa's shouts and sang in a low voice.

Hush, hush,

Somebody is calling my name.

Hush, hush,

Somebody is calling my name.

Oh, my Lord what shall I do.

Massa told his sons to break down the door. The boys were leery of doing this, as they were afraid that Old Free Charlie might have secretly left a gun with Malindy. Cautiously, they moved toward the porch. Mammy and some of the slaves watched them. Sammie and George had not yet come back from the fields and so did not hear the commotion. Massa's sons finally knocked the door in. They shoved the barricade aside, grabbed Malindy by the arms and dragged her out of the cabin. She made it hard for them by fighting back. Some of the male slaves carried torches for light. They had tears in their eyes as they stood by, helpless, as one of their slave sisters fought with all her might. Malindy reassured them. "Don' you worry 'bout me. My Creator, he stands wid me now." In the glow of torchlight, Malindy could see Mammy. Malindy gave her a look that said, "Please save George and Sammie." Mammy understood and had an old man go for them. He detained them with a chore that kept them away from the slave quarters.

Malindy fought Massa's sons all the way to the whipping tree. This tree had played a part in many tragic stories and was stained with decades of slave blood and sweat. That evening, the tree recorded Malindy's story, as she hugged it with her own blood. Trees had always been a source of life and refuge for Malindy. As they tied her to the whipping tree, she said to herself, "Tonight, I'm the tree, strong with my Creator by my side. My ancestors hold me up to the sky." Ellen watched the men

Slaves were often whipped for disobedience.

Wood engraving by Van Ingen Synder, 1864. From *The Suppressed Book about Slavery*, MHS Library.

⊨ MALINDY'S FREEDOM ⊨

tie her mother to the tree. Ellen had left Lara to watch Henry in the cabin, so that she could follow her mother on the arduous journey to the tree. Ellen was afraid that Massa would beat her mother to death. She ran to Massa and cried, "Please, Massa, don' kill my Momma. De Missus hurt baby Henry. Dat's why Momma done what she did."

"Git out of my way, gal, and shut your mouth," Massa growled, brushing by Ellen. The whipping began. Massa hit Malindy again and again. As he whipped her, he said, "Gal, you brought this on yourself!"

"I's a woman, not a gal," Malindy shouted back. Mammy looked at Malindy with tears in her eyes, and said, "Yes, my Malindy, you is a woman." Malindy's thoughts became fixed on her ancestors and her early childhood bravery training with her tribe. The tree she clung to and the memories that clung to her were her weapons, her fortress. No moan came from her mouth, no tear from her eye. Ellen shed enough tears for both of them as she watched blow after blow cut into her mother's body. When the whipping ended, and they untied Malindy from the tree, Ellen's courage gave her the power to help her mother back to the cabin.

Malindy's back was a mass of red blood and lacerated skin. The stud tacks on the whip had bitten deep, creating a road map on her back that she would bear for the rest of her life. When Ellen had removed her mother's torn blouse, the little girl could not stop crying as she looked at the horrible disfigurement of her mother's body. Ellen's anger surfaced and for the first time she herself lost control. Like George, she wanted to kill Massa. For the first time, Malindy saw Ellen's rage. Malindy's motherly impulse was to comfort her child, but she knew that Ellen needed to experience and express her anger. Malindy watched Ellen's agony, and how the child's face seemed to age before her eyes. Slavery made the young old before they ever came into the winter of life.

Despite Malindy's excruciating pain, she comforted Ellen, told her that it was normal for her to feel such rage and pain and held her hand. "My dear chile, one day this meanness gwine to end, en we all gwine to be free. Trust en God en believe in yo'self, Ellen. You's a-gwine to be a fine educated girl one day. You tell de truf' to de worl' 'bout dese white folks." As Malindy spoke, Ellen looked at her in amazement. Her mother was her hero and a saint.

Ellen stood by her mother like a guardian angel. She became the doctor and the nurse in the treatment of Malindy's back. Lara was shaking with fear as she silently observed the dripping wounds. "Gal, you stop dat shakin'," Ellen said, "put some water on de fire fo' tea en warm supper for Sammie en George." Baby Henry was asleep and too young to realize what his mother had risked for him.

Malindy had Ellen wash her back down with cold water mixed with cider vinegar to avoid infection. The vinegar stung her back, already on fire with pain. Malindy had still not shed a tear. Ellen and Lara were both in awe of their mother's courage. She had surpassed the limits of the body and relied on her spirit. Malindy had always told the children that the flesh was weak and could easily fail when things got rough but that they could always depend on their spirit to move the body. She gave this lesson meaning by her own example of enduring suffering. The children never forgot their mother's agony that night.

Ellen put salve on her mother's back. Ironically, the mistress, who was responsible for the cuts on Malindy's back, had given Malindy the salve for burns and cuts. Ellen found it hard to forgive this. Malindy told Ellen not to concentrate on Massa and Missus, because they were committed to keeping the slaves in bondage. "You got to use yo' own stren'th to bring freedom. Let God take care of 'em." Malindy was more concerned for her sons, Sammie and George, than about what the white folk had done to her. "Where's my boys?" she asked Ellen.

"Some of de men done kep' 'em away. Mammy tol' em to. She knowed you didn't want 'em dah." Again, Mammy, her dear friend, had taken care of her. Malindy was grateful that her sons had not seen her punishment.

When Sammie and George walked into the cabin, they were fuming and ready to find a way to harm Massa and his sons. They attempted to keep their voices down, but Malindy heard every word.

"Some day, I's a-gwine to drown both Massa's sons in de creek," George growled.

"Stop dat kind er talk and thank God dat I can speak en see you tonight," Malindy commanded. "Anyway, you'se too small to drown dose big boys. You jis' res' yo' lil' heads now."

Sammie calmed George down and said, "We'll wait for Poppa to come. Dis ain't de time to do nothin' but eat en sleep." Silently, the boys ate supper. George was so exhausted from the fieldwork and witnessing his mother's pain that he ate with his eyes half shut. "Go on en sleep, George," said Sammie.

While the children slept, Malindy remained silent as she tolerated the horrific pain. She would not be able to sleep on her back for a long time. She was proud of her children. Their bravery brought her great hope for the future. They had learned how to thrive and not just survive. Slavery had not devoured their fighting spirits. Fear had not completely shadowed their existence.

In the still darkness of the night, the crackling fire in the fireplace brought Malindy warmth. She thought of how much she missed her Charlie. If Charlie had been there, Massa would never have touched a hair on her head. Then she noticed movement in the room. She thought that everyone had gone to sleep. When she turned around, she saw Ellen wrapped in a blanket sitting in the corner near the fireplace. Ellen was keeping vigil over her. Ellen was mature for her age, watching over her mother for hours. The child's attentiveness overwhelmed Malindy. As tears of happiness streamed from her eyes, Malindy fell into a deep sleep.

Two days after Malindy's whipping, Charlie came back home. As his buggy pulled up to the cabin, his excited children ran to meet him. On their lips were huge smiles, but sadness was in their eyes. As always, Charlie had brought them something good to eat and wear. He was full of stories and news. "Well, how are my children?" he inquired. He was happy to see their faces, but he noticed that something was not right with them.

From the cabin door, Malindy watched her family approach. She considered how she would tell Charlie what had happened to her. She would not have much explaining to do, for as soon as Charlie saw her back, he would know what Massa had done. Malindy worried about Charlie's reaction. He had been the one who taught her to try to forgive her enemies, to walk like Jesus. Always, she listened to her husband, but love for enemies had never yet registered with her. Now, her question was, would Charlie himself be able to control his anger and walk like his Lord?

Over and over, Charlie had drilled into his children's heads the idea that human beings belong only to their Creator, Almighty God. He saw white men profess belief in this God while flouting His laws by holding slaves. Charlie had a difficult time forgiving the United States government for sanctioning laws that protected the slaveholders and fostered the genocide of his Native American and African ancestors. Every day, he witnessed injustice and sadism against his people. Malindy feared that when he saw her condition, it would be the last straw, and he would fight back.

Charlie saw his wife at the cabin door. She looked exhausted and haggard. Her normal radiant glow had faded to pale gray. Charlie couldn't wait to throw his arms around her and hold her tight with his usual big bear hug. He looked at her face as she stood, arms wrapped around her waist, as if holding herself up. Obviously something was wrong with her. He kissed her on the lips and asked, "How is my sweetie? What's been going on around here?" Malindy moved slowly toward Charlie. As she looked into his eyes, tears gushed from her own. Ellen answered for her.

"Poppa, Massa done whup Momma wid de bullwhip en her back is cut all over en sore. Poppa, I seed it all."

Charlie was angry, very angry. But he pushed back his rage and insisted on seeing his wife's wounds immediately. They had stopped bleeding. Quickly, he took out his herbs: comfrey, benzoin gum, witch hazel, myrtle, calendula, yarrow, and horsetail. These were the remedies for wounds, and Charlie mixed them and applied them gently to Malindy's back. His presence soothed the pain in Malindy's back and mind. As he worked, Charlie mumbled silently about his intentions for Massa. This frightened Malindy.

Massa's action was legal, because Malindy had struck his wife, a slaveholder. If Charlie stood up for her, he would be challenging the laws of both the state of Missouri and the U.S. government. But Malindy could no more stop Charlie from trying to protect her than she could stop herself from protecting baby Henry. Charlie's personal honor and his love for his family were the essence of his nature. For a few hours, he sat silently. Sammie and George watched his every move. George wanted Charlie to avenge his mother and was ready to go with his Poppa to the chambers of Hell to get Massa and his sons.

After supper that night, Charlie decided to go to the Big House to attempt to talk the Massa into letting his family go free, and to make arrangements to pay him off over time. Charlie promised Malindy that he would remain cool and sane. Charlie realized that he was not responsible for his family's enslavement, but he felt guilty about it, especially when George wanted to know when Charlie would get them their freedom papers, too. As a free man, Charlie could no longer tolerate the suffering of his family.

Charlie knocked on Massa's back door and stood there, a man striving to save his family. "What do you want out there? Who in the hell is it, anyway?" Massa hollered.

"It's Charlie. I need to talk to you, man to man, about the treatment of Malindy and about freedom for my family."

"You can't talk man to man with me, boy. You free niggers are crazy. Missus, did you hear that? Old Fool Free Charlie thinks he's a man. You know better than to come up here like that. Git away from my house. You hear me, nigger? You're too smart for your own good, talking all uppity," the master railed.

Overwhelmed with anxiety, Malindy waited for her husband. She prayed that somehow he could get them free. But she had watched Massa and Missus for years. She knew that profit, for them, came before anything else. Charlie could not offer Massa the cash he could get from the Dixie Belt. Malindy watched as Charlie returned to the cabin in the light of a full moon, an expression of fury on his face. He was ready to kill. He looked up at the ceiling and then at his sleeping children. All of a sudden, he leaped high off the floor, clicking his heels together three times before they touched the floor again. Then he took down his hunting gun from its hiding place, loaded it, and rushed out of the cabin.

Under the radiance of the moon, the dogs howled in unison. Old Free Charlie lay down at the bottom of the hill, aimed his gun toward Massa's house, and fired. He continued to alarm everyone in the slave quarters and the Big House as he shouted nonstop until daylight. While he shouted, the dogs joined in with more howls. Like deacons in a black church saying amen to everything the preacher says, after each declaration from Charlie, the dogs howled. The dogs had seen Malindy whipped and bore witness to Massa's cruelty. Charlie hollered: "Why don't you white devils be the Christian folk that you claim to be, 'cause justice is close at hand. Justice is now knocking on your doors. You fools are just too low down and stupid to open the door. A surprise waits there for you. Listen and believe me, for God's wrath will surely catch you by the pants and throw you down deep into the pits of Hell where you dern well belong. Repent now! Repent! Trust what I say, for I am a man of God and I can see you burning right here on earth for what you are doing to my family and to all Negroes and Indians. This is your Hell, this so-called land of the free and brave."

Then, Charlie really infuriated Massa when he demonstrated his good education by quoting Robert Burns:

Ye hypocrites! Are these your pranks,

To murder men and give God thanks?

For shame! Give o'er, proceed no further;

God won't accept your thanks for murder!

Charlie continued in this vein for hours, without letting up. "Heaven does not welcome monsters. Hear me, now!" Charlie was amazed and somewhat disappointed that Massa and the overseer did not come for him. He was prepared to blow them away and then die himself. Later on, Charlie figured that God must have decided to save him and the others that night.

At last, the sun rose bright and the dogs quieted down. Charlie stopped to play with them before returning to the cabin. Charlie's behavior that night was the talk of the slave quarters and the Big House for days. White folk said that the moon was full and "a nigger jes' went plumb crazy." Surprisingly, Massa never confronted Charlie about it.

Maybe Massa was concerned about the fact that as a freedman, Charlie had some rights, however few, that were protected under Missouri law. He said that Old Crazy Charlie just liked to blow off steam and that was all he would ever do. The slaves realized that Massa and the overseer were too scared to get Charlie that night, or any night. The slaves joked about how Massa hid under the covers that night from their good friend Old Free Charlie.

While Charlie was home, Massa allowed Malindy to stay in the cabin for a week to heal. One day, she wanted to see the scars on her back. She took a hand mirror and viewed her scarred back through the dresser mirror. Charlie had given her the mirrors. He dreaded the day she would use them to see her scars, for he thought that it would only incite her to more rebellion. But Malindy took an opposite approach. Naturally, she hated the scars on her back, but she thought of more important things. She had to survive and take care of her children. So, instead of seeking revenge against Massa, Malindy determined to keep her anger in check when she returned to the Big House.

Charlie extended his stay at the cabin longer than usual in order to comfort his family as much as possible. Massa did not want him there. However, Charlie simply ignored Massa's order to get off his land. Charlie faced danger on the roads and everywhere; therefore, he could care less about Massa's antagonism. Charlie was going to live and die like a man. He left when he was ready. He had some prospective jobs in Illinois that might mean steady employment, and he left to see about them.

Charlie had worked hard to educate himself. He read everything he could get his hands on. He was handy, a carpenter who could make furniture. He had acquired skills needed in the workplace, but his mulatto status was a barrier that kept him from getting well-paying work. Charlie and his family worked like mules, yet there was never enough money. The only compensation his family received on Massa's farm was a peck of corn and a few pounds of fatback a week, along with the right to live in a cold, damp log cabin. Charlie himself was paid less than a white man doing the same job.

Even in the free states, white folks kept black folks down. Bigoted whites in Illinois disliked the idea of blacks working for wages. The bigots said, "You can make niggers work, but you can't make niggers think." They were wrong. Charlie and many freedmen thought constantly about how to outwit Massa and bring down the edifice of slavery.

When Charlie left, Malindy's wounds had scabbed over but had not yet fully healed. As soon as Charlie was gone, Massa sent word for Malindy to get back to work in the kitchen. Before Malindy fell out with the mistress, they would laugh and talk together when they were in the kitchen. The first blow to Malindy's back changed that. Malindy's good feelings for Missus were whipped out of her.

On the morning Malindy returned to work, the mistress came into the kitchen with a condescending smirk, looking sidewise at her. The mistress didn't dare look Malindy in the eye. As always, the mistress was terrified by the intensity of Malindy's glare. "You deserved every lash and scar on your back," the mistress said hesitantly. "Now you know who's the boss around here. Git goin' and make some of that light bread."

Malindy knew that it was not the regular time to do the baking, and she realized that the mistress was trying to make her suffer more by giving her a heavier load of work. Malindy smiled and prepared the ingredients to do the thing she enjoyed. She recognized her own talents as a skilled cook. Missus and Massa had always praised her good cooking, especially her light breads and buns. Malindy did not need their accolades. She hardly appreciated white folk with praise on their lips and a whip in their hand to beat their slaves.

Despite her whipping, Malindy had ignored the order to leave baby Henry in the slave nursery and had brought him right back into the kitchen. The mistress did not go near him. She simply gave him a fake smile and a hand wave. She had started being curt and distantly polite to all Malindy's children. Malindy sensed from the mistress's coldness that plans were in the making for Malindy's departure from the farm.

Charlie had told Malindy about the booming slave trade in Missouri, the horrors of the slave pens, and the St. Louis slave auction. Fervently, she prayed that it would never happen to her family. She hated the idea that her children would be exposed to that degrading exhibition. As she looked at the white dough in her hands, she envisioned her children holding her tight as the bids for their bodies echoed in their ears. "Goin' for five hundred dollars. Do I hear more? Goin' for a thousand dollars. Do I hear more? Goin', goin', gone. Sold to that gentleman for one thousand dollars." Malindy's fears intensified as the unknown beckoned to her again. But, for the moment, she forgot about her fears and served yet another evening

Slaves' greatest fear was being sold away from their families.
WOOD ENGRAVING, 1849.
FROM *THE NARRATIVE OF THE LIFE AND ADVENTURES OF HENRY BIBB, AN AMERICAN SLAVE*, MHS LIBRARY.

⊰ MALINDY'S FREEDOM ⊱

meal to her masters. Finally, the meal over and the dishes washed, it came time for her to leave her enemies' presence.

Glad that the day was over, Malindy walked to the cabin with her children. It was a warm evening, with the trees dancing to the breeze, while the sounds of nature created a harmonious melody. The fresh breeze caressed Malindy. It refreshed her and cleansed away the stench of hatred in the Big House. Grateful to the Creator, Malindy prayed for acceptance of the unknown. Experience had taught her that in the unknown there is always opportunity. That was some comfort to her.

"If a slave can have a country in this world, it must be any other in preference to that in which he is born to live and labor for another, in which he must lock up the faculties of his nature, contribute as far as depends upon his individual endeavors to the evanishment of the human race or entail his own miserable condition on the endless generations proceeding from him."

—*President Thomas Jefferson*

Chapter Eight

SOLD ON THE AUCTION BLOCK

D oomsday rolled over Malindy Wilson like a volu-
minous dark cloud full of tears. There were signs
that Massa was going to sell Malindy and her
family. The mistress became overly nice to the
children, giving them sweets every day, fattening
them up for sale like pigs. The idea of being sold
tore at Malindy's soul. One hot, humid summer
afternoon, Massa came into the kitchen with a
stern look on his sunburned face.

"Malindy, I want you to git yourself and your children ready by four
o'clock tomorrow morning, hear me, gal?" Malindy hated it when he
called her "gal." When she looked into the mirror, there was no reflec-
tion of a girl, but an image of a worn out, tired, and burdened woman.
Her body became straight and rigid as her unspoken resentment raced
through her mind. Massa continued, "I'm taking you to St. Louis." His
voice sounded urgent. He told her to prepare food for the trip because
it would be a whole day affair, a business trip.

So her time had come. Malindy and her five children, along with
other merchandise, were the business. She and her poor children would
be hauled away like Massa's cows and sold at the market. In the slaves'

quarters, there was always the expectation that their children would be sold one day. It was never a surprise. As part of the upbringing of their children, slave parents prepared them mentally for possible sale. They were always in a state of readiness. Malindy's children might be sold separately and never see any member of their family again.

Malindy hated Massa for imposing this horror on her family. But instead of responding out loud, Malindy simply looked at Massa. Her dark eyes penetrated his soul, and, for once, he said nothing more.

Later, Malindy was preparing dinner and had a chicken in her hand. Massa came into the kitchen, looked at the table where she stood, and saw a big cutting knife. Malindy did not harbor murder in her heart, only sorrow. Yet, Massa did not trust Malindy in that emotional moment with a big knife like that within her reach. At that moment, Malindy could read the fear and suspicion in Massa's mind. Smiling, Malindy picked up the knife and started to cut up the chicken.

As Massa walked out of the kitchen, Malindy muttered under her breath, "Don't worry. I ain't gwine to hurt you, Massa. You ain't worth it. I ain't a-gwine to Hell for killin' de likes of you."

"Gal, did you say something to me? I thought I heard you say something."

"No, sah, Massa," Malindy chuckled, "I didn't say nothin' at all." Her master left, and Malindy continued her reply in her own mind, "I's ready to git away from you en yo' wicked wife." Malindy braced herself and stood straight. She held her tears inside until they flowed through every vein and artery.

She walked slowly back to her cabin. The children were there, waiting. She went straight to the bureau and took out her gunnysack skirt. She had prepared her children for this day long ago. Often the children laughed and joked about the old funny-looking skirt and about how they would have to hold on to it for dear life. Her boys, Sammie and George, even discussed how they could hold on and at the same time support their frail mother, to keep her from falling down.

The children looked at their mother and sensed that something was seriously wrong. Malindy's daughter Ellen saw that her mother's face had a gray cast. Her eyes were clouded with anxiety, and she looked as though she might cry any minute. Malindy drew her children into her embrace. Finally, the tears gushed from Malindy's eyes. The tears and the skirt told the story to come. The future stared the children in the face. They realized their fate. Ellen hugged her mother tightly around the waist.

Slave hunters with bloodhounds made sure that running away was not an attractive option for slaves.
Steel engraving by Van Ingen Snyder, 1864. From *The Suppressed Book about Slavery*, MHS Library.

⊰ MALINDY'S FREEDOM ⊱

"Oh, Momma, please don' let 'em take us away fum you." Malindy looked up at the ceiling of the cabin as if she were asking God for help.

"Hush, chile. It's in de Creator's han's now. We mus' pray fo' help to de Almighty."

"We can run away," George said. "Jis' what we can do."

Malindy looked at George and shook her head. Running away together had been her first thought, but she had no one to help her plan an escape. Furthermore, slaveholders ordinarily had several bloodhounds, useful for tracking down runaways as well as game. Malindy knew what happened when Massa caught a runaway. Runaway slaves were punished severely. Besides, if she ran away, her husband might never be able to find her.

Malindy could not imagine dragging her five children through long stretches of woods, hiding by day and traveling at night, living in caves and holes. For sure, she did not want the "nigger dogs" chasing and mauling her children, or the "white trash" patrollers starving, whipping, or chaining them, clapping them in irons or isolating them in a cell.

George could not understand his mother's reasoning. He tried to persuade her that they could make it. "Momma, I knows we can do it. If I stays here, I knows I jis' kill ol' Massa if he calls me a nigger or whup you agin."

Malindy was angry at Massa for making her carry the burden of wishing to kill him. It was bad enough that she had that burden— she did not want murder in her children's hearts or minds. She said, "Massa catch you runnin' away, he gwine to change yo' name to 'One Foot George.' De only place you gwine to run is to Massa's wagon, you hear me?" The other children laughed and started teasing George and calling him One Foot George. Ellen imitated how he would hop along with only one foot. Even in this ghastly situation, the family was able to joke and laugh.

"We mus' be still en pray," Malindy continued. "We go wid Massa, understan' me, George? No runnin' off! If we goes a-runnin' yo' Poppa will never find us."

Malindy fed the children and got them into bed. The bright moonlight shone in at the window, and she could dimly see their precious sleeping forms. She watched over them tenderly as they slept, but her heart was heavy. She herself could not sleep. Her mind was racing with apprehension and fear of separation from her family. As she looked up at the moon, peaceful thoughts came to her. She remembered the good times, Christmas and Thanksgiving holidays with her family. Charlie and the children had stored black walnuts, hickory nuts, and preserves in the loft for Christmas. Now, she would have to give them all away to friends, along with the furnishings that Charlie had made or bought for her.

When he was on the road, Charlie had no idea of what was happening to his family. Malindy worried about him. Whites in Franklin County were suspicious of Northerners. Preachers, peddlers, and teachers were suspected of being abolitionists. As Charlie was a free black and itinerant worker, he was suspected of working to free slaves as he traveled from place to place. As an herbalist, he was suspected of having skills in witchcraft or engaging in conjure activities. However, Charlie was a good Christian man and did not embrace those aspects of his ancestors' culture.

Malindy went sleepless her last night on the farm. She called out to Charlie in her sorrow. She looked around the room and saw all the things that Charlie had worked so hard for. The bed, bureau, mirrors, chairs, and all the items of comfort had to remain on Massa's farm. Malindy would leave with only the clothes on her back and her children, the most precious gifts Charlie had given her.

Sadness overwhelmed Malindy, but she had work to do. She prepared food for the journey: jelly and butter sandwiches and some pork meat. There was a tin pail of sweets and one with water, along with six tin drinking cups. Malindy got out the children's best clothes. Massa had captured her body, but he had no ownership rights in her dignity. Her children would look their best.

At 4:00 a.m. sharp, Massa and his neighbor pulled up in front of the Big House with his big mule team and wagon. Malindy had the children ready to go, standing close beside her. Massa had a quilt made of old britches spread across the floor of the wagon. Massa and his neighbor loaded the merchandise on the wagon, first Malindy and her children, the human merchandise, then the goods and produce. The goods formed a barricade to prevent the slaves from jumping off the back of the wagon.

Massa surveyed his property and said, "I'm going to make a big killin' at the market today. Big bucks are a-comin'." The early morning was already hot and humid, yet at this remark an icy chill went down Malindy's back.

As the wagon clattered down the road, Malindy took one last look at the birthplace of her children, the only home they had ever known. The children kept looking back, especially Sammie. "No lookin' back, chillen. Keep yo' eyes ahead," Malindy said. "We's comin' to de end. Yes, we's comin' to de end." Sammie, George, and Ellen understood that she was talking about the fact that freedom was coming and that it would be the end for the slaveholders.

Malindy realized that the Massa could have chosen to sell her and the children in Franklin County, but insisted on taking them all the way into St. Louis. There were neighbors in Franklin County who were always buying slaves for their farms, and usually slaves were sold locally. For years, farmers had bought and sold among themselves as they needed more or less help. Now the farmers could get higher prices from the auction block or slave dealers, so more slaves were sold at auction. Malindy's master figured that he would receive more money at auction, especially if the slaves were sold in St. Louis to be sent to the Cotton Belt.

Farmers could get higher prices for slaves at auction than they could selling among themselves.
Wood engraving by Van Ingen Synder, 1864. From *The Suppressed Book about Slavery*, MHS Library.

⊣ MALINDY'S FREEDOM ⊢

It was a beautiful, hot June day. In summer and fall, the slave traders circulated through the Missouri countryside, buying up slaves to offer to the Southern planters who would sell their cotton crops in the fall and have money to spend. Massa had picked a prime time to sell Malindy's family, early in the season, to get the best price. At their ages, Sammie and George were reaching peak value. A prime male hand could bring as much as fifteen hundred dollars. It was ironic that, because Malindy and Charlie had raised good, healthy children, they were more likely to lose them.

Malindy hoped that they would not be sold south on a slave boat. She hoped that a farmer from Franklin County would buy them all, the whole family, so that they could stay together and so that Charlie would be able to find them. In the dim dawn light, Ellen, Lara, and Henry fell sound asleep before the wagon had reached the main road. Sammie and George were too angry to sleep, and Malindy tried to control her own rage. She could see that Sammie and George were ready to jump Massa and his neighbor.

George looked pleadingly at his mother. No words came from his mouth. Malindy looked into his eyes and shared his feeling of entrapment. Like him, she wanted to soar and fly like the birds on wings of freedom. Massa had given them strict orders to be quiet on the journey. Malindy moved her lips in the faintest whisper, "George, hold on, de day's a-comin'. Our ancestors gwine to have de last word." Malindy smiled at her George and began to sing, quietly, so that Massa could barely hear:

He's jis' de same today

When Moses en his soldiers

From Egypt lan' did flee,

His enemies behin' him

En' in front of him de sea.

God raised de waters like a wall

En' opened up de way.

En' de God dat lived in Moses' time

Is jis' de same today.

As they traveled down the road, Malindy continued to sing. She passed out food to the children.

"Gal, what you call yourself singin' back there?" Massa yelled. Malindy ignored him and kept on humming. Finally, when the children were served, she answered. "Massa, you want some good food en water?" The master expected to be served to the very end.

"The gal cooks good food. Don't pay her no mind, just eat," Massa said to his neighbor. "She won't kill us, or even a fly. She's just crazy sometimes."

When Massa said that about Malindy, Sammie looked hard at Massa's back. Malindy shook her head at Sammie with one of her "don' you dare" looks.

The wagon turned onto Manchester Road, the main road from Gray Summit to St. Louis—later Highway 100. They stopped along the way in small towns like Ballwin and Manchester. Sammie and George had never been anywhere except Massa's fields and woods and the Big House. This was an adventure for them. They observed all that was to be seen on the way to the big city. As the wagon got closer to the city, the younger children continued to sleep on the sacks of merchandise. Massa and his neighbor talked and laughed boisterously. "How can Massa laugh and be so happy when he is destroying my family?" Malindy wondered. The master disgusted Malindy. Awake, she stood vigil over her children and sang to relieve her grief. Some slaves sang this song as they were about to be carried to the Dixie Belt on the steamboats:

> See those poor souls from Africa
> Transported to America.
> We are stole and sold to Georgia
> Will you go along with me?
> We are stole and sold to Georgia
> Come sound the jubilee!
>
> See wives and husbands sold apart.
> Their children's screams will break my heart.
> There's a better day a-coming.
> Will you go along with me?
>
> There's a better day a-coming.
> Go sound the jubilee!
>
> O, gracious Lord! When shall it be,
> That our poor souls shall all be free?
> Lord, break them slavery powers.
> Will you go along with me?
> Lord, break them slavery powers.
> Go sound the jubilee!
> Dear Lord, dear Lord, when slavery cease
> Then we poor souls will have our peace.
> There's a better day a-coming.
> Will you go along with me?
> There's a better day a-coming.
> Go sound the jubilee!

Malindy sang all the way to the market, feeling that the spirits of all those slaves who had gone on this journey before sang with her.

When the wagon pulled into St. Louis, Malindy and the children were in complete awe of all the people and buildings. St. Louis was a big city now, having grown in the last twenty years from 5,000 to 75,000 people. Many of the folk were dressed in their finery, as if they were going to a Sunday church meeting. But it was not Sunday.

"Momma, look like dese white folks all gwine to church today," Ellen said.

"Some of dem fancy folk gwine to de auction," Malindy grinned. "Maybe one of dem gwine to be our new massa."

As the wagon moved closer to the courthouse, it seemed that everything was in slow motion. Every detail of that day stood out in Ellen's mind for the rest of her life. Malindy looked at the children and pointed to the gunnysack skirt she was wearing. "Hold on! Hold on!" she whispered to them. Henry was only four years old. He sat on Sammie's lap, looking at his mother with big, sad eyes. Lara looked a lot like Charlie. She had a high yellow complexion, very close to mulatto, and was beautiful like Malindy. Malindy did not want anyone to take her for a potential fancy girl. Ellen held on to her mother's arm, and Lara laid her head on her mother's shoulder, absorbing tender comfort from her. Ellen was worried about Lara. Lara was a weak child and easily frightened.

Malindy carried the weight of her children's love and fear. The possibility of being separated from her children filled her with terror. Hatred for Massa consumed her. Now, she could see the huge dome of the courthouse. It had been built in 1828. It was in this building that the slave Dred Scott sued for his freedom. The St. Louis courthouse was at once a magnificent edifice and a monument to dehumanization. Live human flesh was bought and sold on its front steps.

Now, in 1852, Malindy stood with her family beside those courthouse steps. She wanted justice. She wanted revenge. She refused to be a passive participant in this process. America was her home, her birthplace. Her ancestors had lived on and nurtured this land for millennia. On this dark day the descendants of European immigrants had her up for sale.

As Massa placed her in line, Malindy stood, a full-blood Cherokee, in the midst of black men, women, and children. One woman cried

out, "Oh, my Lord, please let someone buy me en set me free!"
Malindy looked up and down the line into the faces of brave men and
women. They all shared the same pain and wish for freedom from
injustice and the whip. They had heard that antislavery people bought
slaves to free them. They all hoped it would happen to them.

Malindy's prayer was more realistic. She prayed that a good person
would come to her rescue and buy the whole family. She noticed that
many young slaves were in chains, because their masters did not trust
them to stay there. They were sturdy, young, and angry men. Several
masters carried bullwhips. Older male slaves flanked Malindy and her
children on either side. One man's agony poured out in song:

Steal away, steal away,

Steal away to Jesus.

Steal away, steal away home,

I ain't got long to stay here.

The poor man had no tears in his eyes, but Malindy could hear
the tears in his voice. A slave dealer told him to shut his mouth. He
was examined from head to toe. A prospective buyer opened his
mouth to check his teeth. Most of the slaves stood, impassive, while
the crowd jeered and laughed. The auctioneer called the boys "fine
looking bucks" and "strong niggers." Malindy stood straight and did
not flinch.

The auctioneer started the sale with a loud horn. Slave couples were
there. Some were bought together, some separated forever. As their
new masters led them from their mates, spouses pleaded with their new
masters to buy their loved ones. When the sale was over, the old master
simply walked away, without a farewell or backward glance, as if he had
never known the slaves.

Malindy had been moving forward in line and had drawn close to
the steps. Now it was her time to be handled like livestock. Massa
ordered Malindy to move onto the sale steps and line up her children
in a row on one step. Malindy had no intention of lining up her children. As Massa moved closer to her, she and her children moved slowly, clinging together, to the designated step. Some buyers looked at her
and Sammie and George before the auctioneer began the bidding
process. Malindy cringed when she heard someone in the crowd call, "I

Slaves, including Malindy, were sold on the steps of the St. Louis Courthouse.
LAST SALE OF THE SLAVES, *1860.*
OIL ON CANVAS BY THOMAS SATTERWHITE NOBLE, CA. 1871. MHS MUSEUM COLLECTIONS.

⊣ MALINDY'S FREEDOM ⊢

want those fine, strong bucks." She shut down her emotions and concentrated on holding her children above the fray.

Malindy's five children clustered close to her and held on to her skirt for dear life. Lara and Henry cried as Sammie, Ellen, and George made sure that they kept a tight grip on their mother's gunnysack skirt. Malindy had made the skirt from two layers of cloth, with five holes like pockets so the children could hold on to her. Sammie and George kept Malindy anchored so that the tight grips of all five of the children did not cause her to fall.

The auctioneer was furious. "How can the buyers see her body or the children in that position?" he complained to Massa. Massa walked over to Malindy. Malindy gave him a hard look, the look of a mountain lion protecting its young. Massa stopped in his tracks. He knew that if he touched one of her children, Malindy would go completely berserk. Massa could not risk that type of defiance. It could easily spoil his sale and cost him big money. Who would want to buy any of them once they had seen Malindy unleash her rage?

Massa retreated. "You just start the bidding," he commanded the auctioneer.

Malindy stood straight as a warrior and gazed into the crowd. She saw prosperous men grinning in their high top hats, carrying gold-headed canes, and dour farmers dressed in plain clothes. White women stood chatting as though they were at a tea party. The auctioneer screamed at the children, "Let your mammy go." The children tightened their grip and did not budge. They stood firmly connected to their mother. As Malindy gallantly stood her ground, she remembered how she had carried each child in the womb. She saw each umbilical cord that had joined her babies to her. On this day, her gunnysack skirt bound her children to her and to the Creator. No man had the right to sever that cord.

The crowd muttered. They wanted a better view of the merchandise and were outraged by Malindy's disobedience. But the auctioneer was too shrewd to lose the sale. If he couldn't pry them apart, he would try to sell them as a group. "Now what do you bid for this strong, clean, healthy family here?" he called out. "Chillen so obedient to their mammy will be obedient to a master. See how quiet and well behaved they are! Yes, this is a real prize here, five children and a young mammy with more years to breed. Oh, yes, these two fine-looking gals will give you more pickaninnies to come."

He walked over to Malindy and pulled free her straight, black hair. "Who will bid two thousand dollars?" Massa wanted to get more and told the auctioneer that she had a "free nigger" for a husband who helped to support the family. The bids soared. By this time, Malindy was seeing double as she looked down into the crowd. She and the children had been standing in public for hours without being able to relieve themselves. "Hol' on, keep yo' clothes clean," she repeated to the children. "Don' faint now. Don' faint." The sweat ran down their bodies. Buyers came closer to inspect them but stopped several feet away. They could see Malindy's rage, and its intensity drove them back. Her long black hair hung to her waist.

"She ain't no Negro. That's a Injun," one buyer whispered.

"Not for me, that's real trouble there," another replied.

Nevertheless, someone finally did bid an acceptable price and purchased the whole family. Malindy's prayers had been answered, and she smiled as she embraced her family.

The farmer who was Malindy's new master came to the steps for them. Malindy refused to move. She overheard him finalize the transaction with her old master. The new farmer seemed to find it distasteful. "Let's git this done quick," he said. The farmer gave her old master a disgusted look. "Make sure you let her husband know that they are with me now," he said in a gentle voice. When Malindy heard him say that, she was reassured and told the children to release their grip.

The farmer who was now her master told Malindy to follow him to his wagon and said, "I really don't like this slavery business, but this is the only way that I can git help for my farm. I promise you your husband will know where you're at and I'll never sell you or any of your chillen." This was the very first time that any master had spoken kindly to Malindy. He treated her as a person and not as a thing. At that moment, Malindy wanted to trust his words.

"Don' trust dat white man," George said.

"You be quiet, George," Malindy replied. She was overjoyed to have her children with her. This was not the time for distrust. Malindy took a deep breath and looked up to the sky with gratitude to her Creator. Malindy soothed George and hugged him. "George, I knows what you says, but let's give dis man a chance. He seem like a decent man, caught in a web like us." When the farmer told Malindy that his own farm was in Gray Summit like her old master's, Malindy and her children smiled for the first time in many hours, rejoicing at their good fortune. Charlie could find them!

As they hurried toward the wagon, there was an outburst from nearby. A strong man in chains was being whipped by his master, and he sang out in his deep voice:

Go down, Moses,

Way down in Egypt land,

Tell ol' Pharaoh,

Let my people go.

Malindy shooed her children to the wagon, away from that horrid place. Their eyes filled with tears for the young slave they left behind.

His song followed them. The whole horror of this experience and the sound of the auctioneer's voice stayed with them for many years. To Ellen, the St. Louis Courthouse remained forever a wretched place, the symbol of evil.

The new master had promised her that he would never sell her family, and Malindy was happy. Neither private sale nor the auction block would ever affect her life again. The new master gave them food and water on the way back to Gray Summit. Malindy hoped that his promise would hold firm, but in her heart there would always be distrust of white folks.

As Malindy began the long ride back to another slave cabin, she mentally prepared herself for a new life, with a new mistress, a new master, and new friends. New challenges awaited her family. And, because they were going back to Gray Summit, Old Free Charlie would be able to find them. "Stay strong, stay strong, my chillen," were the words the children heard from Malindy as they slipped into sleep.

After many hours of exhaustion, Malindy herself escaped into a deep sleep in the wagon. Her faith and hope surged in her dreams. She dreamed she heard the drums of her children's African ancestors and the chanting of Cherokee women rejoicing in her victory—the victory God had given her family.

"Beat and cuff your slave and keep him hungry and spiritless and he will follow the chain of his master like a dog; but feed and clothe him well, work him moderately, surround him with physical comfort, then dreams of freedom intrude. Give him a good master, and he wishes to become his own master."

—*Frederick Douglass*

⊰ MALINDY'S FREEDOM ⊱

Chapter Nine

MALINDY'S SON
GEORGE DEFIES SLAVERY

ld Free Charlie's journey home from his itinerary in northern Illinois to Franklin County, Missouri, was long and hard. Every year, what had once been a lonely, isolated route had become more crowded. Charlie saw more and more white and black faces thronging the road, while the red ones disappeared. Where prairies full of gophers and jackrabbits once rolled, villages full of white settlers had sprung up. Charlie observed the changes in the land, but the only change in his personal life was that he was older. His family was still enslaved, and he was free in name only. Nevertheless, Charlie was a happy man, secure in his faith and the love of his family and fulfilled by his freedom work. As he traveled, his mind was filled with images of Malindy and the children.

It had been some months since he had seen his family. As he pulled his buggy onto the road into Gray Summit, his heart was stricken with heaviness. He felt that something was wrong. Massa stopped him on the road to the Big House.

"Hey, there, Charlie. What you lookin' for, boy?"

"What do you mean? I'm here to see my family, of course." Charlie looked Massa square in the eye. He had noticed that there was no sign of George or any of the other children, which was unusual.

"Not here any more. Now they live down the road a piece with another master, on his farm. Yes, indeed, boy, I sold your fine family and got a pretty good sum for 'em, too."

Charlie had to control his fury. He took a deep breath. "Lord, give me strength," he whispered. He would not let Massa intimidate him or provoke him to violence. Massa gave him the new master's surname, but no directions to his farm. Charlie turned his buggy in the direction he prayed would lead him to his family.

Malindy had become settled in the new place. The farm was prosperous, and her new cabin was larger than her old one. It had two rooms and a loft. It was a new experience for Malindy to have a mistress and master who appeared to be kind to their slaves. Malindy's new mistress gave her the complete run of the kitchen. Once in a while they had little spats, usually disagreements about how the mistress's children loved to hang around Malindy in the kitchen. Malindy was kind to the white children and playful with them. They were close to her.

Malindy was satisfied that she never heard the word "nigger" from the mouths of the master or his family. These white folk appeared to be respectful and civil. Malindy's children liked the new cabin. It had a wooden floor and a good fireplace and was furnished with beds, cookware, and utensils.

Missus told Malindy that if she or her children became ill, she should send for Missus at the Big House. Missus would provide the medical care or have the doctor come, if necessary. Malindy could not believe her new master's kindness and gentleness. It took away some of the anger she felt about the unfairness of not receiving wages for her labor. She was grateful to her new master and mistress but still did not trust them completely.

Malindy prayed each day for Charlie's safety. She now lived in faith. She had finally accepted Christianity and the value of forgiveness.

George was busy working in the yard around the Big House. He looked up and there came Old Free Charlie in his buggy, driving up to his family's new prison. When he saw his father, George dropped everything and ran yelling, "Poppa, Poppa's here, Momma!" Malindy heard her son and ran out of the kitchen. Missus and Massa told her to go and meet her husband. Jubilantly, she and the children rushed toward the buggy. Charlie saw his family coming toward him with huge smiles on their faces. He had not seen them look so happy in a long time.

Something was definitely different in this new place. His children were all clean and well fed. Malindy made sure of that. Her back was straight, and the gleam was back in her eyes. Seeing his family in improved conditions and looking so well filled Charlie with joy. As Malindy ran closer to him, Charlie cried out, "Malindy! Malindy! I'm so happy I found the other piece of my heart. I thought I'd lost you when I didn't see our children out in the yard at the other place." Charlie stopped the buggy, climbed down, and hugged Malindy. The children gathered around them, and they all clung tightly to one another in one big embrace. Massa and Missus looked on at the joyful reunion. They were impressed by Charlie's appearance, his white-mulatto complexion and stately bearing. His buggy was full of things he had brought for his family.

As Charlie and Malindy walked toward the cabin, George hopped into the buggy and drove it along behind them. He loved his father's old horse and felt proud to be in his free father's buggy, something, along with the horse, that did not belong to Massa. George longed to travel freely like his father. Charlie smiled back at his son. He had no doubt what was on George's mind, but now was not the time to worry about George.

Charlie looked down at his wife. Malindy silently entwined herself with him, full of both happiness and a poignant wish that she could cling to him like this every day. Unlike a white southern belle, a slave woman did not have the luxury of being a clinging vine. She had to be strong, surviving years of agony for her few moments of happiness.

"Poppa, I done prayed to God you'd find us," Ellen said. "I knowed I'd see you again." Charlie looked at his wise daughter, with her bright dancing eyes, and at her brothers and sister. How he loved them all! As the family walked along, they heard Massa's voice.

"Malindy, you gonna tell me your husband's name?"

"Yes sah, Massa, this is Charlie Wilson. Some folks calls him Ol' Free Charlie."

"Looks like a preacher to me," Massa said, looking Charlie over.

"No, sir, I am not a preacher," Charlie replied, "but I do God's work. I am a working man doing God's work."

"Everyone should be about God's business; the world would be a better place," the farmer opined.

"I'm pleased to meet you, sir, mighty pleased," Charlie responded. He resented this man who held his family captive, but the farmer seemed a decent man, as masters went.

"This is your family's home now, and you can come and see them any time," the farmer said. "Since you're a free man, it won't look good for you to stay too long with all the ruckus that's going on now. Don't worry about your family, because they'll be right here with me."

Charlie was surprised by the cordial tone in Massa's voice. Massa almost sounded like some of the abolitionists Charlie had encountered. In general, Charlie did not respect slaveholders, because of their beliefs. Charlie himself was a gentle and godly man, and Massa's considerate behavior moved Charlie to thank him for his kindness.

Behind cabin doors, Malindy and Charlie held on to each other in a lingering embrace. The children snickered; they couldn't wait to hear Charlie's colorful stories about the outside world. This time Malindy told her news first, recounting their experience on the auction block. Charlie jumped up from his chair and paced furiously to and fro, his face tense with anger. The idea of his wife and children being sold sickened him. Eventually, mastering his rage, he sat down, took Malindy's hands in his own, and quietly told her of his recurring dream: "At night, I have dreams of my African ancestors in the crawl space of the ship, crossing the Atlantic on their backs, in chains, lying in their sweat and filth like wild animals. In the dark hold, I see the spirit of the warrior on their faces, their will to live. Their courage keeps me going, Malindy. One day, we will all be free. You must believe this and teach it to the children. We must never stop giving them hope. Malindy, we are here because of God and the will of our ancestors. We must pass that will to Sammie, George, Ellen, Lara, and our little Henry."

Malindy soothed her family into a quieter mood as they ate supper. The room filled with laughter and their love for one another. Charlie marveled at how much his children had grown and thanked God for this moment they shared together. Of necessity, blacks understood the concept of living in the moment and not for the future.

Charlie and Malindy found solace in each other. Their long separation did not divide them. They remained fresh and new to each other in commitment, grace, and love, walking as one with each other and the Almighty. Their union created a sanctuary undefiled by man. Walking through the woods, searching for herbs and speaking to nature, they were one with the sacred beauty of the world.

Malindy and Charlie loved nature and God. Charlie was pleased that Malindy had accepted his teachings about Christianity. He was confident that she would encourage the children in faith. Malindy had no more revenge in her heart. In the pit of Hell, she had learned forgiveness. Her rage had subsided. She loved her enemies, and it brought peace to her spirit. She surrendered her rage and enemies to God, whose wrath would cleanse the evils of slavery not in her time, but in His. Charlie read his family Psalms 35 and 91 for protection. The days passed quickly, and soon it was time for Charlie to leave. He hugged his family close and drove away in his buggy.

Years went by, and Charlie continued to journey back and forth to Illinois, leaving his family in tears and returning to them in joy. Malindy and the children continued to live and work on the farm. The children played with the master's children when they were young but had to do more work as they grew up.

Charlie's sons had grown into young men. Sammie remained Malindy's calm, reliable son, but as George entered his teens, Malindy began having more trouble with him. When George was a little boy, Malindy had noticed how quickly he learned everything. Even as a child he could see the difference between Massa's life and his family's life. By the time he was a teenager, George harbored strong resentment and hatred for white folk. At the age of seventeen he saw blood and wanted revenge for the cruelty his family had suffered. George was a real challenge for Malindy.

George did not have an ounce of forgiveness in his heart for white folk. More than ever, Malindy feared that he would face serious consequences because of his aggressive behavior. Malindy counseled him: "Son, I knows you got plenty cause to feel so bad inside. I knows de pain in yo' heart. But Massa en Missus here ain't like de ones in dat yuther place. Dese is good folk. Dey treats us pooty kind. Son, please do like Massa say en we gwine to be jis' fine here."

George listened attentively to his mother, but he did not change. What stood out most in his mind were the deep, criss-crossed scars on Malindy's slim back and the emotional pain the whole family felt from her whipping.

A freedman like Charlie often had to leave his family to earn his living.
WOOD ENGRAVING, 1849.
FROM *THE NARRATIVE OF THE LIFE AND ADVENTURES OF HENRY BIBB, AN AMERICAN SLAVE*, MHS LIBRARY.

MALINDY'S FREEDOM

"Momma," George responded, "I don' understan' dat kind er nice-ness. Dey so nicey-nicey, why don' dey let us be free like dem?"

Malindy had no answer to this. She simply drew her son close to her and tried to soothe him, "George, jis' pray to God, chile, pray fo' for-giveness en strength. Be patient, son, freedom a-comin'. You gwine to fin' yo' way, son." Malindy knew George's rage ran deep, and she prayed each day that he would find peace. Her heart told her that she would soon be separated from this son.

While Malindy worried about George, Sammie and Ellen were a great comfort to her. Sammie's levelheadedness reminded her of

Charlie and brought tranquility to the family circle. Massa and Missus took a special interest in Sammie, at times giving him work around the house along with Ellen and Lara.

George also worked on the grounds and sometimes in the stable with the horses. Like Malindy, he loved horses, and he enjoyed working with them. Massa was a tobacco farmer, who grew a large crop. He talked about putting George to work in the tobacco fields. Missouri was one of the biggest tobacco-growing states in the country, providing tobacco for the St. Louis cigar factories as well as rivaling Virginia for the export trade to Britain. Massa's livelihood depended on his tobacco crop, and he wanted George to help work it. This did not sit well with George. One day, George told Malindy that he was not going to work in the fields. George's stubbornness had his desperate mother praying to the Lord to protect her son. At times, Malindy found George unbearable and uncontrollable. The only person who could keep George in line was Old Free Charlie. That night, Malindy called out in her sleep, "Charlie! Come now!" The very next day, Charlie did come.

As Charlie drove his buggy up to the Big House, he caught sight of Sammie and George. They had grown tall and strong. His little boys now looked like giants. They were men now, and Charlie was as proud of their healthy bodies and their fortitude as he was of his daughters' lithe beauty.

Charlie alighted from his buggy and looked at George. George was looking down, kicking a stone in the drive. For years, George had seen his father's helplessness, frustration, and anger at his inability to free his family. George shared Charlie's feeling of being trapped, but he added to it a propensity for violence. Charlie worried about George. While he was on the road, Charlie always prayed a special prayer for him:

> My dear Lord, my wife is hot-blooded, and so am I. George is like his Momma and Poppa. I fear that this nature will kill him for sure. Oh Lord, I love him so much. When I am away, please send your angels down to protect him. By the way, Lord, that George of mine needs ten angels, or more.

Now, Charlie said, "Son, what you been doing lately, other than worryin' your Momma? Have you been listening to your Momma, boy?"

Sammie and Ellen watched intently to see how the drama would play out. George was a guarantee of drama, a walking volcano that might erupt at any time. He was wont to speak the truth at any cost. Charlie understood his son's suffering and was tolerant of his ways.

Charlie knew the pain of being "tainted" with African blood, branded with inferiority in the eyes of whites. He understood how George chafed at the limits on his movements and opportunities. Charlie could not ask George to work hard for the good of the master. But Charlie did want to protect his family from beatings and death.

In the cabin that evening, all attention was on rambunctious George. Anything could happen. George rejected Massa's expectation that Malindy would raise obedient and submissive slaves. He forgot that slave parents were often punished for their children's disobedience. His rebellious nature blinded him to the suffering he would bring on his family. Ellen took him to task.

"George, you done seed Momma's back all tore up, de blood, en scars. You 'member her moans dat night. Do you want dat pain for Momma again, or fo' yo'sef? George, stop bein' so crazy en behave. We is slaves en dat's de way it is." Ellen did not trust what George might do. She wanted Poppa to stay with them to keep George in line.

"Think about your family, son," Charlie said.

"I jis' hates bein' a slave, Poppa," George responded. "It jis' ain't right. Dat auction was horrible. Bad, bad. I gwine to die b'fo' I ever go there agin. No mo' auction block fo' me." Tears ran down George's cheeks. "Poppa, please git us free. De Massa, he sho'ly wants me to work in de field wid de tobacco."

Charlie was firm and gentle with George. "Son, your Momma and I love you very much. You know I wish I could be with you all the time. You know I wish I could free you. Well, I can't, and you are old enough to understand why. I admire your courage, but havin' courage is one thing and bein' foolish is somethin' else. If you don't obey, you'll get whipped. We need your help. If you run away, you'll get the whole family whipped. And if you strike the Massa, you could get yourself hanged."

Malindy shuddered. She could easily imagine George dangling from a tree, stone dead.

Charlie continued, "George, I know you are like me and Malindy. I know how you feel. We all got to keep a-hold of ourselves to survive. The white men are fighting each other now. Soon, they will destroy each other. A change is comin', my son. We will be free."

"I tries hard, Poppa," George responded, "but I ain't no slave in my min' or heart. Poppa, I sees you free, why don' you free us?" The room fell silent. Malindy turned from the fireplace, where she was cooking supper.

"Don' you ever speak to yo' Poppa dat way," Malindy scolded George. "Yo' Poppa is a good man, en he works hard to help us."

"You don't know what I go through to be here with you." Charlie raised his voice. "You don't know my pain or trials. Yes, I have these freedom papers, but do I really have freedom? Son, the answer is no. If I were free, you'd be free. I can't even stay here with you." With his usual big mouth, George had hurt Charlie's feelings.

It came time for Charlie to leave again. His buggy was packed and ready. George hated to see his father leave. He wanted to go with him. When Charlie was home, he didn't work for Massa, or show any submission to him as the other black men on the farm did. Charlie was not expected to be obedient to Massa. To George, his Poppa was free as can be.

George grasped everything Charlie taught him except forgiveness and love of one's enemies. As he bid his father farewell, George's thoughts dwelt on freedom. Charlie had tried to help George, but he too sensed that George's temper would take him away from them. For sure, George would journey on a different path than his Poppa and Momma. If need be, George would use violence.

Ellen admired her big brother George's spunky defiance of slavery. He would not go to the fields. He simply refused to obey Massa's orders. Instead, he chose to help take care of the animals, especially the horses. George was so good with the animals that for a while Massa gave him some leeway and did not punish him for his disobedience. However, caring for the animals was not a full-time job. Massa needed the fieldwork to be done, and he needed more hands to do it. Massa thought that if he gave George more harsh tongue-lashings, George would give in and make a good hand for fieldwork. But George remained adamant about not working in the fields.

George had always played with Massa's teenage sons with no problem. They enjoyed being with each other. They played like any young boys and got along just fine. Soon this friendship would cease. One day, Massa had to go all the way to St. Louis on business. Ellen overheard him giving his two sons orders about what they were supposed to get done during the day while he was in the city: "I don't want you hanging around with that lazy, no-'count George. You better see that he works just like everybody else on this farm. I'm tired of his nonsense. You are not to play with him anymore. You can't let these darkies have their own way. After all, they belong to us, anyway. Remember, our future depends on the way we handle these niggers. They are running away, and the dern slave stealers are everywhere. We have to keep our feet on their necks. You better remember what I'm telling you, because if you don't you'll have to clear and work the fields yourselves. Hear me?"

"Yes, sir." His sons had no choice. Their emotions were torn, because they liked George. They had always been told they were better than the darkies, but when they played games with George, his status had not been an issue for them. This day brought a new game with different rules. Massa's sons had to switch their feelings of love for George to hatred, and to experience the pain and ambiguity that would come with that change.

The hurt ripped at Ellen's heart. Massa's harsh words did not reflect the character of the man who had bought her at the auction block. Her disappointment in Massa overwhelmed her. Malindy had always praised Massa for his kindness. Ellen had never heard him call a slave a "darkie" or a "nigger." The sad realization came to Ellen that deep down Massa was no different from the other slave master who had sold her on the auction block. His self-interest and exploitation of the slaves were the same.

Ellen did not want to tell Malindy what she had heard—she knew that it would be like shooting an arrow right into Malindy's heart. Ellen simply kept her composure and watched Massa leave. As Massa waved goodbye to his sons, he yelled, "You better make that George work or I'm gonna punish you two when I get back." Massa's face was distorted and desperate. Ellen decided that she had to tell Malindy.

It was a clear fall morning. Red, orange, and yellow leaves glowed in the bright sun. Malindy smiled as she looked out the kitchen window. She was grateful for the Creator's blessings. Missus gave Malindy her instructions for the day, telling her to go to the woods to collect herbs. The mistress recognized Malindy's talents as an herbalist and had her prepare herbs for sick slaves. From friendly conversations with Malindy the mistress knew how Malindy loved the woods. Missus was respectful to her, and warmth and friendship had grown between them. George derided this respect. "If dey so respectful, dey wouldn' have one slave on dis yer farm. Dey'd pay us some money and let us go to school like dey own chillen."

Ellen had not yet told her mother of the storm that was brewing. Ellen played with her friends, dismissing George's problem from her mind. It was too much for her. The joy of play erased Massa's harsh words. She did warn George when she saw him that morning. "George, you better be careful en do yo' work. Massa tol' his sons to git you."

"Git me? Ain't nobody gwine to git me! Anyway dey my frens. You jis' watch en see, ain't nobody gwine to touch a hair on dis George's head. Be quiet, gal, wid dat silly talk." George jeered at Ellen and ran to the stable.

Ellen pitied George. "Poor George," she thought, "he don't realize that he ain't got his so-called friends no more." A revelation was on its way.

By midmorning, George had finished taking care of the horses and the big Missouri mules that were the farmer's pride. He was sitting under a big shade tree near the farm pond, playing mumblety-peg with his pocketknife. Each time he threw the knife into the ground, it landed exactly where he wanted it to land. He had great skill with his knife; this was his favorite game. He had enjoyed playing it with Massa's sons many times.

Suddenly, George heard voices. He looked up and saw Massa's sons striding across the pasture to him. Their faces were choked with rage, and they muttered to each other. They no longer resembled his childhood playmates. Ellen's warning to George registered in his mind. It was no joke; the threat was real. George became wary. He closed his knife and put it into his pocket; he did not want to cut Massa's sons. As they rushed toward him, George greeted them with his usual big smile.

"George, you git out there right now and work in the field," the eldest son commanded. "If you don't git out there right now, we're gonna give you the whuppin' you should have had long ago."

"You think you can do like us," the younger added. "You're jis' a nigger, and you better remember it. Boy, you belong to us." They had never called George "boy" or "nigger" before. Now they taunted him, "darky, darky, nigger."

George's warrior blood was stirred. He rose up like a giant, laughing. "You never gwine to be my Massa," he declared. Enraged by his defiance, Massa's sons grabbed him and dragged him into the pond. They ducked his head under water and held it there. Ellen had run down to the pond to see what all the fuss was about. George's head stayed under a long time. Ellen was afraid he would drown. She started jumping up and down on the bank of the pond, yelling, "George, you can git 'em! Git 'em, George!" Just then, George's head popped up. He took a big breath. He heard Ellen's voice, and it gave him strength to fight harder. He twisted from the sons' choking grip, grabbed both of them and butted their heads together. George fought vigorously as they all tumbled deeper into the pond. Massa's sons kept trying to hold George's head under water, but he was too tall and strong for them; he gained the upper hand. He kept butting their heads together and holding them under the water. For a long time, he held their heads underwater with a strong grip.

Fortunately, the sounds of the fight and Ellen's yells had drawn a trusted old slave down to the pond. He rushed to the rescue of Massa's sons.

"George, turn those boys a-loose," he hollered. "Turn 'em a-loose right now. You hear me?"

As he was struggling to get air and keep from drowning, George's rage had become uncontrollable. "How dare they order me aroun'?" he thought. He wanted to kill his so-called masters. The words repeated themselves over and over in his head. "How dare they lay a hand on me?" He fought furiously, roused to a blind, killing rage.

"George, stop dat right now. You gwine to git us all whupped to def' when Massa comes home," the old slave pleaded. "You, George, jis' stop it now."

With the wise words of the old man ringing in his ears, George dragged his enemies out of the water and dumped them on the bank. Ellen was terrified when she thought of what the consequences would be for her brother. She thought the boys were dead, but they took big, shuddering breaths and scrambled away from George toward the white-haired slave. Massa's sons stood up and shook their fingers at George. They were so out of breath they could hardly talk.

"You had your last chance," the elder son's voice croaked like a pond frog. "Now, Poppa's gonna whup you when he gits back home."

"After he whups you, you're gonna be a good slave like old Pops here," the younger son added. The old slave bowed his head and followed his young white masters as they rushed up to the Big House to tell their story to their mother.

"We's in big trouble now, George," Ellen said. George saw only one option for himself: to get out of there. He was sure to be whipped, anyway, so he might as well run away. Ellen could read his thoughts. "George, please don' leave me," she begged. George smiled tenderly at his little sister. His anger was gone. He and Ellen ran to the cabin. Ellen watched tearfully as George stuffed his few clothes in his knapsack. As he fled along one of the old Indian trails, toward the secret cave where Charlie had often taken him to talk, Ellen ran after him.

"Ellen, go on back now. You can't come wid me." George also had tears in his eyes. Ellen stopped and looked at her brother as he ran. When he was almost out of sight, he turned to look back and wave at her. Ellen waved back. She watched intently until her brother disappeared down the trail. It was as if he had left the trail and walked into the turquoise sky to disappear behind a cloud.

Malindy was busy ironing in the laundry room when she heard the shouts of the master's sons coming toward the house. "Momma! Momma!" they called. Malindy walked to the door to see what the commotion was about. The boys were a sight. Their clothes were all wet and muddy, their faces dark red and covered with mud, like beets just pulled from the soil.

"Take a good look at what your lazy son did to us."

"He like to drownded us, that's what." In a frenzied clamor, the boys told Malindy what had happened. It sounded serious. She listened in alarm, reminding herself that this was just their side of the story, that George would tell her his side.

"Well, don't jes' stand there looking silly," the eldest boy said. "Git in the house and bring us some clean clothes. Right now!" Massa's sons had never spoken to her in that way before. She was stunned and frightened by their tone.

Formerly, the boys had taken Malindy's part and had snickered behind their mother's back when the mistress had little spats with Malindy. Malindy had convinced herself that this white family was better than the ones in her past. Today, she was disappointed to realize that slavery was the same everywhere. The smiles and friendliness of Massa and Missus did not change the fundamental fact that she was still a slave to be exploited, a thing to serve their self-interest. Malindy held her tongue. Quickly, she fetched changes of clothes for Massa's sons, who, in one day, ceased to be her friends and became her new masters.

After giving the boys their clothes, Malindy ran down the hill to her cabin to find George. She was ready to hear his side of the story.

Hotheaded though he was, George had never started a fight with anyone before, especially one with Massa's sons. Malindy remembered how well they had always gotten along, and how they had always enjoyed playing with each other. When she entered the cabin, Malindy found it empty of people, but full of the scent of fear.

Malindy's mind filled with questions. She rushed back to the Big House. All her children except Henry seemed to have disappeared. Where were they? What would she say to the mistress about this incident? Malindy thought it best to keep still. She understood a mother's fears and realized how frightened and angry the mistress must be. From the point of view of the mistress, George had just tried to kill her sons. Malindy hoped that the mistress would have compassion for her and spare George. When Malindy entered the kitchen, the mistress greeted her calmly and gave her instructions about preparing supper. She spoke quietly to her.

"Malindy, the boys told me what happened. They said George tried to kill them. It is better that we do not say anything about this until my husband returns home. I'm sure that he will settle the problem in his own way. It is best that you stay out of it."

Malindy froze. She could not say a word. She nodded her head and prayed that her son would escape the severe punishment that lay ahead for him. Malindy had visions of blood, scars, and hanging ropes. Maybe Massa would show mercy. With each breath, Malindy groaned. She dreaded Massa's return to the farm. Missus had instructed Malindy to do what no true mother could do. How could a mother stay out of it? Malindy resolved that she would do everything humanly possible to help George. Where was he? Where was Ellen?

Finally, Ellen came running into the kitchen. "Momma, dey done tried to drown George to his very death in de pond. I saw it wid my own eyes."

"Hush, Ellen," Malindy whispered, "we kin talk about it in de cabin."

"I sho' wish Poppa was here."

"So do I, chile, so do I."

Massa arrived home just in time for supper. As Malindy served the meal, Massa and Missus discussed what to do about George. They talked freely, ignoring Malindy, as though she were not there, or George was not an important person to her. Ellen waited fearfully in the kitchen. Malindy moved mechanically, expressionless. She pretended to be uninterested in their discussion. She felt invisible, a nonentity. She started when Massa spoke to her.

"Malindy, where is that George?"

"I don' rightly know, Massa," Malindy responded. In the kitchen, Ellen overheard the question and shivered. She was the only one who knew that George was hiding in the cave. She knew there were all kinds of critters in the cave, but it was safer there than being with mean old Massa.

"Malindy, when you git to your cabin, send that George to me."

"Yes, Massa," Malindy coughed through her tears.

In the slave quarters, George's story spread like a brush fire. Sammie, Lara, and Henry waited in the cabin for Malindy and Ellen. George's survival was in doubt. How would he get out of this mess?

"Where's George?" Lara asked. "I hear he's in tur'ble trouble."

"I don' know, Lara," Sammie replied. He had noticed, however, that George's knapsack and some of his clothes were missing. George had often told Sammie that he was going to run away. Malindy rushed through the cabin door.

"Where's dat brother of yours?" Sammie silently pointed to where George's clothes and knapsack usually hung on pegs.

"Oh, my Lord, my baby done gone, my poor George!" Malindy dropped to her knees and moaned, hugging a chair to her trembling body.

"George is over yonder on de ol' Injun trail, Momma," Ellen said. "He done gone hours ago. He's way gone fo' sho'."

Malindy's first impulse was to withhold the details of George's disappearance from Massa. She would send Sammie to Massa to tell him that George had run away. She knew Ellen could keep the secret of George's whereabouts. In the end, Malindy decided that she did not want her other children to bear the additional burden of a lie and a secret. Once she had calmed down and gotten her emotions in check, she instructed Sammie and Ellen to go and bring George back.

George was still in the cave. He listened to his brother and sister. "George, ef you don' come back, Massa sho' 'nuf gwine to whup Momma," Ellen said. George realized that he could be facing death as a punishment for hitting the Massa's sons, but Malindy was so deep in his heart that he would rather risk death than cause her suffering. George did not want his family, especially his mother, to suffer reprisals for his disobedience. He returned to the cabin with Sammie and Ellen.

As soon as George walked into the cabin, Malindy grabbed him and held him tight, murmuring, "George, I loves you so. Don' do dat agin."

"Massa gwine to make sho' I don' have no mo' chance to do it," George joked in a shaky voice, looking over her shoulder. "He gwine to kill me dis time." Malindy turned and looked out the window to see Massa and his sons coming up the walkway to her cabin. Tears ran down her cheeks.

The farmer pushed open the cabin door with his foot. He had his shotgun.

"Give me that no-good nigger," he said. "Give him to me now."

George came to the door, standing straight and tall despite his fear. He saw the master's sons, hanging back on each side of their father. He saw the farmer, enraged by the danger to his sons.

"George," the Massa said, shotgun cradled in his arm, "I want you off this farm. I ain't a-goin' to whip you, but you got to get off this place. Go, and don't come back."

Malindy screamed at the top of her voice and fell to her knees. She crawled toward the Massa. "Massa, please don' sen' my chile away fum me," she begged. "I'll make him change, sho' 'nuf. Where will he go, Massa?"

The farmer pushed her aside. "You better be glad I don't have a rope for him," he said. Malindy got up from her knees and told George to go with Massa's sons. She gathered some food into a bag and held it out to him.

"Don't you dare give my food to that lazy nigger," Massa said. "He's on his own now." Massa ordered his sons to walk George off the property, all the way to the main road. Malindy and the other children huddled together in a tight group as they watched George walk away between the brothers.

Malindy was terrified that George was on the road to a quick death. A black person without freedom papers faced acute danger on Missouri roads. Surely, George needed a miracle to survive. Days passed, and Malindy mourned for her son. Every night, the family prayed for his safety and protection. They had no idea where George was or what had happened to him.

George had always been lucky, and his luck held out. Some would say it wasn't luck, but God's protection of one of his children. George did get a miracle that first day on the road. When he had gone only a few miles from the farm, which was farther than he had ever been alone in his life, three white men on horses rode up to him. George was startled and afraid, because he thought they were slave hunters.

"Whose boy are you?" one of the men asked.

"My momma's massa done put me off de farm," George replied.

"What work can you do?" The men seemed downright friendly, and George thought they must be abolitionists. George grinned.

"I kin blacksmith en work with hosses. I cooks en does other things," he answered.

"Well, then, we can use your help," one of the men said, and the others nodded in agreement.

"Come on." One of the men reached a hand down to help George mount up behind him. He gave George a drink from his canteen. George held tightly to the rider as they trotted down the road. They came to a cave. Once lived in by the first Native Americans, Missouri caves were now home to runaway slaves, freedom fighters, and outlaws. This cave was stocked with food and supplies. The men gave George food, drink, a blanket, and a place by the fire. Only one day after leaving Malindy and life on the farm, George had a new home and a new life. George thanked the Creator for this miracle, and Malindy and Charlie for all their prayers for him. He missed Malindy, but he was excited by this adventure and overjoyed because now he called no man Massa. Finally, George felt free.

To George, the white men were his friends and different from the slaveholders. They wanted him to be part of the group. George thought he would finally make some money for his labor. His new friends told him stories about the abolitionists and about the dangers on the roads resulting from the struggles between proslavery Border Ruffians and antislavery Jayhawkers on the Kansas border. The men told him that they themselves were cautious in their movements because of the Border Ruffians. Old Free Charlie had told George that freedom was near for all the slaves, and these men told him the same thing.

The terror on Missouri roads made it far more difficult for Charlie to visit his family. It was safer for him in Illinois. The Missouri Ruffians had no tolerance for free blacks. So Charlie was separated from his family for longer than usual and had no idea of George's banishment or Malindy's grief. Malindy knew that she would see Charlie again, but she feared that she would never see George again. Although Malindy had chosen nonviolence, she still admired George for protecting his integrity. She believed George would be avenged by a higher power. She told her children that at least the auction block was over for him.

Malindy believed Massa's promise that the auction block was over for her and her other children, too, although Ellen doubted that Massa would keep his promise. Malindy felt that God and the spirits of her ancestors were touching her with sparks of energy to help her survive. Every day, she put her arms around Ellen, filling her with hope.

Every day, too, Malindy prayed to God to protect her son George from the patrollers on the road. For consolation, she sang him a song of freedom, "Fly my chile, high my chile, you can run to the Lord." As she worked in Massa's kitchen, she spoke to George under her breath, "Run, my son. Run, George, run." Malindy believed that if she concentrated hard enough, she could communicate with George and transmit her thoughts directly into his brain. Her thoughts did reach George. He heard her, and he ran. With his strong will, Malindy's prayers, and God's protection, George survived for several years.

As the years passed, the tension over slavery in Missouri continued. Malindy and her other children continued to do Massa's work on the farm. Sammie worked closely with Massa and traveled with him across Missouri. Massa gave Malindy no more trouble. The damage was done: He had given her a grieving heart.

"You'll be free or die!"

—Harriet Tubman

⊰———•———⊱

from "the Wanderer of Switzerland"
Welcome wanderer as thou art,
All my blessings to partake;
Yet thrice welcome to my heart,
For thine injured country's sake,

. . . .

Wanderer, whither would'st thou roam?
To what region far away?
Bend thy steps to find a home,
In the twilight of thy day,

. . . .

Where a tyrant never trod,
Where a slave was never known,
But where Nature worships God,
In the wilderness alone.

—James Montgomery

Chapter Ten

THE NATION BECOMES DIVIDED

Some years after Massa drove seventeen-year-old George from the farm, Malindy and the children still wondered what had happened to him, where he was, and whether he was safe. They prayed for his safety.

Sammie had become a great support for the family. Now in his twenties, he had grown into a fine young man, kind and loving. He protected his family as much as he could, warning the male slaves to stay away from his sisters. Sammie adored his sisters, who had grown into beautiful teenage girls. They loved him dearly.

Sammie worked with the horses and drove the master's carriage. Sammie got along with everyone. For years, he spent time playing with Massa's sons. They liked him. At Sammie's age, Massa usually found a male slave a wife. Malindy looked forward to seeing Sammie married.

One day, Malindy was in the kitchen when the master and mistress were rejoicing about the upcoming marriage of one of their sons. Smiling, Massa said, "Malindy, our boy's gettin' him a fine wife. We are going to have some big wedding for him!"

"Yes, Massa, I's bakin' a big beautiful cake, en cookin' plenty of good food, everythin' Missus wants for dis yer grand party." Missus

Sammie and his wife, Frances Burch, at their home on Papin Street in St. Louis, undated.
PHOTO COURTESY OF THE AUTHORS.

talked with Malindy about what food to prepare for the party and about some of the wedding gifts she and Massa were giving their son.

Along with his mother and Ellen, Sammie worked hard to prepare for the wedding party. Finally, the wedding day dawned. So many white folks came to the party that it looked like Massa had invited the whole county. Of course, Massa's slaves were dressed in their Sunday best. Malindy, Ellen, and Lara had everything laid out beautifully for the reception. As the band played and the guests danced, Ellen and Lara looked on, tapping their feet to the music. There was singing and laughter and plenty of food—much joy in the Big House that day.

When the party was almost over, Massa came in as Malindy was cleaning the kitchen. He spoke to her in a firm, low tone. "Malindy, did Missus tell you that I'm giving Sammie to my boy for a wedding present?" Malindy began to tremble in her knees. Her jubilant spirit turned to a fog of disillusionment and sadness. Malindy remembered Massa's promise when he bought her family. He had promised never to sell her or any of her children, and he had kept the letter of his promise. Yet now, in a split second, he robbed her of the company of her firstborn, her precious Sammie, by giving him away.

Massa saw her grief and anger. "Don't you worry about Sammie. He's only goin' to St. Louis. Remember, he's with my son. That's still in the family. When he comes to visit with my son, you'll still get to see him."

Malindy pushed back her tears and asked one question. "Massa, when's my Sammie leavin' me?" She was about to faint. She braced herself, holding herself up with her arms wrapped around her, clutching at her waist. Charlie had always had to travel for a living. To lose George was hard, yet she had always anticipated that some day she would be separated from him. Malindy had never thought she would be separated from Sammie. Sammie never gave anyone any trouble. He followed the rules. As his reward, he became a gift for Massa's son.

"Massa, how's I gwine to tell him he's leavin' me?"

"You don't have to tell Sammie. He knows already. My boy told him. He's gonna drive the carriage for my son in the big city. He'll be a coachman, all dressed up fancy."

Malindy could not look at Massa. With bowed head she prayed to herself: "Dear Lord, how much do I have to bear? First George is gone, now Sammie. Leastways, I know where my Sammie's going and I'll see him sometimes." That gave Malindy some comfort, but she hated not being able to control her life or protect her family. Losing Sammie increased her hostility toward Massa and her distrust of him.

In the cabin, Malindy did her best to comfort her children and be at peace. Ellen and Lara saw their mother's grief and anger on her face. Nevertheless, that last night with their big brother was full of fun. They joked with him about going to the big city with a fancy suit on his back. They thanked God, ate supper, sang songs, and laughed. They filled the cabin with prayers for Sammie's safety in St. Louis.

Sammie promised Ellen that someday he would return for her. He told his sisters and brother never to give up the dream of freedom, because freedom was on its way. Sammie was grateful that he did not have to labor in the fields. He recognized that the best way to help his family was to obey his masters until the freedom bell rang. He believed Old Charlie's assurance that freedom was coming, and he encouraged his family to hold on to the dream.

Morning came. The family woke with the sunrise. Sammie was all packed and ready to go. Ellen stood distraught. Lara hated the fact that her big brother was leaving. Now she and Ellen would have to protect themselves from the males, white and black, on the farm.

Malindy solaced her fragmenting family with a cheerful smile.

"Everythin' gwine to be jis' fine, Sammie. Don' you worry about us. You jis' take care of yo'sef. Remember we loves you. Remember yo' Poppa's promise. Freedom's a-comin'." Malindy smiled at Sammie, and he hugged his mother, tears shining in his eyes.

"Look at dat! Big brother cryin'!" Ellen joked. "Better not let Massa see dat. He keep you here en you have to work wid dose nasty hogs!" Ellen looked admiringly at Sammie. "I jis' can't wait to see you in dat coachman's suit. I's gwine to tell Poppa, 'Yes, that Sammie's up in St. Louis, bein' all fancy en proper en sich.'"

The family walked Sammie up to the Big House, helped him load up the buggy, saw him take his place on the driver's seat, and waved as he drove away. Silently they stood watching until the buggy disappeared down the road.

Now Ellen had no doubt that her owners saw slaves not as real people but as mere things. How else could they dare give a human being as a gift? Now she had a better understanding of Charlie's struggle.

Charlie's next homecoming was tinged with sadness by the loss of Sammie from the family circle. Charlie felt his second-class status, as though degradation were tattooed on every inch of his skin. He had been robbed of his manhood as his children were torn from the loving embrace of his wife. His children wore the badge of a transient people with no true home. His firstborn, Sammie, did not even bear his own surname of Wilson, but would be known all his life by the last name of Burch, which he picked for himself.

Charlie saw the lively gleam fade from Malindy's eyes, to be replaced by sadness. The images of her missing sons, Sammie and George, crowded her thoughts. She stopped asking Charlie if he was ever going to buy their freedom. As it was, the slave laws of Missouri already put enough pressure on her husband. She would not add to it.

Now Ellen was the oldest of Malindy's three remaining children at home. She worked closely with her mother in the Big House. As Ellen matured, she understood more of the conversations she overheard there. She had her parents' gift of insight. She could read people and size them up the minute she saw them. She observed Massa's fears mount as abolitionists and the Underground Railroad advanced the cause of freedom.

Malindy saw Sammie when he drove Massa's son out to the farm from St. Louis. She was always happy to see Sammie all dressed up as a coachman. At least as a house slave he was not dirty from hard toil in the fields, she thought. Like his father, Sammie always brought gifts.

The first time Sammie came back to Massa's farm, Malindy inquired, "How dey treatin' you up there, son?"

"Right good, Momma, right good, but I'm still a slave. I don' ever forget dat or my brothers in de hot fiel's," Sammie replied. "Momma, dey's free black men en women in St. Louis. They have a Baptist church." Sammie spoke low to his mother about freedom, telling her the news he got from freedmen in St. Louis.

As for George, all the family knew was that if he were still alive, he was out there somewhere. Missouri roads had become full of guerillas. This made Charlie especially concerned about George's safety.

In fact, however, George was living with his white companions. His mother's love remained with him. He had no doubt that he would see her someday. He planned to free his whole family with the help of his friends. He often wished that he would run into his Poppa on the hidden trails where he and his friends rode secretly from place to place. Since George did not have freedom papers, his white friends told whites they met in the towns or on the roads that he was their slave. George never felt like a slave with them—he knew that they said this to protect him.

Despite the murky nature of his activities, George had a sense of accomplishment. He had his own horse, good clothes, and money in his pocket. Plus, he had outwitted the slaveholders by escaping from a life of slavery.

The white men with George were poor. Like George, they felt that the ruling classes oppressed them. Also, like some other poor whites, they felt that the slave owners deprived white laborers of wages for work by using slave labor. To their minds, slave labor robbed the bread from their own children's mouths. These white men thought that they were entitled to use any means necessary to take back something for themselves from the ruling classes. George's companions refused to be shackled by the lords of the land. They charted a map to secure their manhood in a society that they saw as built on deception, fraud, and blood. They chose vengeance and fought the slaveholders on their own terms. George's band was one more flame consuming the burning tower of Missouri.

Malindy was always eager for her children to become educated. Charlie could read well, but he could not stay in Missouri long enough to teach her or the children how to read more than a little. So most of what his family learned was by word of mouth.

Lately, everyone on Massa's farm had been talking about the Dred Scott case. Scott was a slave in St. Louis who had sued for his freedom in 1846. In 1857, the U.S. Supreme Court held that because he was a slave he could not be a citizen. That meant that he could not sue as a citizen in federal court. He had no right to be there. The Court also said that even though his master had taken him into the free state of Illinois, and into free federal territory, Dred Scott remained a slave. Whatever the Court said, Dred Scott became a hero in slave yards nationwide. His effort to take his master to court was a beacon of courage.

The country's economy was faltering amidst the political turmoil, and Old Free Charlie felt the pain of worsening poverty. How could he protect his family? He shared his wife's concern as their two daughters developed into beautiful young women who could at any point be taken from Malindy's side and forced into separation or marriage.

"God, please don' let Massa take another one of my chillen," Malindy would cry as Charlie comforted her in his strong arms. As he looked around the cabin, the faded images of George and Sammie tugged at his heart. His wife was crushed by their loss, and he could not promise her anything but his own love. He was helpless. It was the law: There was nothing he could do.

Ellen loved her father, and she never doubted his love for the family. She understood the difficulties he faced. Like Malindy, Ellen always showed gratitude for everything Charlie did for the family. Malindy did not allow the whites' power to cloud Charlie's image in the children's minds. She always praised Charlie to the children and explained to them that he was doing the best he could for them, under the circumstances.

When he was at the farm and sat with them around the fireplace, Charlie told them that the white men were fighting among themselves now and that the politicians were saying that the thunder of war would soon roll across the nation. Charlie took the threat of war seriously. He prepared his family for the worst.

One day, he and Malindy went for a walk in the woods. Charlie said, "Malindy, I know it's comin'. I can see a dark cloud of smoke over the hills of Missouri. I may not be able to see you in wartime. Malindy, you must stand strong. Our family will get through this and be truly free. Our ancestors will be avenged. Justice is on its way." Malindy felt Charlie's intensity. Every word came from the depth of his being. He was a man who truly walked in the spirit. Malindy thought of being reborn as a free woman. As Charlie stood before her he said, "God is in control. He is goin' to set us free, soon. Be patient, Malindy, and obedient to God. Like Moses, God will carry us across the waters."

Malindy was grateful for her husband's cheering words, grateful that today, at least, he was walking beside her, holding her hand. "I knows God will save us," she responded. "As the tree stands tall en strong, I's gwine to be like de oak tree en be strong."

The next day, Charlie, the wanderer, prepared to leave again. He was confident that his wife's strength and courage would prevail. Silently, Malindy walked Charlie to his buggy. They embraced each other. Malindy tried to hide her sadness, but Charlie could see it in her eyes and her mechanical movements. She could never fool him.

Ellen handed Charlie a pail of food to take with him. This was the first time she had ever cooked for her Poppa. Her pride shone out all over her. Ellen was the considerate child. She loved to be of service to her family. Charlie was proud of Ellen, Lara, and Henry. They were good folk like Malindy. He was grateful that Ellen understood obedience and saved her family from unnecessary trouble.

The family waved goodbye, holding back their tears until Charlie was out of sight. As he pulled onto the road on that hot, humid day in the summer of 1858, Charlie was thinking of George. He sensed a presence, and he had a weird feeling that George was near.

Malindy and Ellen spent the rest of the day canning fresh vegetables and fruits for the winter months. The master raised everything but sugarcane and cotton. He kept beehives, and they produced lots of honey. Little Henry loved honey. His curiosity sometimes got him in trouble. Ellen tried to keep him out of the honey and safe from bee stings. She was the protector of the younger children. She had a big heart and a natural air of authority. Her siblings thought she was a skinny, bossy giant with a loving heart. Malindy saw herself in Ellen and remembered her own youth and innocence. Ellen always worked hard beside her mother in the kitchen of the Big House and in the cabin.

As usual, it was nighttime when Malindy and Ellen left the Big House for the cabin. As they walked home together, they chatted about the events of the day, the Massa's life and business. Life revolved around Massa and his family's needs and desires.

"I's so tired, so tired of livin' my life for white folk," Malindy exclaimed. "Some day, my chile, you gwine to have a life 'thout de Massa en Missus breathin' down yo' back. Believe me, you'll see."

Ellen smiled. She said, "I sees myself wid my long, pretty dress en bonnet jis' a-walkin' wid my umbrella all over dat big St. Louis, free as free, Momma. I's gwine to go to school en learn somethin', learn a lot, like Poppa. Oh, I already miss Poppa so much.."

When Charlie went on his journeys, the family missed his views on the outside world and the stories he read them. Without Charlie, they had no books, and no time to read anyway, as they worked from dawn to dusk and had no lanterns.

The night was simmering hot, and Malindy and Ellen were dead tired when they reached the cabin. Henry was hungry. Malindy cooked supper, and they all ate silently. Malindy and Ellen were strangely preoccupied with thoughts of George. After supper, they laughed and talked on the porch for a while before going to bed. Bright moonglow surrounded the cabin, so that only the most brilliant stars were visible. The cabin seethed with heat, even with the windows unshuttered. There was no breeze that night, no rustling leaves, only the sounds of frogs and crickets. Lightning bugs surrounded the cabin like a ring of dazzling diamonds.

"Wid all dat fuss de frogs makin', I reckon dey's gwine to be a lot of rain tonight," Malindy said.

"We sho' could use some rain 'roun' here right now," Ellen replied.

"Well, when I was a little gal, my folk done tol' me dat de chorus of de frogs is a sign fo' rain." Malindy put her arm around Ellen. "You gwine to be a fine woman, Ellen, I jis' knows it. Charlie, he always talkin' 'bout you bein' de storyteller. 'Dat Ellen listen to every word en breath,' he says. 'Her big ears gwine to serve dis family well. I hear talk of Negroes writin' books and newspapers. Some day, all our chillen gwine to be in school.' Poppa tol' me that, en I believe my Charlie." Malindy beamed at her daughter.

As she looked at Ellen, Malindy grew thoughtful, remembering the ways of the Cherokees she was taught as a child. Among them, education was encouraged. Many Cherokees could read and write. Malindy had received bits and pieces of information about her people from Charlie over the years. She knew that the Cherokee Nation was prospering. Tahlequah, their new capital in the Oklahoma Territory, had elegant neoclassical public buildings and a library. Books, pamphlets, and a newspaper, the *Cherokee Phoenix and Indians' Advocate,* were printed in the Cherokee language, which had its own alphabet and was taught in the Cherokee public schools.

Ellen saw that Malindy was lost in thought. She shook her mother's arm. "Momma, listen to me. Sammie say he's comin' fo' me some day. We'll take care of you. Don' worry."

Lara and Henry were sound asleep on their pallets on the cabin floor. Henry liked to sleep in the loft, but the loft was far too hot tonight. Both Ellen and Malindy were exhausted. As they were getting ready for bed, they heard a noise outside. It sounded like horses' hooves. A bridle jangled. Footsteps crossed the front porch to the cabin door.

Ellen clung to her mother. Malindy put her arm around Ellen's shoulders. They both prayed that it wasn't the patrollers, the bad men that scoured the roads, coming to search the cabin for runaways. Startled and silent, they waited. There came a quick, sharp knock at the door. Someone was in a hurry.

"Momma, open de do' en let me in. It's me, George." His voice rasped deeper, but Malindy recognized it. The way he said "Momma" was just the same as she remembered it. Malindy's heart jumped. She and Ellen ran to the door to let George in. The lost son had returned. They all were overwhelmed with joy. Malindy stepped back, holding George by the shoulders, and turned his face to the moonlight to see him better. There he stood, so very handsome, tall, with shoulder-length, black, wavy hair. His eyes shone with pure excitement. He was very nervous. Now, he held his mother at arm's length.

"Momma, Momma, I done come here to take you outen dis Hell to freedom! Hurry en git ready. We got to go right away." George's voice shook with urgency. Now Malindy could see over his shoulder. He was not alone. Some rugged-looking white men on horseback were behind him. Malindy looked at her grown-up son apprehensively.

"Hush, chile. Jis' let me look at you. Calm down, chile, en jis' let me look at you." Malindy pulled George close to her again.

"You got to hurry. Right now, Momma!" George repeated. Ellen woke Lara and Henry. They were happy and surprised to see their big brother.

"Ellen, gal, you're a tall one, en pretty, too," George said, his voice warm with love. "Now get dressed 'cause I'm takin' you straight to freedom." He turned to Malindy again. "Dey ain't no time fo' 'splainin'. Jis' trus' me. I got a buggy hid away on dat hidden trail. I got plenty supplies. Please, Momma, hurry en git ready now."

Malindy froze as she caught sight of blood on George's coat sleeve. Her joy congealed into fear. Her son was before her, tall and strong, but he was bleeding. Now she saw the gun in a holster in his belt. She realized that he had been wounded. "George, you let me take a look at dat arm," she insisted.

George stood by the window looking around the little cabin as if nothing were wrong with him. Pain radiated down his arm, but he was so concentrated on his goal of freeing his family that he payed no attention to it. He saw only how much Malindy had aged, the toll that the pain and torments of slavery had taken on his beloved mother. Seeing her so worn out hurt him more than his own physical pain. For George, freedom for his mother took precedence over everything else.

Malindy said, "Ellen, run git me de herbs en some water en clean cloths." Working by the light of the moon pouring through the cabin window, Malindy peeled back George's shirt, washed the wound, put a poultice of herbs on it and held the herbs in place with strips of clean cloth. As she dressed her son's arm, years of worry tumbled out in questions.

"Son, where you been dese seven years? How you been livin? What you been doin'? Who are dese men? Where dey come from?"

"I been wid dese men since de first day I lef' here. I uz about ten mile up de road when dey run into me. Dey ask me where I's a-goin' en whose boy I is. I tol' 'em I didn't have nowheres to go, 'cause my Momma's massa done run me off his lan'. I tol' 'em straight out dat my name was George en dat I could shoe hosses en take good care of 'em. One of 'em said, 'George, kin you cook?' I tol' him I could do 'bout anythin'. Dey took me wid 'em en from dat day I wasn't never called 'boy' or 'nigger' no mo', jis' 'George.' Dese men are my fren's. I lives with dem in caves en all over, Momma. I done seed a lot!" George's eyes glowed and he spoke quickly in his excitement.

Ellen, Lara, and Henry listened, eyes wide, fear of the unknown sending chills running down their spines. Ellen prayed that Massa and his sons would not get wind that George was in the cabin. She felt hot and cold all over. She loved George so much. She was thrilled about his freedom, but terrified of the danger. She remembered the stories Old Free Charlie told about the bloody battles on the Missouri and Kansas borders.

Ellen wondered whether these white men were abolitionists. She had heard that abolitionists were mostly men of Christ and gentlemen. Ellen peeked out the window at these men, slouched easy in the saddle, as though they were part of the horses. They were unshaven and unkempt, hair straggling under their wide brimmed hats. The moonlight showed the wear on their rough clothes and gleamed on their revolvers, gunbelts, and rifles. These men looked like they had never seen the inside of a church and wore far too many handguns to be gentlemen. Most white men had hunting guns for hunting, but handguns were for something else.

Of course, Massa's gentlemen friends went to church and then went right home and whipped their slaves. Churchgoing gentlemen like Massa did not help George, but these men had. Ellen was grateful to George's friends for keeping her brother safe all these years. She was ready to go with George.

George looked at Malindy and pleaded with her. "Please, Momma, hurry. Everythin's ready. Trus' me. Please. My fren's will keep us safe. Dey done kep' me safe all dese years. Dey don' believe in slavery. Please git ready." George's voice became strained as he tried to convince his mother. "Come wid me, Momma. I kin take you to a free state. Hurry en come."

"No, son, we ain't never gwine to be free 'til the gov'mint says we's free. Den we goes our own way en lives in peace." Malindy shook her head sadly at George. "You ain't free now, only yo' spirit's free. You's in hidin', en in great danger ridin' 'round wid no freedom papers. Missouri is bad now. Wicked men is killin' en stealin' en dey got dogs everywhere. I love you, George, en I thank you, but I can't put dese chillen in danger. I mus' live by de law 'til freedom come. I knows life here on Massa's farm, but I don' know yo' life en what's out dere. I has to keep dese chillen safe. We got to stay here for Poppa, so's he can fin' us."

George burst out crying. His dream for his family was not to be realized. He had come all this way and been shot, and now his Momma wouldn't come with him. He couldn't carry her to freedom.

One of the white horsemen called out, "Hurry up, George. We gotta git the hell out of here right now. If you're comin' with us, come on." George started for the door. He turned to Malindy and reached out to give her some gold coins from his pouch.

"I love you, George, but I can't take dat gold," Malindy said softly. For George, it was as if the wings of his will had been clipped; no winds of the spirit could support him to soar. He felt like someone had kicked him hard in the knees. He shoved the money in his pocket. In pain and sorrow, he reached out to hug Ellen, Lara, and Henry one last time. As George turned to leave, they cried out, "Don' go, don' go." Lara held tight to little Henry. Ellen and Malindy sobbed.

"I don' know when I ever kin see you all agin," George's voice showed his anger. He shouldered the burden of rejection. He strode out the door and mounted his horse. "Yes Momma, I'm free, an' that's what I want for you," George cried out, with his hand on his gun. He was ready for Massa and his sons. "I ought ter go up dere en kill all dose white folk fo' what dey done to my family."

George thought of himself as a freedom fighter and was tormented by his failure to liberate his own family. Ellen felt her brother's bitter disappointment but wanted to stay with Malindy, no matter what. Gloom hung over Ellen like a shroud as she peeped out the window to get one last look at George. The three white men sat tall on their big horses. Their wide-brimmed hats shadowed their faces, and their dark, shining coats hung long. Ellen could hear the creak of leather and the deep breathing of the horses, then only the sound of hooves as George and his friends disappeared into the night.

Now, Malindy had still another tragic memory. This had become the saddest night of her life. What had happened to her beloved son? Who was he now? Had he forgotten altogether about God and forgiveness? These white men did not look like abolitionists and freedom fighters. Malindy had heard Massa and his friends talking about the border wars. She knew that freedom fighters like John Brown used guns to free slaves, but George had too much gold for a freedom fighter.

George's belligerent attitude, his handgun, and his wound gave Malindy an idea where the gold coins must have come from. She surmised that George and his friends were outlaws. She had terrifying visions of what George's life must be like. She fell to her knees crying and calling on God to have mercy on George's life and his choice to ride with such dangerous men.

Ellen always remembered the night that George came home. George had fulfilled his dreams—he was free. The white men rode with him to save his family and waited for him outside. There he was with a pocket full of gold and his own horse. This represented freedom to Ellen. He loved his family, and he risked his life to save them. George was Ellen's hero.

George had given Ellen hope that someday she would be free. Afterwards, she and Lara talked often about freedom, and how they would live in a big house like Massa. In the meantime, Ellen helped her mother with the kitchen work and looked after her younger siblings to keep them out of trouble.

Malindy worked hard in the Big House. Ellen and Lara both helped her now. Even playful little Henry was old enough to work in the Big House. They had little time for leisure, but every night, Malindy made supper in the cabin and had a meal with her three children. Then they said their prayers and went to bed.

Old Free Charlie continued to fend off the dangers on the roads to return to his family. Though making a living was hard, he still managed to bring them things. Malindy told Charlie all about George's effort to set them free. Charlie was proud of George's courage.

John Brown was an abolitionist who "liberated" slaves by killing their masters and transporting the slaves out of Missouri.
WOOD ENGRAVING AFTER A PHOTOGRAPH BY J. W. BLACK AND COMPANY, N.D. MHS PHOTOGRAPHS AND PRINTS.

"Malindy, our son tried to free you. I've never been able to do that for you. It hurts me to my very soul that I can't give you an ounce of freedom. Don't worry about our son, or judge him. He has friends and God. Are Massa and Missus our friends? No!"

"I jis' don' want our son on dat road to hell, Charlie, wid dose outlaw men."

"All our life, Malindy, we've bowed our heads down—'Yes, sir; yes ma'am; yes, Massa; yes, Missus'—to the biggest outlaws in the land. Our son doesn't have freedom papers like me, but he has friends that risked their lives to come help him free his family. Let's not judge them, but pray for them."

As always, Charlie's words refreshed Malindy. It made her secretly happy that George had friends who would fight for him, and against slave owners, though she herself was committed to living under the law.

"When I uz young," Malindy explained, "my people taught me to obey de laws of de tribe. I knows slavery is wrong, but it's de law. We's jis' like a mountain lion wid a paw caught in a trap, but we's gwine to git loose. We'll be free someday. I knows I won't never see my George agin, but he's in my heart. Thank God I knows where my Sammie is. Charlie, we's blessed, we knows where four of our chillen is."

For Malindy the political turmoil which was dividing the nation and separating fathers, sons, and brothers from one another reflected her own life. From the time she was seven years old, she had known the agony of separation from her loved ones. First she was stolen from her parents and her Cherokee people, then she was sold away from her surrogate parents, then her two older sons were sent away. Malindy felt that slave owners had declared ceaseless war on her person. She lived each day with an internal war, struggling to keep peace with Massa and Missus for the sake of her family.

Charlie told Malindy about John Brown, the abolitionist who "liberated" slaves by killing their masters and then transporting the slaves out of Missouri. Soon, the whole country would burst into the flames of war. After the federal government offered a reward for his capture, John Brown fled Missouri and returned to the East. His raid on the federal arsenal at Harpers Ferry, Virginia, in October 1859 ended with his capture by Robert E. Lee, then a colonel in the United States Army. John Brown was subsequently tried for murder and treason and hanged by the state of Virginia. Because his intention was to end slavery, John Brown was regarded by Malindy and the other slaves as a martyred hero.

Slaves were surrounded by death and struggled to keep their spirits alive. But Malindy continued to move across Massa's yard with dignity and grace. Her eyes stayed on the prize, her children's freedom. In times of distress, she saw visions of her ancestors. She remembered the faded faces of her parents, her mother's love, and the feeling of safety in the clan's protection. Malindy's clear recollections of her mother enabled her to be the best possible mother to her children. Every day she lived, every breath she took was dedicated to the Creator and her children.

No merciless master, no wretchedness of slavery ever overwhelmed Malindy's spirit. She refused to feel inferior to anyone. Her refusal to accept slave status made her life more difficult. She aged rapidly as she expended her energies working for Massa, controlling the defiance rumbling in her heart, and yearning for her menfolk.

Ellen saw how worn out her mother had become. Ellen wished that Old Free Charlie, Sammie, and George were with them. She remembered the sound of the horses' hooves as George and his white companions had galloped away, drifting into the moonlight. As Malindy aged, Ellen was burdened with increased responsibility. Fortunately, Lara and Henry were quiet types, obediently following Ellen's direction.

Ellen longed for George and the outlaws to come back and rescue her from under the hammer of slavery. She looked at her mother and the other older slave women. She did not want to be like them and live out her life as a slave or see her children born into slavery. She prayed for freedom every night. But Ellen knew that, even if George did come back to free her, she could never leave Malindy. Malindy saw that her daughter was deep in thought and tried to comfort her.

"Gal, you jis' do too much thinkin'. Now, don' you worry yo' min' too much. Everythin' gwine to be all right."

"Momma, when's Poppa comin' to see us? He's been away so long. It look like somethin's wrong. I hope Poppa's not dead."

"Don' you worry about yo' Poppa. Dey ain't nothin' he can't handle. He'll be 'long soon's he can." Ellen smiled at her Momma, appreciating her reassurance.

Ellen loved to talk and chattered nonstop in the kitchen with her

Momma. She worried about what would happen to her.

"Don' you fret, Ellen," Malindy said. "You'll be free someday, en you'll have a fine husban' en plenty of chillen."

Malindy wanted her children to feel safe, but she realized how vulnerable they were. Missouri slaveholders were still renting out slaves to other farms in Missouri or selling them south. Everything was up for grabs in Massa's world. Malindy hoped Massa would keep his promise not to sell her and her family.

Charlie always reassured Malindy. He encouraged her with stories about Abraham Lincoln, a good man working against slavery. "As I would not be a slave, so I would not be a master," Lincoln said. He was the presidential candidate of the "nigger-loving" Republican Party that stood against slavery. He won the election and became the sixteenth president in 1861. Slave owners feared that he would take their slaves by force, and they became more militant.

People said that Lincoln liked trees and felt kinship with them. Lincoln knew that a person's character is revealed by trials, as wind and lightning expose the heart of a tree. Malindy felt she could trust a man who understood trees. She wondered if Lincoln would plant the tree of freedom. Would she ever have the right to stand with the hard maple, pine, cedar, spruce, and cypress, and say, "Oh, yes, I am free. We are all free"?

"Liberty came to the freedmen not in mercy, but in wrath, not by word choice, but by military necessity, not by generous action of the people among whom they were to live and whose good-will was essential to the success of the measure, but by strangers."

—*Frederick Douglass*

———————

"A man who won't die for something is not fit to live."

—*Dr. Martin Luther King Jr.*

Chapter Eleven

FREE, FREE AT LAST

A s soon as Lincoln was elected, trumpets blew across the land in the form of orations from politicians, preachers, and journalists. They spoke of slavery and secession. The violence they heralded was soon to occur and define a dark period for Missouri and the whole nation.

Malindy and the other slaves bore the brunt of the burden of increased tensions in the Big House. Massa and Missus were more upset than ever. The life they knew seemed doomed, and they would fight to save it.

Charlie was traveling home to Malindy in Missouri while the new president was on his way to Washington. Both men were in great danger from the partisans of slavery. While both men traveled with faith in God and divine protection, only Lincoln had armed bodyguards.

On the dark roads, where ruthless guerillas roamed, Charlie prayed for peace and freedom for his family and country. He understood the mentality of the slaveholders and the great challenge facing the new president. Despite the fact that the slave laws plagued Charlie's family, he still had compassion and forgiveness for the whites. Charlie loved a country that did not love him.

Even when he traveled in the so-called free state of Illinois, Charlie could never let his guard down. Around his neck perpetually hung the Black Law of Illinois, adopted in 1853 to prevent black immigration into the state. Under this law, similar to those in other free states, any free Negro or mulatto from another state remaining within the borders of Illinois for ten days was subject to a fifty-dollar fine, with the fine increasing by fifty dollars for each repeated offense. Blacks unable to pay the fine were to be sold at public auction, for a short period of servitude, to anyone who would pay their fine. Persons who helped blacks settle in the state could be fined five hundred dollars and imprisoned for up to a year. Even though Charlie was a free man, he could be temporarily enslaved for want of fifty dollars, a large sum at that time.

Slave auctions continued in Missouri. Every week, Malindy heard of slave daughters and sons from neighboring farms who were sold to the Deep South. She saw the hatred intensify in the white folks' faces as their anxiety deepened. The fear of losing their slaves made the whites more suspicious of them. Now, Missus had few friendly conversations with Malindy.

Slaves continued to praise John Brown's memory. Ellen was curious about Lincoln. She wanted to know whether he would save them. Ellen wondered whether Lincoln was like John Brown: "Momma, who is dis man Lincoln? Missus en Massa sho' don' like him a bit. Dey talkin' 'bout him all de time. I guess he's pooty important. I knows fo' sho', whoever he is, he's got Massa right by de tail. Massa is rightly scared out of his britches. It look dat way to me. Momma, all dem white folks is scared to death. Dey talkin' 'bout war. Nothin' but mo' trouble, Momma. Seems like dem white folks knows how to fin' trouble for everybody. We all may be killed."

"Don' worry," Malindy reassured Ellen. "God knows what He's a-doin'. De time is here fo' white folks to pay. God picks de time, remember dat my chile. God says, no mo' of dis yer slavery. Let my people go. Massa en his frien's better listen, or it gwine to be jis' too bad for dem."

Malindy prayed that her children would remain with her, and that her boys and Charlie would not get caught up in the white men's war. She prayed, too, that Charlie would come home and stay with her and their children. Malindy told Ellen: "God always win, watch en see. Dis man Lincoln, Poppa says he's a good man who hates slavery. Maybe we can trus' him. White folks 'roun' here says all kind of bad things about him. They call him 'nigger lover' en a bastard en say bad things 'bout his granny en his momma. Some say he looks dark. He bein' dark is a good thing 'cause most white folks I see cause me only pain en trouble. We jis' has to pray fo' him every day. He need all de prayers he can git to deal wid dese debbils."

Some in the proslavery camp claimed that Lincoln was a mulatto. His mother, who was described as tall with a dark complexion, was said to be the illegitimate child of a Virginia gentleman and a mulatto woman. The rumor that Lincoln himself had African ancestry was intended to demean him, but it was a sign of hope to Malindy.

During this period, Massa had many visitors. Much debate about secession occurred. Ellen and Malindy listened intently to everything. Hostility toward the slaves mounted. One day Massa said, "I need to sell all these niggers, before they run away with the Yankee abolitionists. We have to watch every move they make."

Massa and Missus were growing old. They had enough money for themselves, but they wanted to secure their farm and slaves for their heirs. When Massa talked about his property, Malindy understood that she and her children were part of the inventory of his assets. The commotion over secession made it more difficult to liquidate these human flesh assets. The slaveholders who visited Massa mourned over their projected economic losses.

Malindy encouraged her three children to keep the faith and ignore the talk. "Don' you let on dat you knows what all's happenin'," Malindy said. "You can't smile at Massa's misery. We knows dat freedom is comin'. Let's pray dat de evil men don' kill us. Don' you go in de woods or out on de road. You stay close to de Big House en de cabin, hear me?"

Malindy's prayer was answered. Old Free Charlie did come home. He knew of the imminent perils to himself and his family, so he decided to stay closer to his home. In the midst of turmoil, Charlie would bring Malindy some peace with his love.

Massa did not mind Charlie staying with Malindy. Massa believed that Charlie would not break the law of the land. For his family's safety, Charlie would stay in his place. In addition, Charlie supplied the mistress with herbs and helped the slaves do their chores. He still continued to bring things home from his travels to improve his family's slave cabin.

Malindy's spirits were always higher when Charlie was on the farm. Ellen and Lara were glad to see their mother happy for a change. At night, Charlie would go from cabin to cabin in the slave quarters, visiting the menfolk and telling them stories of his travels. To the ones he trusted, he spoke of politics and the possibility of war. He had great faith in the new president. Charlie often said, "This man, Lincoln, I hear, is an honest man who wants freedom for all of us."

Ellen, Henry, and Lara walked in the woods with Charlie to gather herbs. He passed on to them his knowledge of herbs and medicines. Many cold nights in the cabin, Charlie kept the fire going in the fireplace and watched over his family.

Most of the time, however, Charlie felt helpless. Sometimes, he thought of defiance, but he realized that any aggressive behavior would only cause more problems. Even if he could take his family away, where would he take them? He had no money and lived in a country that hated him. What alternative was there to life in the slave cabin? While he kept up the image of strength, his internal struggle tormented him. Malindy could see her husband's pain. Every day he spent on the farm challenged his manhood to the core. Smiling and grinning when he was with Massa, who held Charlie's family prisoner, only aggravated his sense of injustice.

One night, Malindy spoke to Charlie as she lay in his arms. "You don' have to stay here. We'll be all right. Go on back to Illinois. Try to make more money. We'll need money when we's free. We done traveled a long, hard journey, but de road ahead still goes far over de mountain. God got us here. He takes us yonder. We'll git there, Charlie."

Charlie told her how much he loved her and appreciated her courage. He said, "My place is here now with you. I'll go to farms in Missouri to sell herbs, and do some work with freedmen in St. Louis. We'll have some money when freedom comes. Malindy, you and our children won't starve." Charlie's words of encouragement gave Malindy a sense of security and peace.

With the first shot fired on Fort Sumter, on April 12, 1861, the Civil War began in earnest. During the summer and fall of 1861, the struggle to hold Missouri in the Union became raw-boned warfare, embroiling civilians in its toils and pointing a menacing finger toward the specter of future devastation. The battle of Wilson's Creek, near

Springfield, Missouri, on August 10, 1861, was considered a draw. It resulted in the first death of a Union general, Nathaniel Lyon. Guerilla warfare, long concentrated on the Kansas border, spread throughout the state.

The widespread civil unrest made it even more difficult for Charlie to make a living at home in Missouri. He decided, reluctantly, to leave his family again for a short period and go back over to Illinois to earn money.

Missouri was at war with itself. For every Missourian who fought for the Confederacy, three fought for the Union. Families across the state had some members loyal to the Confederacy and some loyal to the Union. Their slaves made clothes for soldiers on both sides of the conflict. In the Big House, Malindy and her daughters also sewed clothes for both armies. Malindy and her family understood what was happening around them. Although Massa strove to keep his slaves ignorant of the war, news reached the slave quarters quickly.

Old Free Charlie heard the news about the war on the roads and in the towns of Missouri and Illinois. He told Malindy that the Confederates had tried to take over Missouri, so as to use St. Louis as a port for war activity. Malindy was happy to hear that the Union Army prevented the takeover and that Union soldiers were stationed at Jefferson Barracks, near St. Louis. One day, as she was working up at the Big House, Malindy was humming and smiling, for in her mind she could smell freedom.

"What you got to smile about, gal?" Massa asked.

"Jis' prayin' for dem boys down yonder, Massa, we want 'em back home wid us," Malindy replied. She did not lie. She always prayed for Massa's sons. But it was Union Army victories that brought joy to her heart.

On September 22, 1862, shortly after the Union Army had turned back the Confederate Army's incursion into Maryland at Antietam, President Lincoln relied on his war powers to issue the Emancipation Proclamation. This document offered the Confederate States the chance to keep their slaves if they would lay down their arms and return to the Union in the next one hundred days. The Confederates did not trust this offer and rejected it. Therefore, on January 1, 1863, the Emancipation Proclamation took effect, freeing all slaves in those states that were in rebellion as of that date.

News of the proclamation spread like wildfire. But the Emancipation Proclamation did not free slaves in the Union states and Tennessee and the other border states of Delaware, Maryland, Kentucky, and Missouri. Malindy did not understand why Missouri slaves were not freed, but she rejoiced for her fellow slaves. She had faith that her own turn would come.

Although the Proclamation did not free his own family, Old Free Charlie, too, was happy for the slaves who were emancipated. He had always had faith that God would do this for his people. Charlie warned Malindy to be careful, because now the slaveholders in Missouri would become more repressive.

"Massa's so mad, I don' rightly know what he's a-gwine to do next, Charlie," Malindy said.

"Just keep doin' your work and don't mind Massa." Charlie encouraged her. "I don't think he'll do anythin'. He's not as bad as some of 'em 'roun' here. They're scared of the future, Malindy. We have to pray for freedom, that it'll come soon to Missouri."

"How come we don' git our freedom wid de others?" Malindy asked, tears of disappointment in her eyes. "We jis' knowed Lincoln was gwine to free us all."

Charlie couldn't answer her question, for he had no idea. That freedom came only to some slaves confused many people. Charlie could only console his wife. He also warned the other slaves to be watchful, because Missouri was soon to be draped with a cloak of justice, and the freedom bell would ring for Missouri slaves too. Charlie said that in the near future, "It'll get harder for us; stay still or run." Charlie was right.

Masters infuriated by defeat in war, who felt that they would lose their slaves and other livestock anyway, had little incentive to restrain their rage or to care for their slaves.

After the Emancipation Proclamation, blacks were officially allowed to enlist in the Union Army. Malindy and her family were proud of their free brethren who fought for them. They all had faith that soon Massa's foot would be torn from their necks and the shackles would fall from their bodies. On the farm, the slaves were encouraged by the news that free blacks were fighting for them and that many slaves had escaped to freedom.

The campfire song of the black soldiers echoed in the slave yards. The slaves sang the verses under their breath, smiling to one another.

O yes, over there, I lay dis body down,

I'll walk in de graveyard, I'll walk thru de graveyard, to lay dis body down.

I go to judgment in de evening of de day, when I lay dis body down.

Slaves talked of the black soldiers that they had seen on the roads. "Momma, I hear dey's colored soldiers in President Lincoln's army. Maybe George is wid dem," Ellen suggested hopefully to Malindy.

Malindy hoped that her son was fighting for a good cause and not with an outlaw group. "Chile, dat George could make a right good soldier, he ain't a-scared of nothin'. I pray dat my boy be all right. We has to pray for all dose young boys fightin' for freedom, and even for dem who don' know what's right, down South. I sees blood in my dreams all over de place. Dey's even talk 'bout some Injuns fightin' in de war. Some of my folk could git killed in dis mess. Lord, I have to pray for my folk too."

The Cherokees needed all the prayers in the world. Doom was on their doorstep. Once again, they were pawns in a white conflict. The Cherokee principal chief, John Ross, attempted to keep the Cherokees neutral, but they were forced to go to war, to their ultimate ruin. Cherokee chief Stand Watie raised a regiment, the Cherokee Mounted Rifles, for the Confederacy. For a while, Principal Chief John Ross and his men also fought for the Confederacy.

At the Battle of Pea Ridge, Arkansas, March 7–8, 1862, the largest battle fought west of the Mississippi, Watie's men captured a Union battery. Ross's men were captured. They turned coats and subsequently fought for the Union. After Pea Ridge, Confederate major general Earl Van Dorn moved most of his men and matériel back east over the Mississippi, effectively abandoning the lands west of the river to the Union.

After John Ross switched sides, Stand Watie entered the Cherokee capital, Tahlequah, and ordered Ross's home burned to the ground. On December 7, 1862, the loss of the Battle of Prairie Grove in northwest Arkansas halted uniformed Confederate attempts to retake Missouri for two years, though bitter guerilla warfare continued throughout the state. Watie and his men continued to fight for the Confederacy in the Indian Territories.

Starving and freezing, Oklahoma Indians fled north to Kansas and Missouri to escape the fighting. More Cherokees died of privation than

After the Battle of Pea Ridge the Confederates did not threaten Missouri.
THE BATTLE OF PEA RIDGE, ARKANSAS, MARCH 8, 1862. WOOD ENGRAVING FROM *HARPER'S WEEKLY*, 1862.
MHS PHOTOGRAPHS AND PRINTS.

MALINDY'S FREEDOM

in combat. At the war's end, Brigadier General Stand Watie, the only
Native American general on either side, whose Cherokee name means
"Stand Firm," was the last Confederate general to surrender, at
Doaksville, Indian Territory, on June 23, 1865.

Old Free Charlie had been able to find some work in Illinois, and
he had saved up a little more money. He missed his family, however,
and once again decided to return to Missouri.

Wartime had made it harder and more dangerous than ever for him
to travel back and forth between Missouri and Illinois. Early in the
Civil War, the federal authorities in Missouri declared martial law
throughout the state. Travelers within the state and across state lines
had to obtain passes, without which they were subject to arrest.

Gangs of outlaws, motivated solely by greed, infested the Missouri
countryside. The Jayhawkers, Kansas abolitionists, regarded all
Missourians as Southern sympathizers and swarmed across the border

to wreak havoc in western Missouri. Poorly trained, undisciplined Union militia, many drawn from free states such as Kansas, Iowa, and Illinois, terrorized and, on occasion, murdered Missouri citizens suspected of supporting the Confederate cause.

The well-armed, pro-Confederate Bushwhackers wore civilian clothing or captured blue Union uniforms. They paid no attention to military discipline or the laws of war. Using hit-and-run tactics, they committed atrocities the length and breadth of the state. The Bushwhackers made a real contribution to the Confederate war effort in the West. Guerilla warfare appalled all Missourians and touched many of them.

In time, freedmen became disillusioned about Lincoln. They felt that he should speak out against slavery everywhere, including the border states. But Lincoln had openly stated that the war was being fought not to end slavery but to preserve the Union. Lincoln admitted he did not have the constitutional power to free the slaves in the border states, and he did not want to antagonize the border states into secession by trying to do so. Charlie feared that the war would not free his own enslaved wife and children.

Nevertheless, Charlie thought well of Lincoln. Charlie told his children, "You can't always judge a man by what he says and even by what he does. Listen behind the words, to what is not said, and you can hear his heart speaking." Charlie believed that Lincoln had a good heart that was caught in nets of political necessity in a deep sea of woe. Charlie believed that in God's good time slavery would be ended by one whom God chose to lead. Maybe it would be Lincoln.

While Charlie was traveling, the slaves on the plantation could not wait for their Old Free Charlie to come home. He was the man with the news. Often the slaves would communicate forbidden information in code. For example, when a slave told another slave he was "looking greasy," he or she had war news to pass on. Some slaves referred to Lincoln as "Old Rideup."

Massa sometimes said to the slaves, "You think that Lincoln's gonna free you? You're wrong. You're going to stay right here."

Malindy and her family paid Massa no mind. Malindy said that Massa was "downright scared to his bones." She heard of the thousands of slaves who ran away from their masters to fight in the Union Army. To their understanding, the war was being fought over slavery, and there

Abraham Lincoln, the nation's sixteenth president.
PHOTOGRAPH BY JULIUS GROSS AFTER ALEXANDER GARDNER, 1863. MHS PHOTOGRAPHS AND PRINTS.

MALINDY'S FREEDOM

were no ifs, ands, or buts about that fact. Many slaves believed that if white folks wanted to kill themselves over slavery that was their own business. Sometimes, the family sat on the porch and made jokes about it. Bad as their situation was, they managed to laugh about it. God would free the slaves in His own good time. It was always obvious whom the slaves were rooting for; it was too hard to hide.

No matter how tired she was Malindy had to deal with Massa's and Missus's depression. Her ears tired of Massa's bellowing about the war. He blamed the "darkies" for all the trouble with the government. He intentionally spoke loudly to intimidate the slaves. "What would all these niggers do without us good white folks? We take dern good care of 'em. They're too ignorant to make it on their own."

When Charlie heard these comments, he wanted to harm the master. He was outraged. He remembered how he had returned to Gray Summit one day, after traveling around other parts of Missouri. Malindy told him the news: "Two of Massa's boys done gone to fight wid dey relatives down South. Massa jis' so proud dey aim to fight to keep us slaves." Malindy thought of how she had cared for Massa's two sons. How could they become Confederates? "I jis' don' understan' dat kind of thinkin'. We don' mean nothin' to 'em, Charlie. When will it pass? Let it pass." Malindy spoke low, her voice trembling in distress.

One day, on returning home from Illinois, Charlie looked at his daughter Ellen and saw something strange. Her eyelids were swollen and sore. Missus had made her knit socks and gloves for hours and hours. She was not allowed to go to sleep. When Ellen became sleepy and nodded, Missus propped her eyes open with pieces of broom straw between her eyelids. It was painful and left marks on Ellen's eyelids for the rest of her life.

Charlie stared at Ellen's injured eyelids. Ellen became frightened when she saw the expression on her father's face, which had turned the flaming red of sumacs in the fall. Charlie was furious and ready to charge Massa to avenge the mistreatment of Ellen. "How dare they put marks on my daughter," Charlie shouted. "I can't take any more. They rob me of my family and the right to live as a man. No more, no more. Now, they got her knittin' socks for the dern Confederates."

"Poppa, please don' go up to de Big House," Ellen cried out. "Dey'll kill you, Poppa. Dey so angry now 'bout de war, Poppa. Please, Poppa," Ellen cried, the tears pouring from her sore, deformed eyelids.

Malindy did everything she could to soothe Charlie and calm him down. "Charlie, I knows you's a man, but you can't stan' up to Massa now," Malindy said. "It's too dangerous. Massa is jis' a-lookin' for any reason to git even wid free Negroes. Massa en his friends, dey always talkin' 'bout free Negroes causin' de war 'long wid de white nigger-lovers."

Charlie understood her clearly. It was extra hard for free blacks now, especially those who worked for white folk. The whites blamed free blacks for the division in the country.

"Massa en Missus is so upset 'bout de split of dey family," Malindy said, "wid de boys way down yonder wid de Confederates. Dey already taken dis war out on us enough. Don' make it no worse, Charlie, please."

"They're the ones who caused all this sufferin' and hell," Charlie responded. "They're just concerned about their money. If they're concerned about the loss of life, and their sons, why don't they just free my family and all the slaves from all of this sufferin'. No, they're just too greedy and stupid. They know that God didn't make us to be another man's slave."

Ellen was proud of her father's courage. She didn't like to see him get angry, but she was always amused when he did his Indian whoop. No matter how old he became, his anger still propelled him into a high jump as he clicked his heels three times together before he touched the floor. He floated in the air like a well-trained dancer.

Sometimes, Ellen and the other children attempted to perform Charlie's jump. They never could do it. Ellen said, "Maybe I got to git real angry b'fo' I can fly up in de air like Poppa." Charlie wanted Ellen to fly—not by anger, but by freedom.

Malindy continued to grieve for her lost son, George, not knowing whether he was alive or dead. She and Charlie did not fear for Sammie. He was still in St. Louis and could get word to his family that he was safe and healthy. He came to see the family regularly. He and his father would discuss what they had seen and heard while traveling.

Sammie said, "Poppa, do you ever think of George? I hope he ain't in no trouble out there. When I's on de road wid Massa, I sees de troops en de whole dern lot. A white man done tol' me dat I'll never be free. I hear dat masters are killin' black folks like mad. I knows Massa won't kill us. He ain't dat kin' of man." Charlie looked at his son.

"We don't know what the white folks'll do," Charlie said. "We must pray that God keeps Massa's wrath from our heads."

"Massa won't mess wid you, Poppa. He's scared of you, Poppa."

"He's not scared of me, he's scared of himself. He's got the law in his hands and on his side. It's his guilty conscience scares him to death, and God's wrath is in his face now. Remember, son, Missouri is a place of trouble and confusion. Slavery is still law. Son, it's comin' to an end, soon. When it does, I want you to take Ellen to St. Louis and put her in school. She is a smart girl; she must have a chance."

"Poppa, don' you worry none about Ellen," Sammie promised, "I'll take good care of her."

Despite the riots that were occurring in some cities over the draft and between anti- and proslavery partisans, Sammie did not fear any danger in St. Louis. Union soldiers had secured the city under martial law. Malindy and Charlie did not mind if their son decided to serve in the Union Army, but they did not want him to be killed in a meaningless riot in the city.

Ellen was anxious, for she loved Sammie and did not want him harmed in any way. She had set her sights on St. Louis and freedom, and she welcomed Sammie as her guardian.

Her deformed eyelids made Ellen furious with the slaveholders. She never forgot the cruelty of the broom straws propping open her eyes during the long nights she spent without sleep, knitting for the soldiers. Where were the Union soldiers to free her? She wanted to be free. When she looked into the mirror, Ellen was tormented by the thought of the pain she had endured and the knowledge that she was scarred for life.

One day Malindy asked Charlie about the Cherokees. He told her that some of the Cherokees were still fighting for the Confederacy, though some were now fighting on the Union side. She understood that many of her people would die. She never understood how any of the Cherokees could fight for the Confederacy, even if some of them did own slaves. She told Charlie that she wanted to find her family. Yet, even as she said this, in her heart she knew that it would be impossible. Her people had been scattered from her childhood home. The Cherokee Nation lost more than a third of its people, over 7,000 out of a population of 21,000, as a result of the Civil War. No state in the North or South came close to this proportion of loss.

Confederate Major General Sterling Price crossed from Arkansas into Missouri on September 16, 1864, hoping to drive the Federal forces from Missouri. This campaign was intended to capture St. Louis and close the Mississippi River to Union shipping. In several battles in central Missouri during September and October, Price was driven back out of Missouri by Federal forces that included black Union soldiers stationed at the Rolla camp. One of those black soldiers was Nelson Buckner, of Lexington, Kentucky, who was serving with his brother.

As Ellen worked hard on the farm with her mother, she too prayed for freedom and dreamed of starting a family that lived as free folk. Ellen's destiny was woven with Nelson Buckner's. One day, they would meet.

Old Free Charlie heard that the war was turning in favor of the Union. The black troops had made a difference. He praised them to his family. "We must pray for these boys every day. They still have a hard time, yet they carry arms to protect us from the Confederacy. Let's not forget that we live under the Union flag, even though the Confederacy is in Massa's heart." Charlie did not feel that the master would kill his family, yet he remained watchful and kept his shotgun well hidden. He was prepared to use it at any moment, if need be.

In the last days of 1864, the destiny of Malindy's family and all black folks floated on the tides of war. Would millions of slaves in the Northern and border states ever be freed? If so, what would become of them? The Negro in many quarters was viewed as the inevitable Sambo, the everlasting "nigger." Popular feelings about slavery and the alleged inferiority of Negroes went deep, on both sides of the battle lines. Malindy felt the chill as Massa pondered how to keep her enslaved.

Some days, Malindy wanted to run away. She had never committed a crime; she was herself the victim of the crime of kidnapping, yet it was she who was imprisoned. Her labor guaranteed Massa's children an inheritance of wealth. Her labor pains from the birth of her firstborn, Sammie, enriched Massa's own firstborn son. White folk, the ones who robbed her of her true Cherokee identity, called her "nigger." Like her own Cherokee people, Malindy was a pawn in the white people's hands. Over and over, Malindy asked the Lord to change the tide.

On April 9, 1865, General Robert E. Lee surrendered the Army of Northern Virginia to General Ulysses S. Grant at Appomattox Court House, Virginia. Though the last significant engagement of the war was fought at Palmito Ranch, Texas, on May 12-13, 1865, the war was effectively over by April 14, 1865, when Abraham Lincoln was assassinated.

Missouri held a constitutional convention which abolished slavery on January 11, 1865. However, it was not until December 6, 1865, with the ratification by the requisite number of states of the Thirteenth

State of Missouri

Executive Department.

City of Jefferson January 23ᵈ 1865

Henceforth and forever, no person within the jurisdiction of this state, shall be subject to any abridgement of liberty, except such as the law shall prescribe for the common good, or know any master but God.

Thoᵈ C. Fletcher
Governor of Missouri

The first Governor of the free State of Missouri

The document signed by Missouri governor Thomas C. Fletcher abolishing slavery in Missouri, 1865.
Courtesy of Stuart Symington, Jr.

Amendment to the Constitution of the United States, abolishing slavery, that most Missouri slaves gained their freedom.

The year 1865 brought Malindy's family both good and bad news. At last the day of freedom came for Charlie, Malindy, and their children. "Old Free Charlie" Wilson no longer had to carry freedom papers at peril of being enslaved. He was free to travel and do business wherever he pleased. Yet, with freedom came great anxiety. When Massa told them they were free, his face was grave and sad: "Well, you got your freedom now; I guess you're happy."

The slaves stood silent. The expected jubilant outburst did not occur. No one seemed to be uplifted by the news of freedom. Both the slave master and the freed slaves now had a problem. Massa still needed help to work his land. The main concern for the slaves was: with no money and no property, where would they go? Where would they live? How would they eat? What would their future be in a bitter world still controlled by whites? Where were the forty acres of land and a mule that Abraham Lincoln planned to give to newly freed Negroes? Would former slaves have an active part in the government in Washington?

As the slaves stood there, they looked at Massa and Missus and at each other. Massa's farm had been their home for years. Now separation was upon them. Much healing would be needed to cure their broken hearts. They were torn by conflicting emotions. Some of the slaves both hated and loved their oppressors. Massa was part of their being.

Charlie looked into Malindy's face and smiled at her. She rejoiced that she could count on Charlie and God. She had sympathy in her heart for Massa, who was not the worst master in Missouri. She had experienced far worse masters in her early years. Sometimes, Massa had acted like he didn't like slavery. Poor man, he lived a Dr. Jekyll and Mr. Hyde existence. Like it or not, Massa saw his slaves as a workforce necessary for his own family's survival.

Massa asked Charlie and Malindy and the family to stay and work for him on the farm. He promised to pay fifty cents a day. He said they could live there as long as they wanted to. "This is your home," he said. Charlie and Malindy decided to accept Massa's offer, because they felt that it would be best for the children, until things settled down. Malindy felt a sense of peace.

The death of Abraham Lincoln saddened Malindy and her family. The fact that Lincoln died on Good Friday seemed to them a symbol of

Lincoln's goodness. His death was not merely an assassination, but a martyrdom in expiation of the sins of his beloved, guilty country. Black Americans came to regard Lincoln as a perfect, personal emancipator and kept pictures of him posted on the wall above the mantelpiece. To deeply emotional and religious slaves, Lincoln was an earthly incarnation of the savior of humankind. Walt Whitman wrote of him:

O' powerful, western fallen star,

the sweetest, wisest soul of all my life

and days and lands.

As soon as the war ended, Union soldiers moved swiftly into slave states to take the census and evaluate property damage. One day, Ellen heard a bugle. Three horsemen in Union Army uniform were riding up the road to the farm. The rider in the middle carried a United States flag. Charlie gathered his family together as the riders approached the Big House. Massa was running toward them, frightened.

"Hurry," Massa ordered, "git in the cellar." Massa had heard horror stories about the brutality of Union soldiers. "The war is over," he said, "but we can't trust these Yankees." Massa looked at Malindy, who kept her children huddled close to her.

Charlie faced the scared white man and said, "No, Malindy is not a slave and she is not going down into the cellar. Malindy is free now. Today she will be counted as a person, a human. We have nothin' to hide. Now, we shall all be counted as United States citizens."

Seeing that Charlie meant business, Massa said, "You're all free now. I don't want no more trouble with the government."

The three soldiers rode up to the Big House and told everybody to stand in a line. The newly freed women, men, and children were counted right along with the whites. Ellen held her mother's hand tightly.

Malindy looked to the sky reverently and gratefully. She said, "We done made it this far, Lord, I knows we can go yonder." The spirits of her Cherokee ancestors surrounded their orphan, lost child as she emerged into freedom once more, on the land her forefathers loved. Freedom's price had been paid in blood. Malindy's descendants would know freedom for all generations to come.

For thirty-eight of her forty-five years, Malindy had carried the knot of slavery in her stomach, twisted together from threads of fear

Ellen Buckner and her granddaughter Blanche, undated.
PHOTO COURTESY OF THE AUTHORS.

and anger. As she looked at Massa and Missus, she saw in them all the masters who had debased her emotionally, spiritually, and physically. She prayed, "How bad can folks be? Oh, God, how bad? I's so tired en' I mus' forgive 'em all. Please, God, let me forgive."

No matter how much the ex-slaves prayed to be forgiving, it would be a difficult journey, because the white men's own destructive behavior made it harder for the ex-slaves to forgive the whites. Despite emancipation, the hearts of many whites, north and south, were still frozen in attitudes of discrimination and oppression.

Charlie looked at his wife and understood her pain and her thoughts. He took her by the hand and said, "We must never forget the past. It must be remembered and passed on for generations to come. But, we must move forward. We are free of the white man's slavery. Now, we must be free of our own hatred of them, too, or it will enslave us. We must forgive these sad white folk, Malindy. We will move on and be who we truly are on God's earth.

"Malindy, you were never robbed of your soul. You kept it alive and free. Your strength and courage will move through the winds of time. The foundation that we have built will grow in our children. The generations will soar like eagles. Oh, my sweet Malindy, we are free!"

Malindy said, "Now, Charlie, we'll see our chillen grow tall en strong like a tree. A tree is free en it knows de lan'. Our chillen will be free en know dis lan' too."

Charlie put his arm around Malindy's waist as they walked peacefully, without malice, back toward their cabin and their future, the unknown.

"A New Song"

I speak in the name of the black millions
Awakening to action.
Let all others keep silent a moment.
I have this word to bring,
This thing to say,
This song to sing:

> Bitter was the day
>
> When I bowed my back
>
> Beneath the slaver's whip;

That day is past.

> Bitter was the day
>
> When I saw my children unschooled,
>
> My young men without a voice in the world,
>
> My women taken as the body-toys
>
> Of a thieving people.

That day is past.

—Langston Hughes

AFTERWORD

By the time freedom for all rolled across the country to Missouri, Malindy was forty-five years old, worn, tired, and sick. Yet, her will remained strong as she prepared for the future. Her marriage to Charlie, which as a slave marriage could not be legally recognized until slavery ended in 1865, continued to be the strong foundation of her life. Now, Malindy and Charlie Wilson lived together as a married couple. They were concerned about the welfare and education of their children.

The years of struggle had taken a toll on the family. Since that dramatic night before the war, when her son George Wilson rode up with his companions to try to carry Malindy and her children to freedom, George was never seen or heard from again. Perhaps Malindy's refusal to accompany him had seemed a rebuff that severed George's relationship with his family. Perhaps the rough men he rode with in the night were the outlaws Frank and Jesse James, who reputedly used nearby Meramec Caverns as a hideout, and perhaps George had met an outlaw's end. Perhaps George Wilson joined the Union Army and lost his life helping to free his family and all his people. Malindy continued to love and miss him and to pray that, somewhere, her George was safe.

When he was grown, Henry Wilson, Malindy's youngest son, also left the farm and disappeared from the family.

Ellen Buckner

Elizabeth, ca. 1902

Ophelia

Malindy and Charlie's three other children presented them with a total of eleven grandchildren. Malindy herself did not live to enjoy her grandchildren. Worn out by her grief for her people, years of hard labor, and recurring illnesses, she died shortly after 1870. Her husband, Old Free Charlie Wilson, went on to live a long life, enjoying the company of some of his grandchildren and teaching them about herbs.

Malindy's two eldest children flourished after the war. Sammie Wilson (called Sammie Burch) took Ellen to St. Louis to work and to go to school. In St. Louis, there was a curfew to prevent disorder and riots from postwar social upheaval. For newly freed blacks, it was still a dangerous place to be. Sammie prospered, married a woman named Frances, and remained in St. Louis. They had two children, Samuel Burch Jr. and Walter Burch.

Ellen endured, worked, and attempted to go to school, but it was difficult. In St. Louis, she met and married Nelson Buckner, a former slave, who with his brother had come out of Kentucky through the Underground Railroad and joined the Union Army.

Lara Wilson, Malindy's youngest daughter, lived with Ellen Wilson Buckner and Nelson Buckner and died at an early age, leaving one

Milton

Mollie in Los Angeles, ca. 1924

George, age 15

daughter, Liza. Ellen raised Liza like one of her own children. Liza, who was mulatto, left the family when she was a teenager and was never heard from again.

Ellen Wilson Buckner had eight children: Clarence, Elizabeth, Ophelia, Edwina, Milton, Mollie, Cora Belle, and George. These children flourished and gave Ellen a total of thirty-four grandchildren. Elizabeth had seven children, two girls and five boys. Ophelia had fifteen children, six girls and nine boys. Edwina had one daughter. Milton had six children, four girls and two boys. Cora Belle had two daughters. George Buckner had three children—Mildred Buckner Johnson and Theresa Delsoin, the authors of this book, and a son, Paul.

George Buckner, served overseas in the U.S. Army during World War I. George's son, Paul, served in the U.S. Army in World War II. Ellen's daughter Ophelia's eldest son, Sylvester, served in the U.S. Army in World War I. Five more of Ophelia's sons served in the U.S. Army in World War II. Some were decorated. All returned home safely.

After the privations of the Civil War, Nelson Buckner was a sickly man and died relatively young. Ellen Wilson Buckner, however, with the strength of her Cherokee, African American, and Irish American forbears and the freedom her husband had helped to win, lived a long life, rich in the blessings of her many descendants.

As Old Free Charlie Wilson had predicted, Ellen had almost total recall of all that had happened to her and to her family in slave times. As Malindy had instructed, Ellen told her children, grandchildren, great-grandchildren, and great-great-grandchildren the stories of their ancestors. It was at Ellen's knees that her granddaughter, Mildred Buckner Johnson, heard the story of her family. Ellen raised Mildred. In the evenings, when Mildred would comb out Ellen's hair, which was beautiful and long like Malindy's hair, Ellen told Mildred about her family, especially Malindy. Ellen encouraged Mildred to put this story in writing for future generations. Secure in the knowledge that the story of Malindy's life would be preserved, Ellen Wilson Buckner died in 1941 at the age of ninety-seven.

Malindy and Charlie Wilson left their family a rich legacy. Above all, they gave them a profound belief in God. They taught them, too, to revere Mother Earth and to respect their ancestors and know that their ancestors watched over them and loved them. By their love for each other and for their children, Malindy and Charlie planted a seed of love and close family ties that has flourished from one generation to the next. Malindy and Charlie prized education and encouraged their children to work hard. By their own example, they showed that any task should be performed to the best of a person's ability as a matter of integrity and self-respect.

In their own lives, Malindy and Charlie demonstrated that even surrounded by hatred and evil, a soul can choose not to hate. When freedom came for Malindy, she and Charlie were more than free on paper, and free from physical slavery. Their faith enabled them to walk through the fires of slavery unscorched, with no flame of malice kindling in their hearts. Malindy's prayers to be forgiving were answered, and with this power Malindy freed herself and all her descendants.

Malindy and Charlie's descendants have worked hard to build their lives on this strong foundation. Among them they have amassed bachelor's, master's, and doctoral degrees. They are skilled craftsmen, entrepreneurs, medical professionals, poets, writers, educators, social workers, laborers, and just plain honest hard-working folk. It was an arduous journey for the ancestors; the journey continues in their descendants.

Malindy and Charlie's generations enjoy a family reunion picnic on July 26, 1975, at Kirkwood City Park.
PHOTO COURTESY OF THE AUTHORS.

⊣ MALINDY'S FREEDOM ⊢

The descendants of Malindy and Charlie recognize all their ancestors, Cherokee, white, and black. The blood of all runs in their veins. Many did what was right for this country. Some did not fare too well. We must never forget either the atrocities or the many acts of human kindness through the years. Without that human kindness, blacks might still be slaves.

We salute our black ancestors with a poem by Robert E. Hayden:

"We Have Not Forgotten"

We have not forgotten the prayers you prayed,

Black fathers, O Black mothers, kneeling in

The cabin-gloom, debased, yet in your hearts

Bearing high springtime pageantries of faith.

We have not forgotten your morning hope,

More burning than the sun of cottonfields,

Upon dark, shackled limbs, nor songs your anguish

Suckled.

These are the vital flesh and blood

Of any strength we have; these the soil

From which our souls' strict meaning came — where grew

The roots of all our dreams of freedom's wide

And legendary spring.

And if we keep

Our love for this American earth, black fathers,

O black mothers, believing that its fields

Will bear for us at the length a harvesting

Of sun, it is because your spirits walk

Beside us as we plough; it is because

This land has grown from your great deathless hearts.

In remembrance of our Cherokee ancestors and celebration of all peoples in the world are these words of Shirley Loatman Pharis, 1995:

"In Remembrance of The People"

In remembrance of The People as they were
of Customs, of Pride, of Rituals

In remembrance of the Animals as they were
of Substance shared, of Teachings offered

In remembrance of the Birds as they were
of Grace, of Majesty, of Mystery

In remembrance of the Insects as they were
of Living Wisdom, of Necessary order

In remembrance of the Plants as they were
of Flowers, of Grasses, of Trees

In remembrance of the Reptiles as they were
of Eerie Beauty, of Natural Purpose

In remembrance of the Heavens as they were
of Clarity, of Seasons, of Spirit World

In remembrance of the Waters as they were
of Abundant Life, of Sacred Purity

In remembrance of the Lands as they were
of Freedom, of Harmony, of Oneness

Appendix

201: 1790–1850, Slave Population of the United States

Missouri became a slave state when it was admitted to the Union in 1820. In 1821, there were approximately 10,000 black slaves in Missouri. In ten years, the number of slaves almost tripled. The 1840 census listed 322,888 whites in Missouri, 58,240 slaves, and 1,574 freedmen. The 1850 census listed 529,004 whites, 87,422 slaves, and 2,618 freedmen in Missouri.

202: 1850 U.S. Census, Schedule of Slave Inhabitants, Franklin County, pp. 631 and 639 (2 pages of 17)

In Franklin County in 1850, there were some 249 slaveholders and 1,506 slaves, 126 of whom were specifically identified as mulattoes. These two pages—of seventeen—show the names of slave owners followed by the number of slaves owned and their age, sex, and race, but not their names. The *M*s, for mulattoes, are circled. As Abraham Lincoln said in a speech in Springfield, Illinois, on June 26, 1857, "In 1850, there were in the United States 405,751 mulattoes. Very few of these are the offspring of whites and free blacks. Nearly all have sprung from black slaves and white masters."

204: 1870 U.S. Census, Schedule of Inhabitants in Bonhomme Township, St. Louis County, p. 31

Lists Charles Wilson, age 40, "working on farm"; Malinda, age 40, "keeps house"; Laura, age 11; and Ellen, age 17.

206: 1880 U.S. Census, Schedule of Inhabitants in Bonhomme Township, St. Louis County, p. 20

Lists Nelson Buckner, age 45, "farmer"; Ellen Buckner, mulatto, age 27, "keeps house"; Clarence, age 6; Elizabeth, age 3; Ophelia, age 3 months; and Charles Wilson, mulatto, age 54, "works on farm."

1880 U.S. Census, Schedule of Inhabitants in St. Louis City, p. 10

Lists Samuel Burch, mulatto, age 40, "laborer," birthplace Franklin County, MO; Francis H. Burch, age 38, "keeps house"; Samuel A. Burch, age 3; and Virnum Varnum, age 69, father, "keeps house."

TABLE LXXI.—*Slave Population of the United States.*

STATES AND TERRITORIES.	1790.	1800.	1810.	1820.	1830.	1840.	1850.
Alabama...............	....	....	....	41,879	117,549	253,532	342,844
Arkansas...............	....	....	....	1,617	4,576	19,935	47,100
California...............	....	....	....	....	....	....	....
Columbia, District of...........	....	3,244	5,395	6,377	6,119	4,694	3,687
Connecticut	2,759	951	310	97	25	17	....
Delaware...............	8,887	6,153	4,177	4,509	3,292	2,605	2,290
Florida...............	....	....	....	....	15,501	25,717	39,310
Georgia...............	29,264	59,404	105,218	149,654	217,531	280,944	381,682
Illinois...............	....	....	168	917	747	331	....
Indiana...............	....	135	237	190	3	3	....
Iowa...............	....	....	....	....	....	16	....
Kentucky...............	11,830	40,343	80,561	126,732	165,213	182,258	210,981
Louisiana...............	....	....	34,660	69,064	109,588	168,452	244,809
Maine...............	....	....	....	....	2	....	....
Maryland...............	103,036	105,635	111,502	107,397	102,994	89,737	90,368
Massachusetts...............	....	....	....	....	1	....	....
Michigan...............	....	....	24	....	32	....	....
Mississippi...............	....	3,489	17,088	32,814	65,659	195,211	309,878
Missouri...............	....	....	3,011	10,222	25,091	58,240	87,422
New Hampshire...............	158	8	....	....	3	1	....
New Jersey...............	11,423	12,422	10,851	7,557	2,254	674	236
New York...............	21,324	20,343	15,017	10,088	75	4	....
North Carolina...............	100,572	133,296	168,824	205,017	245,601	245,817	288,548
Ohio...............	....	....	....	..	6	3	....
Pennsylvania...............	3,737	1,706	795	211	403	64	....
Rhode Island...............	952	381	108	48	17	5	....
South Carolina...............	107,094	146,151	196,365	258,475	315,401	327,038	384,984
Tennessee...............	3,417	13,584	44,535	80,107	141,603	183,059	239,459
Texas...............	....	....	....	....	....	....	58,161
Vermont...............	17	....	....	....	....	....	....
Virginia...............	293,427	345,796	392,518	425,153	469,757	449,087	472,528
Wisconsin...............	....	....	....	....	....	11	....
Territories. { Minnesota...............	....	....	....	....	....	....	....
New Mexico...............	....	....	....	....	....	....	....
Oregon...............	....	....	....	....	....	....	....
Utah...............	....	....	....	....	....	....	26
				1,538,125 * less 87			
Aggregate................	697,897	893,041	1,191,364	1,538,038	2,009,043	2,487,455	3,204,313

SCHEDULE 2.—Slave Inhabitants in *District No. 31 being* **in the County of** *Franklin* **State of** *Missouri*, **enumerated by me, on the** *5th* **day of** *October*, **1850.** *E. F. Brown* **Ass't Marshal.**

63 1

	NAMES OF SLAVE OWNERS.	Number of Slaves.	Age.	Sex.	Colour.	Fugitives from the State.	Number manumitted.	Deaf & dumb, blind, insane, or idiotic.	
	1	2	3	4	5	6	7	8	
1		4	7	7	m				1
2		5	1	7	m				2
3	Beasley William	1	70	6	B				3
4		2	40	m	B				4
5		3	30	m	B		7		5
6		4	30	m	B				6
7		5	16	m	B				7
8		6	30	7	B				8
9		7	20	7	B				9
10		8	14	7	B				10
11		9	14	m	B				11
12		10	4	m	B				12
13	Hart Albert G	1	21	7	m				13
14		2	1	7	B				14
15	Bell William	1	42	m	B				15
16		2	12	7	B				16
17	Robertson John R	1	40	m	B				17
18	Right Thomas	1	36	7	B				18
19		2	15	m	B				19
20	Steines Frederick	1	40	m	B				20
21		2	19	7	B				21
22	North William	1	36	m	m				22
23		2	38	7	B				23
24		3	25	7	B				24
25		4	16	m	m				25
26		5	14	7	m				26
27		6	8	7	B				27
28		7	7	7	B				28
29		8	6	7	m				29
30		9	6	7	m				30
31		10	6	7	m				31
32		11	4	m	m				32
33		12	4	m	m				33
34		13	4	m	B				34
35		14	4	m	B				35
36		15	3	7	B				36
37		16	3	7	m				37
38	Smith Nathan	1	14	6	B				38
39		2	3	7	B				39
40	Searight John S	1	25	m	B				40
41		2	21	7	B				41

	NAMES OF SLAVE OWNERS.	Number of Slaves.	Age.	Sex.	Colour.	Fugitives from the State.	Number manumitted.	Deaf & dumb, blind, insane, or idiotic.	
	1	2	3	4	5	6	7	8	
1		4	18	m	B				1
2		5	2	m	B				2
3	Perkins Harold	1	50	7	B				3
4		2	25	m	B				4
5		3	23	m	m				5
6		4	25	7	m				6
7		5	21	m	B				7
8		6	20	m	B				8
9		7	20	7	B				9
10		8	2	m	B				10
11	Perkins John M	1	13	7	B				11
12	Daniel Alexander	1	50	7	B				12
13	Bell Andrew	1	21	m	B				13
14		2	14	7	m				14
15		3	9	m	B				15
16	Walker Eaves	1	48	7	B				16
17		2	16	m	B				17
18		3	5	m	B				18
19	Roberts Samuel R	1	88	7	B				19
20		2	50	m	B				20
21		3	42	7	B				21
22		4	35	m	B				22
23		5	30	m	B				23
24		6	24	7	B				24
25		7	22	7	B				25
26		8	20	m	B				26
27		9	11	7	B				27
28		10	1	m	B				28
29	Macy Stephen T	1	25	m	m				29
30		2	20	7	B				30
31		3	16	7	B				31
32	Vosper L G	1	35	m	B				32
33		2	9	7	B				33
34		3	15	m	B				34
35		4	6	7	B				35
36		5	6	7	B				36
37		6	3	7	m				37
38	Green Catharine	1	16	7	B				38
39		2	7	m	B				39
40	Sanderling John	1	22	7	B				40
41		2	2	m	B				41

SCHEDULE 2.—Slave Inhabitants in _District No. 34 being_ in the County of _Franklin_ State of _Missouri_, enumerated by me, on the _27th_ day of _October_, 1850. _C. T. Brown_ Ass't Marshal.

	NAMES OF SLAVE OWNERS.	Number of Slaves	Age	Sex	Colour	Fugitives from the State	Number manumitted	Deaf & dumb, blind, insane, or idiotic		NAMES OF SLAVE OWNERS.	Number of Slaves	Age	Sex	Colour	Fugitives from the State	Number manumitted	Deaf & dumb, blind, insane, or idiotic
		1	2	3	5	6	7	8		1	2	3	5	6	7	8	
1	Eubanks Phillip	1	31	m	B				1		6	1	f	B			
2		2	24	f	B				2		7	5	f	B			
3		3	9	f	B				3	Bigby George M	1	11	m	B			
4	Cheatham Pharos	1	60	m	B				4	Cabell John	1	30	f	B			
5		2	19	f	B				5		2	31	m	B			
6		3	13	m	B				6	Lund J. C.	1	33	m	B			
7		4	12	m	B				7		2	15	f	B			
8	Coleman John G	1	45	m	B				8		3	6	f	B			
9		2	19	f	B				9	Roarke Nancy	1	63	m	B			
10		3	11	f	B				10		2	20	f	B			
11		4	18	f	B				11		3	3	m	B			
12		5	5	f	B				12	Obannon John	1	44	m	B			
13		6	3	f	B				13		2	40	f	B			
14		7	1	f	B				14		3	44	f	B			
15		8	½	m	B				15		4	30	m	B			
16	Childs Alfred M	1	35	m	B				16		5	20	m	B			
17		2	20	m	B				17		6	18	m	B			
18		3	12	m	B				18		7	18	m	B			
19		4	25	f	m				19		8	16	m	B			
20		5	8	f	B				20		9	10	m	B			
21		6	4	m	B				21		10	10	f	B			
22		7	2	m	B				22		11	8	f	B			
23	Gibson Joseph	1	10	m	B				23		12	6	f	B			
24		2	40	f	m				24		13	3	f	B			
25		3	30	m	B				25	Herrman William	1	30	f	B			
26		4	30	f	m				26		2	8	f	B			
27		5	27	f	m				27		3	6	f	B			
28		6	14	f	B				28		4	4	f	B			
29		7	10	m	m				29		5	4	m	B			
30		8	7	m	B				30		6	1	f	B			
31		9	6	m	B				31	Ogden Susan	1	30	m	B			
32		10	6	m	m				32		2	21	f	B			
33		11	4	f	B				33		3	7	m	B			
34		12	2	m	B				34		4	3	f	B			
35		13	1	m	B				35	Brown James B	1	60	f	B			
36	Goode Phillip	1	21	m	B				36		2	55	m	B			
37	Bridges William	1	17	m	B				37		3	40	m	B			
38	Bridges Andrew	1	30	m	B				38		4	24	m	B			
39		2	46	f	B				39	Jones Richard	1	55	m	B			
40									40		2	40	f	B			

Page No. *31* Inquiries numbered 7, 16, and 17 are not to be asked in re

SCHEDULE 1.—Inhabitants in *Bonhomme*

of *Mo* , enumerated by me on the *23* d

Post Office: *Ballwin*

					DESCRIPTION.				VALUE OF OW
20	4	4	Weeds Charles	40	M	C		"	
21			Malinda	40	F	C	K	house	
22			Laura	11	F	C		at home	
23			Ellen	17	F	C		"	
24	5	5	Watts Jerry	45	M	C	working on farm	

d in respect to infants. Inquiries numbered 11, 12, 15, 16, 17, 19, and 20 are to be answered (if at all) merely by an affirmative mark, as /.

_____ *Twp* _____, in the County of _____ *St. Louis* _____, State

_____ day of _____ *June* _____, 1870.   **15**

            E. L. Dasenbach, Ass't Marshal.

LUE OF READ ESTATE OWNED.				PARENTAGE.					EDUCA-TION.		CONSTITUTIONAL RELATIONS.	
			Virg						/ /			**20**
			"						/			**21**
			Mo						/			**22**
			"						/			**23**
		/	"						/		/	**24**

Page No. _____ 20

Supervisor's Dist. No. 1

Enumeration Dist. No. 183

Note A.—The Census Year begins June 1, 1879, and end

Note B.—All persons will be included in the Enumerati

June 1, 1880, will be OMITTED. Members

Note C.—Questions Nos. 13, 14, 22 and 23 are not to be

SCHEDULE 1.—Inhabitants in *Bonhomme Township*

enumerated by me on the ___

In Cities.				Personal Description.			Civil Condition.	
18	124 182	Burdash Hebson	B M 45					Fa
19	—	Ellen	W F 27	Wife			Kep
20	—	Clarence	W M 6	Son			
21	—	Elizabeth	W F 3	Daugh			
22	—	Orpha	W F 1/2	Mar Daugh			
23	Nelson Charles	M M 54	Father L			Work

Page No. 10

Supervisor's Dist. No. 1

Enumeration Dist. No. 117

Note A.—The Census Year begins June 1, 1879, and ends

Note B.—All persons will be included in the Enumeration

June 1, 1880, will be OMITTED. Members of

Note C.—Questions Nos. 13, 14, 22 and 23 are not to be as

SCHEDULE 1.—Inhabitants in *St. Louis*

enumerated by me on the

11		Burch Samuel	M M 40	Neighbor	1	Labo
12		Elizabeth	W F 38	Wife	1	Ke H
13		Samuel L	W M 3	Son		
14		Konum Venum	B F 64	Father	1	Ke H

[1-260.]

... May 31, 1880.

... who were living on the 1st day of June, 1880. No others will. Children BORN SINCE ... of Families who have DIED SINCE June 1, 1880, will be INCLUDED.

... asked in respect to persons under 10 years of age.

...6 , in the County of *St. Louis* , State of *Missouri*

21st & 22nd day of June, 1880.

Richard A. Hadbin

Enumerator.

Occupation.		Health.		Education.		Nativity.		
						Tenn	Mo	Mo
...inus	B					Ky	Ky	Ky
...inghouse						Mo	Va	Va
				✕✕		Mo	Ky	Mo
				✕✕		Mo	Ky	Mo
						Mo	Ky	Mo
...on farm	✓					Va	Va	Va

... May 31, 1880.

... who were living on the 1st day of June, 1880. No others will. Children BORN SINCE ... of Families who have DIED SINCE June 1, 1880, will be INCLUDED.

... asked in respect to persons under 10 years of age.

City

, in the County of *St. Louis*, State of *Mo*

3th day of June, 1880.

Laborer				Franklin Co. Mo
...				Bolis Co. Mo
				St. Louis Mo
... House				Va

SELECTED BIBLIOGRAPHY

Baringer, William E. *A House Dividing: Lincoln as President Elect.* Springfield, IL: The Abraham Lincoln Association, 1945.

___. *Lincoln's Rise to Power.* Boston: Little, Brown, 1937. Reprint, St. Clair Shores, MI: Scholarly Press, 1971.

___. *Lincoln's Vandalia: A Pioneer Portrait.* New Brunswick, NJ: Rutgers University Press, 1949.

Barton, William E. *The Lineage of Lincoln.* Indianapolis: Bobbs-Merrill, 1929.

Basler, Roy P. *Abraham Lincoln: His Speeches and Writings.* Franklin Center, PA: Franklin Library, 1979.

___, ed. *The Collected Works of Abraham Lincoln.* New Brunswick, NJ: Rutgers University Press, 1959.

Bassett, John S. *The Southern Plantation Overseer as Revealed in His Letters.* Northampton, MA: Southworth, 1925. Reprint, New York: Negro Universities Press, 1968.

Bennett, Lerone. *Before the Mayflower: A History of Black America.* 6th ed. Chicago: Johnson, 1988.

___. *The Road Not Taken, Colonies Turn Fateful Fork by Systematically Dividing Races.* Highland Park, MI: International Committee Against Racism, n.d.

Blankenship, Bob. *Cherokee Roots.* Cherokee, NC: Author, 1992.

Blassingame, John W. *The Slave Community.* New York: Oxford University Press, 1979.

___, ed. *Slave Testimony: Two Centuries of Letters, Speeches, Interviews, and Autobiographies.* Baton Rouge: Louisiana State University Press, 1977.

Botkin, B. A., ed. *Lay My Burden Down: A Folk History of Slavery.* Chicago: University of Chicago Press, 1945. Reprint, New York: Delta, 1994.

Bradford, Sarah H., ed. *Scenes in the Life of Harriet Tubman*. Auburn, NY: W. J. Moses, 1869. Reprint, Salem, NH: Ayer Company, 1988.

Bremer, Fredrika. *The Homes of the New World*. Translated by Mary Howitt. New York: Harper and Brothers, 1853. Reprint, New York: Johnson Reprint, 1968.

Brown, William Wells. *The American Fugitive in Europe: Sketches of Places and People Abroad*. Boston, 1854. Reprint, Freeport, NY: Books for Libraries Press, 1970.

___. *The Negro in the American Rebellion: His Heroism and His Fidelity*. Boston: Lee & Shepard, 1867. Reprint, New York: Citadel Press, 1971.

Buckley, Gail. *American Patriots: The Story of Blacks in the Military from the Revolution to Desert Storm*. New York: Random House, 2001.

Buckmaster, Henrietta. *Let My People Go: The Story of the Underground Railroad and the Growth of the Abolition Movement*. New York: Harper, 1941.

Captain Shoe Boots to the National Council, October 20, 1824. Cherokee Nation Papers, Book of Records, 1837.

Carter, George E., and C. Peter Ripley, eds. *Black Abolitionist Papers, 1830-1865*. Sanford, NC: Microfilming Corporation of America, [1981?]. Reprint, Ann Arbor, MI: UMI, 1993.

Carter, Samuel, III. *Cherokee Sunset: A Nation Betrayed*. New York: Doubleday, 1976.

Catton, Bruce. *Mr. Lincoln's Army*. New York: Doubleday, 1951. Reprint, New York: Anchor Books, 1990.

___. *Terrible Swift Sword*. Vol. 2 in *The Centennial History of the Civil War*. New York: Doubleday, 1963.

Chambers, Bradford, ed. *Chronicles of Negro Protest: A Background Book for Young People, Documenting the History of Black Power*. New York: Parents' Magazine Press, 1968.

Christopher, Henry E. *Forever Free: From the Emancipation Proclamation to the Civil Rights Bill of 1875*. Philadelphia: Chelsea House, 1995.

Commager, Henry Steele, ed. *The Blue and the Gray: The Story of the Civil War as Told by Participants*. New York: Meridian, 1994.

Connelly, Thomas L. *Army of the Heartland: The Army of Tennessee, 1861–1862*. Baton Rouge: Louisiana State University Press, 2001.

Douglass, Frederick. *Life and Times of Frederick Douglass*. San Francisco: Phillips & Hunt, 1882. Reprint, New York: Gramercy Books, 1993.

___. *My Bondage and My Freedom*. New York: Miller, Orton & Mulligan, 1855. Reprint, Urbana: University of Illinois Press, 1987.

___. *Narrative of the Life of Frederick Douglass, an American Slave, Written by Himself*. Boston: Anti-slavery Office, 1845.

Dubois, W. E. B. *The Suppression of the African Slave-Trade to the United States of America, 1638–1870*. New York: Longmans, Green and Co., 1896. Reprint, Baton Rouge: Louisiana State University Press, 1969.

Ehle, John. *Trail of Tears: The Rise and Fall of the Cherokee Nation*. New York: Anchor Books, 1989.

Eisenschiml, Otto, and Ralph Newman. *The American Iliad: The Epic Story of the Civil War as Narrated by Eyewitnesses and Contemporaries,* Indianapolis: Bobbs-Merrill, 1947.

Five Hundred Thousand Strokes for Freedom. New York: Negro Universities Press, 1969.

Fogel, Robert William. *Without Consent or Contract: The Rise and Fall of American Slavery*. New York: Norton, 1989.

Foner, Jack D. *Blacks and the Military in American History: A New Perspective*. New York: Praeger, 1974.

Forbes, Jack. *Africans and Native Americans: The Language of Race and the Evolution of Red-Black Peoples*. Urbana: University of Illinois Press, 1993.

Franks, Kenny. *Stand Watie and the Agony of the Cherokee Nation*. Memphis, TN: Memphis State University Press, 1979.

Furry, William, ed. *The Preacher's Tale: The Civil War Journal of Rev. Francis Springer, Chaplain, U.S. Army of the Frontier*. Fayetteville: University of Arkansas Press, 2001.

Gaines, W. Craig. *The Confederate Cherokees: John Drew's Regiment of Mounted Rifles*. Baton Rouge: Louisiana State University Press, 1989.

Genovese, Eugene D. *Roll Jordan Roll: The World the Slaves Made*. New York: Pantheon, 1974.

Glatthaar, Joseph F. *Forged in Battle: The Civil War Alliance of Black Soldiers and White Officers*. New York: Free Press, 1990.

Guelzo, Allen C. *Abraham Lincoln, Redeemer President*. Grand Rapids, MI: Eerdmans, 2000.

Gutman, Herbert G. *The Black Family in Slavery and Freedom, 1750–1925*. New York: Pantheon Books, 1976.

Halliburton, R. *Red over Black: Black Slavery among the Cherokee Indians*. Westport, CT: Greenwood Press, 1977.

Hansen, Joyce. *Between Two Fires: Black Soldiers in the Civil War*. New York: F. Watts, 1993.

Hargrove, Hondon B. *Black Union Soldiers in the Civil War*. Jefferson, NC: McFarland, 1988.

Hay, John. *Lincoln and the Civil War in the Diaries and Letters of John Hay*. 1939. Reprint, New York: Da Capo Press, 1988.

Herndon, William H., and Jesse W. Weik. *Herndon's Lincoln: The True Story of a Great Life*. Springfield, IL: Herndon's Lincoln Pub. Co., [1888?]. Reprint, 1921.

Hoyt-Goldsmith, Diane. *Cherokee Summer*. New York: Holiday House, 1993.

Hurt, Douglas. *Agriculture and Slavery in Missouri's Little Dixie*. Columbia: University of Missouri Press, 1992.

Index to Compiled Service Records of Volunteer Union Soldiers Who Served with U.S. Colored Troops in the Civil War, 1861–1865. Washington, DC: National Archives and Records Service.

Jacobs, Harriet A. *Incidents in the Life of a Slave Girl*. Edited by L. Maria Child. Boston: Author, 1861. Reprint, Cambridge, MA: Harvard University Press, 2000.

Jefferson, Thomas. *Notes on the State of Virginia*. New York: Furman & Loudon, 1801. Reprint, New York: Palgrave, 2002.

Johnson, James Weldon, ed. *The Book of American Negro Spirituals*. New York: Viking Press, 1925.

Kavasch, E. Barrie. *Enduring Harvests: Native American Foods and Festivals for Every Season*. Old Saybrook, CT: Globe Pequot Press, 1995.

Keckley, Elizabeth. *Behind the Scenes*. New York: G. W. Carleton & Co., 1868.

King, Duane H., ed. *The Cherokee Indian Nation: A Troubled History*. Knoxville: University of Tennessee Press, 1979.

Leech, Margaret. *Reveille in Washington, 1860–1865.* New York: Grosset & Dunlap, 1941.

Leedom, Tim C., ed. *The Book Your Church Doesn't Want You to Read.* Dubuque, IA: Kendall/Hunt Publishing Company, 1993.

Lindsey, David. *Americans in Conflict: The Civil War and Reconstruction.* Boston: Houghton Mifflin, 1973.

Malinowski, Sharon, et al., eds. *The Gale Encyclopedia of Native American Tribes.* Detroit: Gale, 1998.

May, Katja. *African Americans and Native Americans in the Creek and Cherokee Nations, 1830s to 1920s.* New York: Garland, 1996.

McLaurin, Melton A. *Celia, a Slave.* Athens: University of Georgia Press, 1991.

McLoughlin, William G. *After the Trail of Tears: The Cherokees' Struggle for Sovereignty, 1839–1880.* Chapel Hill: University of North Carolina Press, 1993.

___. *The Cherokee Ghost Dance: Essays on the Southeastern Indians, 1799–1861.* Macon, GA: Mercer, 1984.

___. *The Cherokees and Christianity, 1794–1870: Essays on Acculturation and Cultural Persistence.* Athens: University of Georgia Press, 1994.

___. *Cherokees and Missionaries, 1789–1839.* New Haven, CT: Yale University Press, 1984.

Merkel, Benjamin G. *The Antislavery Controversy in Missouri, 1819–1865.* St. Louis: Washington University, 1942.

Miers, Earl Schenck, ed. *Lincoln Day by Day: A Chronology, 1809–1865.* Washington, DC: Lincoln Sesquicentennial Commission, 1960.

Mooney, James. *Myths of the Cherokee: And Sacred Formulas of the Cherokees.* Nashville, TN: C. Elder-Bookseller, 1972.

The Negro in the Military Service of the United States: 1639–1886. Washington, DC: National Archives and Records Service, 1973.

Nevins, Allan. *The Ordeal of the Union.* New York: Scribners, 1947.

Newby, I. A. *The South: A History.* New York: Holt, Rinehart and Winston, 1978.

Nicolay, John G., and John Hay, eds. *Abraham Lincoln: Complete Works.* New York: Century Co., 1922.

Northrup, Solomon. *Twelve Years a Slave*. 1853. Reprint, Baton Rouge: Louisiana State University Press, 1988.

Novak, Daniel A. *The Wheel of Servitude: Black Forced Labor after Slavery*. Lexington: University Press of Kentucky, 1978.

Oakes, James. *The Ruling Race: A History of American Slaveholders*. New York: Knopf, 1982. Reprint, New York: Norton, 1998.

Oates, Stephen B. *Abraham Lincoln, the Man behind the Myths*. New York: Harper & Row, 1984.

Olmstead, Frederick Law. *A Journey in the Seaboard Slave States*. New York: Dix and Edward, 1856.

Paine, Thomas. "African Slavery in America." *Pennsylvania Journal and Weekly Advertiser*, March 8, 1775.

Perdue, Theda. *The Cherokee*. New York: Chelsea House, 1989.

___. *Slavery and the Evolution of Cherokee Society, 1540–1866*. Knoxville: University of Tennessee Press, 1979.

Potter, David M. *Lincoln and His Party in the Secession Crisis*. 1942. Reprint, New York: AMS Press, 1979.

Quarles, Benjamin. *Black Abolitionists*. New York: Oxford University Press, 1969.

___. *The Negro in the Civil War*. Boston: Little, Brown, 1953. Reprint, New York: Da Capo Press, 1989.

Raboteau, Albert J. *Slave Religion: The "Invisible Institution" in the Antebellum South*. New York: Oxford University Press, 1978.

Randall, J. G., and David Donald. *The Civil War and Reconstruction*. Boston: Heath, 1961.

Rawick, George P., ed. *The American Slave: A Composite Autobiography*. Westport, CT: Greenwood Press, 1972.

Redpath, James. *The Public Life of Capt. John Brown*. Boston: Thayer and Eldridge, 1860. Reprint, Freeport, NY: Books for Libraries Press, 1970.

Register of Letters Received by the Office of Indian Affairs, 1824–1880. Washington, DC: National Archives and Records Service.

Robinson, Randall. *The Debt: What America Owes to Blacks*. New York: Plume, 2001.

Roger, J. A. *Africa's Gift to America*. New York: Author, 1959.

Rollins, Richard, ed. *Black Southerners in Gray: Essays on Afro-Americans in Confederate Armies*. Murfreesboro, Tenn: Southern Heritage Press, 1994.

Sandburg, Carl. *Abraham Lincoln: The Prairie Years and The War Years, in Three Volumes*. New York: Dell, 1959.

Stampp, Kenneth. *The Peculiar Institution: Slavery in the Ante-Bellum South*. New York: Knopf, 1956.

Stowe, Harriet Beecher. *The Key to Uncle Tom's Cabin*. Boston: Jewett, 1853.

Taylor, Yuval, ed. *I Was Born a Slave: An Anthology of Classic Slave Narratives*. Chicago: Lawrence Hill Books, 1999.

Terrell, John Upton. *The Arrow and the Cross: A History of the American Indian and the Missionaries*. Santa Barbara, CA: Capra Press, 1979.

Thomas, Benjamin P. *Lincoln Day by Day, 1847–1853*. Springfield, IL: The Abraham Lincoln Association, 1936.

Thomas, Emory M. *The Confederate Nation, 1861–1865*. New York: Harper & Row, 1979.

Thomas, Velma M. *Lest We Forget: The Passage from Africa to Slavery and Emancipation*. New York: Crown Trade Paperbacks, 1997.

Thornton, Russell. *The Cherokees: A Population History*. Lincoln: University of Nebraska Press, 1990.

Trexler, Harrison Anthony. *Slavery in Missouri, 1804–1865*. Baltimore: Johns Hopkins Press, 1914. Reprint, New York: AMS Press, 1986.

Truth, Sojourner. *Narrative of Sojourner Truth: A Bondswoman of Olden Time*. Grand Rapids, MI: Candace Press, 1996.

Unger, Steven, ed. *The Destruction of American Indian Families*. New York: Association on American Indian Affairs, 1977.

U.S. Census Office. *Seventh Census of the United States, Slave Schedules*. Washington, DC: National Archives and Records Service, 1850.

U.S. Census Office. *Eighth Census of the United States, Slave Schedules*. Washington, DC: National Archives and Records Service, 1860.

U.S. Commission to the Five Civilized Tribes. *Final Rolls of Citizens and Freedmen of the Five Civilized Tribes in Indian Territory, 1907-1914*. Washington, DC: National Archives and Records Service, 1907.

Walker, Margaret. *Jubilee*. New York: Bantam Books, 1967.

Walker, Robert. *Torchlights to the Cherokees: The Brainerd Mission*. New York: Macmillan, 1931.

Ward, Andrew. *Dark Midnight When I Rise: The Story of the Jubilee Singers, Who Introduced the World to the Music of Black America*. New York: Farrar, Straus and Giroux, 2000.

White, Deborah Gray. *Ar'n't I a Woman? Female Slaves in the Plantation South*. New York, Norton, 1985.

Wildins, Thurman. *Cherokee Tragedy: The Ridge Family and the Decimation of a People*. Norman: University of Oklahoma Press, 1986.

Williams, G. W. *A History of the Negro Troops in the War of the Rebellion, 1861–1865*. New York: Harper & Brothers, 1888.

Wills, Garry. *Lincoln at Gettysburg: The Words That Remade America*. New York: Simon and Schuster, 1992.

Wish, Harvey, ed. *Ante-bellum Writings of George Fitzhugh and Hinton Rowan Helper on Slavery*. New York: Capricorn, 1960.

Woodson, Carter G., ed. *Free Negro Owners of Slaves in the United States in 1830, Together with Absentee Ownership of Slaves in the United States in 1830*. New York: Negro Universities Press, 1968.

Woodward, C. Vann, ed. *Mary Chestnut's Civil War*. New Haven, CT: Yale University Press, 1981.

Wright, J. Leitch, Jr. *The Only Land They Knew: The Tragic Story of the American Indians in the Old South*. New York: Free Press, 1985.

Yenne, Bill. *The Encyclopedia of North American Indian Tribes*. New York: Crescent Books, 1995.